THE QUEST FOR RESPONSIVE GOVERNMENT
AN INTRODUCTION TO STATE AND LOCAL POLITICS

L. HARMON ZEIGLER

University of Oregon

and

HARVEY J. TUCKER

University of Oregon

DUXBURY PRESS

North Scituate, Massachusetts

Library of Congress Cataloging in Publication Data

Zeigler, Luther Harmon, 1936–
    The quest for responsive government.

    Includes index.
    1. Local government—United States.
    2. Political participation—United States.
    I. Tucker, Harvey J., joint author.   II. Title.
    JS331.Z38   320.9'73   77–13830
    ISBN 0–87872–145–2

Duxbury Press
A Division of Wadsworth Publishing Company, Inc.

The Quest for Responsive Government was edited and prepared for composition by Dianne Zolotow and Martha Gleason. Interior design was provided by Richard Spencer and the cover was designed by Ann Washer.

L.C. Cat. Card No.: 77–13830
ISBN 0–87872–145–2
Printed in the United States of America

1 2 3 4 5 6 7 8 9 – 82 81 80 79 78

To Pat
and Sandy

CONTENTS

CHAPTER 5
The Politics of Educational Governance   189

CHAPTER 6
Barriers to Responsiveness   255

CHAPTER 7
Epilogue   319

Index   329

PREFACE

OUR PURPOSE in writing this book is to develop and explore the theme of responsiveness in government at the state and local level. Most people would agree that responsiveness is the key to American democracy: government should do what the people want. But how often can and do state and local governments adopt the policies the people want? Can we say that a majority of governments are responsive to a majority of the people in a majority of decisions? What factors promote and inhibit responsiveness? Are governments equally responsive to all citizens, or are they more responsive to enfranchised citizens, voters, taxpayers, the politically active, or to those most affected by the policy in question? Clearly, the question of government responsiveness is important. Unfortunately, it is also extremely complex.

As the reader will see, our goal of analyzing responsiveness in government has caused us to write a rather unorthodox text. We have not attempted to provide encyclopedic coverage of all topics related to state and local politics and government. In fact, we have consciously sacrificed breadth of coverage. However, we believe that we have succeeded in raising some important questions that frequently are overlooked in traditional courses in state and local government. For example, state and local governments are presumed to be either more responsive, or potentially more responsive than the federal government, because they are closer to the people. Are they? Is physical proximity the most important factor affecting governmental responsiveness? How shall we decide if governments are responsive or unresponsive? Our conclusion is that state and local governments are generally unresponsive in the broadest sense. Governments are responsive but only very selectively.

In teaching these materials, we have noticed that college students tend to identify themselves with the underdogs, the underrepresented masses. Many are shocked when we point out that they are, or will become, the elite in relation to state and local governments. We attempt to challenge the notion that government responsive to the masses is either attainable or desirable. In all honesty, we must report that our arguments here have failed to convert the most fervent believers in broadly defined governmental responsiveness. Whether you agree or not, we hope you will finish this book not with a feeling of pessimism, but with the desire to learn more about how political systems actually operate.

The following individuals provided guidance, suggestions, and assistance on the project: William Eubank, John Grumm, Frank Hoole, Gordon King, Leroy N. Rieselbach, Barry Siegel, Sandra Tucker, Ron Weber, and L. A. Wilson II. Students at the University of Oregon helped us sharpen our ideas and presentation. Virginia Williams was our secretary. Dr. Tucker would like to acknowledge his intellectual debts to Ronald E. Weber, Francis W. Hoole, Leroy N. Rieselbach, and Bernard S. Morris. Dr. Zeigler would like to acknowledge his long-standing intellectual debt to Heinz Eulau. We gratefully acknowledge this support. Naturally, the final product is the sole responsibility of the authors.

1

RESPONSIVENESS IN STATE AND LOCAL GOVERNMENT

THE THEME of this book is responsiveness: how responsive state and local governments are to demands made on them, and to whom state and local governments are most responsive. Generally speaking, most people, whether active in politics or not, assume that government "should do what the people want"—that is, government should be responsive. However, an apparent tendency in American public opinion—exacerbated by the Watergate scandal—is a growing feeling of inability to influence the content of governmental policy. A study commissioned by the U.S. Senate Committee on Government Operations to measure "public perception of the responsiveness of government at the federal, state and local levels and to explore ways to increase the responsiveness and efficiency of government at all levels" found that a majority of the adult public felt "profoundly impotent to influence the actions of their leaders."[1] Presumably, as such comments imply, it is "bad" for elites to be unrestrained by the expectations of masses.

1

Leaving aside for the moment whether, as implied in the instructions of the committee, responsiveness and efficiency are equally possible in the same governmental unit, let us recall some of the more revealing testimony surrounding Watergate. One of Richard Nixon's most deeply felt frustrations was his belief that federal bureaucracy was not under direct presidential control. As is now well known, one target of his anxiety was the Internal Revenue Service. The White House sought, with varying degrees of success, to harass enemies by persuading the IRS to audit their taxes. When he learned of the agency's reluctance to be used for political purposes, John Dean lamented in a memo to Nixon, that the Internal Revenue Service was "unresponsive and insensitive."

Although both the Senate Committee on Government Operations and John Dean seemed to be concerned about responsiveness, it certainly is a fair guess that they had different definitions of responsiveness in mind. On the other hand, both seemed concerned about a common problem: lack of influence. Looking closer at the problem, Dean's lament may be less outrageous than it seems at first glance. He served as the representative of a president elected by a landslide. Nixon apparently felt his election provided more of a mandate than it actually did, but clearly, Dean's anger was based on the assumption that nonelected government agencies should be held accountable—that is, responsive—to elected officials who spoke for "the people." Thus, both Dean and the Senate Committee on Government Operations believed that responsive government required a linkage between "the people" and their elected representatives.

Public officials are not alone in their confusion about the conditions of responsive government. Scholars are equally perplexed. Virtually no one argues that governments should not be responsive. As the authors of a recent study of city councils put it, "in a democracy, the degree to which the governors are responsive to the preferences of the governed is the *sine qua non* of whether democracy in fact exists."[2] Similarly, Sidney Verba and Norman Nie argue that "responsiveness is what democracy is supposed to be about. . . ."[3]

MODELS OF RESPONSIVE GOVERNMENT

BEYOND AGREEMENT on responsiveness as the key to democracy, however, there is no clear agreement about how one decides whether a government is in fact responsive. There are two schools of thought on this matter: the "representational" school and the "congruence" school.

The representational school argues that responsiveness is a relationship between leaders and led. In this relationship the people make demands—that is, they actively communicate their expectations to decision-makers. Decision-makers, in response, attempt to satisfy demands. Decision-makers—if they are responsive—hear what is being said, develop a series of alternative means of satisfying demands, mediate conflicting demands, and ultimately reach a decision that is formulated in response to the most dominant set of demands. The key concept here is activity; both making demands and responding to demands are required.

Thus, according to the representational concept, decision-makers are unresponsive if they do not comply with—or at least consider—preferences expressed to them directly by their constituents. In a superb description of such nonresponsive city councils, Eulau and Prewitt write: "These councils appear to be altogether immune to pressures emanating from the public; no identifiable public voices, whether sporadically or permanently organized, intrude into their deliberations. These councils may or may not be acting in the interests of the represented, but they are clearly not acting in response to the represented."[4] Such councils are deemed nonresponsive because they ignore constituent demands. Obviously, constituent demands are a necessary element of representational responsiveness. Without demands there can be no response. According to the representational school, decision-makers, regardless of their desires, cannot be responsive until they are presented with constituent demands.

The representational school assumes the existence of demands that are communicated from constituents to governments. This requirement is rather strict and is frequently not met in the real political world. The congruence school of thought proceeds from less severe requirements. The congruence model of responsiveness assumes merely that constituents hold general political attitudes and expectations. Responsiveness exists when the policy actions of a government reflects the attitudes and expectations of its citizens. Responsiveness under the congruence model may be a result of shared attitudes between rulers and ruled; for example: "We judge a legislature to be more representative of [read responsive to] its citizens if the opinions of the representatives on a broad spectrum of relevant issues closely parallel those of the citizens on the same issues."[5]

Of course, it is also possible that representatives will, on occasion, act according to what they perceive to be the wishes of citizens, even though they personally do not agree. Such actions would have the same effect as actually sharing values. In either case, however, leaders must accurately perceive citizen expectations, must either agree or suspend personal judgment, and, by implication, must become active in implementing citizen preferences.

All these acts might be undertaken without any of the various forms of political communication so vital to the representational model. City councils, for example, might be quite free of demands from interest groups, informal organizations, or interested individuals. Unresponsive in the first sense (that is, not responding to communications), they could be quite responsive in the second sense (that is, the actions they undertake are compatible with the expectations of constituents). Indeed, one could argue that precisely because they are so responsive, in the sense of accurately perceiving the priorities of citizens, there is no need for the communication so crucial to the representational model.

There is a third notion of responsiveness that we will not consider in this text: a government is responsive to the extent that it detects and responds to problems and needs whether or not those problems and needs are perceived by citizens. The representational and congruence models both posit responsiveness as a relationship between citizens and government. This third school posits responsiveness as a relationship between government perceptions and government response to those perceptions. There is no necessary relationship between rulers and ruled in this third model. Whatever the merits of this model of responsiveness, it is clearly irrelevant to a discussion of democratic governance.

Both the representational and congruence models will be subjected to empirical examination in this book. For the moment, let us consider some questions which each model raises, regardless of the empirical accuracy of each.

The Representational Model

The first issue the representational model raises is that it is biased appreciably in favor of active participants. That is to say, responsive government is defined solely on the basis of its receptivity to active communications. How well do the active participants reflect latent public opinion or even opinion within the strata for which they speak? Consider, for example, the typical city council or state legislature. Suppose we find, in each case, that certain types of interest groups, such as business and professional groups, are substantially more vocal than civil rights and minority groups. Even if we found such a city council or state legislature responsive (in that it heeded the views of such active groups), would we be satisfied? According to the representational model, our satisfaction is automatic, because activity—the expression of political expectation—is the sole input into the decision-making system. To take another example, how would we judge a state legislature in which— because of the concentrated economy of the state—a single interest group dominates communication?

Examples of single-interest domination occur most frequently in the histories of company towns, but can also be found at the state level. In Montana, for instance, the Anaconda Company once achieved a near monopoly of political resources. "Its strength rests not only in its wealth and resources, but also in its elaborate network of relationships with key citizens, banks, legal firms, and business organizations throughout the state. Rare is that unit of local government—county, city, or school district—that does not have among its official family an associate, in some capacity, of the Anaconda Company."[6] Of alleged equal dominance in other states are oil in Texas and Louisiana and the Du Pont Company in Delaware.

In such cases, even if the decision-making body is responsive to (or dominated by) a single dominant interest, it is certainly not responsive to any recognizable diversity in the petitioning process. It is responsive only to the active vocal *minority*. We will demonstrate that the entire process of communicating with government is largely a middle- to upper-class act. Thus, the representational model is a model of response to a limited, unrepresentative sample of the broader spectrum of community priorities. As one city council member puts it: "Most of the time we bow to the wishes of the people, not necessarily the majority of the citizens, but the majority of the people who are interested."[7] This majority is in fact a small minority.

Most people not only do not communicate with state and local government officials, but have only the vaguest understanding of (or interest in) what is going on. In one of the most intriguing findings of the Eulau–Prewitt study of city councils, there was a pronounced tendency for "responsive" councils to believe that they often took stands counter to majority preferences. Thus, those councils who engaged in regular communication with formal organizations, or those who interacted even with hastily formed and quickly disbanded groups, recognized the minority origin of these communications. Somewhere "out there" was a majority in whose interests the "responsive councils" did not presume to speak. In contrast, the "unresponsive" councils—those who deliberations occurred in isolation from interest groups—believed that they seldom took stands in opposition to the wishes of the majority. Thus, the unresponsive councils were those with decidedly majoritarian self-images!

A basic problem of the representational model of responsiveness is ascertaining the generalizability of expressed demands. Should one assume that the active minority represents the varied interests of the general public? Clearly not. Does one follow editorial opinion, letters to the editor, and so forth? Perhaps, but it is quite likely that in neither case will one achieve a body of demands from the general population, nor will letters from constituents provide a more reliable sample of demands. Those who initiate communication are disproportionately more educated and affluent than those who do not.

Two striking illustrations of the distorted quality of legislative mail can be cited. In both instances a comparison of the opinions of those who claimed to have written public officials (about 15 percent) with a sample of the general population revealed noticeable differences. In the first illustration, if "letter opinion" is perceived as public opinion, Senator Goldwater held an appreciable lead midway through the 1964 campaign. Goldwater's apparent belief that there were hidden conservatives waiting for the chance to vote for him was based on his unjustified confidence in the representativeness of letter writers.[8] In the second illustration, if public officials had relied on their mail to assess opinions about the Vietnam war, they would have concluded that the population was more than one and a half times more "hawkish" than it actually was.

THE ATTENTIVE PUBLIC   Such distortions are probably repeated at the state and local level, particularly because state and local officials seem to place more reliance on mail than their national counterparts. Additionally, state and local officeholders have a greater opportunity for wandering among the grass roots. However, the same problem of biased communications appears during such wandering through the district. Legislators, naturally, will talk to people who know and care about politics, the attentive public.

The attentive public exhibits roughly the same characteristics as political influentials usually do: they are of higher socioeconomic status, not only in comparison to the general public, but also in comparison to the legislators themselves. Further, attentive publics typically have occupied public office, usually at the local level. Thus, their high interest in—and knowledge of—the political process stems not only from their high economic status, but also from their active involvement in governmental affairs.

As linkage mechanisms between the mass public and the legislature, the attentive publics leave much to be desired. They communicate frequently with the political elite—state legislators or local public officials, for example—but they rarely talk with the nonelite—the portion of the public that normally is inattentive to governmental affairs. Though attentive publics perform one-half of the linkage function quite well, that of transmitting expectations to decision-makers, they do not do very well at articulating the desires of the mass public. As Kingdon explains, the mass public is excluded in such a communications system: "Many respondents [to Kingdon's survey], for example, judged voter interest in the campaign by reference to various phenomena at the elite level, such as the number of people who volunteer to campaign. Even when asked directly about them, some politicians treat rank-and-file voters as a comparatively unknown realm and interpret statements concerning them in the light of phenomena closer to themselves: the elite, mass media, party activists."[9] Kingdon later describes the process of "mingling among the people" as an "elite cognitive world, largely isolated from rank-and-file voters."[10]

The Congruence Model

The congruence model of responsiveness holds that constituents and governors usually hold common attitudes and expectations. Furthermore, when attitudes are not congruent, governors defer to the wishes of their constituents. For governments to be responsive, they must be able to identify what their citizens desire.

We have seen that both written and oral communication is dominated by elitist or unrepresentative populations. What about the ultimate expression of public opinion: voting? Here the prospects for responsiveness are slightly better. The core of voters is somewhat larger than the articulate public because it takes less effort to vote than to engage in acts of direct communication. However, 80 to 90 percent of the people habitually do not vote in local elections. Only citizens who are intensely committed to the community are likely to vote in local elections. Nonvoters are drawn disproportionately from the poor and uneducated. Although the voting public is larger than the attentive public, it is also an inaccurate representation of the general public.

Other problems prevent elections from serving as gauges of public opinion. Most elections are for personnel, not policy. Those referenda elections that do decide policy attract even fewer participants than elections for personnel. When a voting population elects a representative, or when a serving representative is reelected or defeated, what sort of a policy mandate exists? The message is, at best, ambiguous. For elections to serve as a policy mandate according to the congruence model, several explicit conditions must be satisfied: (1) competing candidates should offer clear policy alternatives; (2) voters must be aware of and concerned about questions of public policy; (3) representatives should be able to ascertain majority policy preferences by examining election results; (4) elected officials should be bound by the position they assumed in the campaign.

In fact, these conditions do not apply to most state and local elections. Candidates, whether competing in partisan or nonpartisan elections, more often than not try to blur differences because they are competing for the votes of the active electorate—votes that tend to be disproportionally drawn from the middle and upper classes. Moreover, even within the active electorate, policy considerations are not the normal mode of choice. The traditional party identification and candidate image are far more important.

Given these conditions, it is quite risky to infer a policy mandate from the election of a particular candidate, even if differing policy perspectives are articulated during the campaign. Of course, the inferential leap from the position of an elected official to an electorate position is exactly the sort of inference that everyone, especially journalists, make. Candidate A, let us say, is strongly opposed to capital punishment. He wins, and therefore, it is inferred that the electorate is equally opposed. However, such a deceptively easy inference is misleading.

A study of the 1962 Wisconsin gubernatorial campaign illustrates the danger of inferring electorate preferences from elite behavior. In this case, tax policy dominated the campaigns of both candidates. The question was whether to increase the income tax, the incumbent Democrat's position, or to extend the sales tax, the Republican position. Each position attracted committed supporters. The Democratic candidate won. Could he thus conclude that a mandate to raise the income tax was provided? He should not, not only because a substantial number of voters failed to become aware of his position, but because his majority included many people who disagreed with his policy as well as many who voted for him for reasons unrelated to the tax issue. Although the election centered upon a single issue, its results did not reflect a wish by the majority to increase the income tax.[11]

Of course, the problem is complicated further when a single issue does not command the attention of both candidates. Even assuming that most voters were aware of the various positions taken and made their choice according to issue preference (which is not the case), how would the successful candidate decide whether voters supported each position, or whether some issues were more salient to voters than others? Without very sophisticated opinion polling techniques, successful candidates are free to provide whatever interpretation to electoral success they choose. As Flanigan notes: "It is perfectly appropriate to attribute policy significance to an election on the basis of the policy preferences of the winning candidate, as long as it is not implied that the voters had these policy implications in mind when they voted."[12] Indeed, this sort of inference is fairly common among politicians, especially successful ones who obviously wish to attribute their victory to the good sense of the electorate. According to Kingdon, "the winners tend to believe more than the losers that the voters in their district decided how to cast their ballots not by blind party voting, but according to the issues of the election and the man who was seeking the office."[13]

The development of sophisticated polling techniques presents another source of information to the decision-maker who wants to be responsive according to the congruence model. Certainly the use of polls is increasing, more at the national than subnational level, but even in some states and communities there is a thriving business in polling. On the face of it, public opinion polling might solve some of the dilemmas we have encountered so far. Unlike any other form of public expression, polls can be representative—that is, it is possible to create a microcosmic public. If a few people who accurately reflect the beliefs of the larger public can be selected, then the description of what they are thinking is reasonably accurate. Once the distribution of opinion is ascertained, the responsive public official need only do what the people want.

Unfortunately, even with reliable sampling techniques, the problems are considerable. There is, of course, the problem of cost. Though statewide candidates, such as those for governor, can afford polls, candidates for lesser offices frequently cannot. Thus, the wealthier candidates obtain more than their usual advantage. Additionally, polls are rarely used between campaign periods. In the interim period when policy choices are being made, polls (except those regularly conducted at the national level and in a smattering of states) are unavailable.

THE AGENDA   But such practical considerations beg the question. What if state and local governments made regular, systematic use of the polls? An initial and major problem is setting the agenda: who decides what the issues are? It is entirely probable that the issues that absorb the attention of elites are far removed from the daily concerns of the common person. Setting the agenda is more than a problem of response, it is also a problem of *power*. As Schattschneider explains: "political conflict is not like an intercollegiate debate in which the opponents agree in advance on a definition of the issues. As a matter of fact, *the definition of the alternatives is the supreme instrument of power. . . .* He who determines what politics is about runs the country, because the definition of alternatives is the choice of conflicts, and the choice of conflicts allocates power."[14]

Because public officials communicate mainly with articulate minorities, the agenda they develop will differ from an agenda prepared by the masses. Such articulate minorities are generally more "public-regarding"—that is, they adopt a substantially more community-oriented view of society. As active participants in the governing process, they view the goals of the policy in a more long-term fashion than do the masses. By the very nature of their existence they are "out of touch" with the masses. Because they think a good deal about governmental problems, the decision-makers and their attentive publics have no trouble in listing priorities and developing alternatives.

For the general public, the list is not so simple. In fact, it is by no means certain whether or not substantial portions of the public actively hold an opinion until the issue is raised by elites; it is equally uncertain to what extent their opinions about alternatives, as well as the issues to be debated, are developed by the actions of elites.

We really cannot be certain whether public opinion influences public policy, or whether public policy influences public opinion. We are speaking not only of conscious governmental attempts to influence public opinion, but also of the act of debating policy alternatives. Such debates may create opinion where none existed before. As Key explained: "One can never be certain of the extent to which the parallelism of governmental action and public preference results from governmental influence on opinion and to what extent it results from the adjustment of public policy to bring it into accord with public opinion."[15]

THE INSTABILITY OF ATTITUDES   If opinion flows from elite to masses, then other characteristics of mass opinion become understandable, even while they cloud the issue of responsive government. If many respondents really have no opinion until someone asks, it is likely that their opinions will be unstable. A rather large portion of the public provides what Erikson and Luttbeg call "doorstep" answers to questions in opinion polls.[16] Rather than appearing uninformed, they provide some sort of answer, even if the opinion they hold is weak or actually nonexistent. Such spontaneous responses result in high degrees of instability of opinion. A person will provide an answer, but when asked the same question at a later date, may fail to recall the earlier response and provide the opposite answer. One might argue that such instability is, in reality, a change of mind. However, most of the opinion changes appear to be random. One study estimates that less than 20 percent of the public hold meaningful opinions on a given issue, even though two-thirds offered an opinion when asked in a survey.[17]

Not only do "opinions" among the less interested vary randomly, they are also subject to variation in accordance with the wording of questions. On questions of public policy, "the wording of the question can often determine the apparent majority position on the issue."[18] Again, apparent rapid changes in public opinion may result from the wording of the question interacting with a weakly held attitude. For instance, people without definite opinions are likely to agree with statements more often than not, no matter what the content of the statement. This tendency to agree can produce contradictory "majorities" on the same issue. Erickson and Luttbeg provide an example:

> For instance, compare the response of two rather opposite statements about academic freedom that were presented to respondents in a 1968 California poll. When asked whether they agreed or disagreed with the statement, "professors in state supported institutions should have freedom to speak and teach the truth as they see it," Californians appeared to support academic freedom by a ratio of 52 to 39. But when opinions were sought on the statement, "professors who advocate controversial ideas or speak out against official policy have no place in a state supported college or university," the same ratio of 52 to 39 was found, but this time the majority was on the side favoring restrictions on academic freedom.[19]

The difficulties of surveys should not suggest that they are worthless, but merely flawed, in some cases, seriously. Unlike other forms of communication (such as from interest groups and articulate publics), they are representative. However, the fact that the information was sought rather than volunteered exposes surveys to the problems outlined above.

CAN REPRESENTATIVES REPRESENT?

WE HAVE examined two general models of responsive government: representational and congruence. The difficulties of each bring us to a question, the answer to which is by no means apparent: can representatives represent? That is, can they either respond to a sufficiently diverse set of demands or act on an accurate perception of constituent attitudes and expectations? If we start with the assumption that the need for representation arises because a relatively large number of people cannot participate directly in governance, then the question becomes: can a small group make the choices that the large group would make if it could?[20] Everything we have said so far indicates that such representation is impossible.

Theories of representation generally revolve around the dilemma, first articulated in the eighteenth century by Edmund Burke, as to whether a representative ought to act in strict accordance with his constituents' wishes (a delegate) or in obedience to his "unbiased opinions, his mature judgment, his enlightened conscience" (a trustee). The dilemma is, of course, false. The delegate style of representation is clearly impossible. There is no mandate to follow. Whatever the representative thinks he is doing, the linkages with constituents are simply not adequate: "Despite all the oratory of the politicians, they cannot possibly be responsive, in the traditional sense, to individual constituents whose numbers are in the hundreds of thousands or millions, whose interests are enormously diverse, and whose understanding of the complexities of public policy is minimal."[21]

For a government to be responsive, then, there must be a reasonable amount of linkage between (1) mass opinion, (2) elite articulation, and (3) governmental response. Though there may be agreement between 2 and 3, evidence suggests there is little agreement between 1 and 2 or 1 and 3. If for no other reason, the substantially higher socioeconomic status of those who occupy positions 2 and 3 makes them remote from 1.[22]

Representatives at the state and local level of government—legislators, city councilmen, school board members, and the like—appear to have adopted a role orientation suitable for behavior in a system without clear mandates. We distinguish between two approaches to the job of representation: the trustee, who sees himself as unconstrained by constituency opinion, and follows his own personal judgment, and the delegate, who feels he should follow the wishes of his constituents even when he does not agree with them.

Most representatives feel more comfortable with the trustee role. In fact, the smaller the government unit, the more dominant becomes the trustee role. Though subject to considerable variation, local officials seem somewhat more paternalistic than do their colleagues at the state level. In both cases, however, the dilemma of representation—what does one do when one's conscience and one's constituents differ—is easily resolved: when a difference occurs, the public should be ignored. Moreover, in at least one case, the minority of legislators who described themselves as delegates were noticeably more inaccurate than the self-described trustees in predicting constituent preferences.[23] Although public officials are quite confident that they can ascertain majority opinion, they are frequently wrong. Thus we have a majority of officeholders—trustees—willing to ignore a public mandate and a minority—delegates—wishing to follow a mandate, but being unable to define that mandate accurately: "Thus the hope and assumption of representative democratic theory that legislative institutions provide an adequate means to insure legislative responsiveness to public opinion—the minimal condition for representative democracy—does not appear to be met."[24]

PUBLIC OPINION AND PUBLIC POLICY

THERE IS, of course, the additional question of policy. No matter what representatives think and say they do, if their actual policy decisions are congruent with what the majority wants, then the content of policy could be considered responsive, regardless of the process by which the policy was created. Suppose, for instance, that representatives thought and acted as though they were unconstrained by popular mandate but reached decisions that were actually in accord with the majority. There is very little direct evidence that such accidental congruence occurs very often.

At the national level, the relation between a congressman's vote and his constituency's opinion is very low, except for the extremely salient issue of civil rights.[25] We can assume that the same rule applies at the subnational level of governance: on most issues, there will be little if any relation between mass opinion and the content of policy; on the occasional highly emotional issue, congruence will improve.

By estimating the opinion in each state, it is possible to provide an educated guess as to how often policy follows mass preferences. Ronald E. Weber and William Shaffer have provided a fifty-state estimate of public opinion on five areas of policy: (1) discrimination in public accommodations, (2) aid to parochial schools, (3) right-to-work laws, (4) teacher unionization laws, and (5) firearms control laws. By matching the actual legislation on these policies with what the public wanted, the authors found no appreciable congruence between policy and opinion in four out of five policy areas. Discrimination in public accommodations provides the exception, as did the civil rights issue in Congress.[26]

Frank Munger, using the same techniques of estimation, concludes that the probability of a state's policy matching the preferences of its citizens is only slightly better than the fifty-fifty ratio generated purely by chance.[27] Public opinion does not appear to make any difference in public policy except when the issues are extremely emotional. At other times, elites are free to do what they wish.

The threat of electoral reprisal is minimal; incumbents are routinely returned if they wish to be. The low salience of politics for the masses guarantees that elections largely legitimate decisions, not punish unresponsive legislators. Unless misrepresentation is very serious (for example, on civil rights), the public is disinclined to punish anyone.

A governing system, then, is one of intraelite communication. It is in this communication that one can find some understanding of the problem of responsiveness. As V. O. Key says, "The longer one frets with the puzzle of how democratic regimes manage to function, the more plausible it appears that a substantial part of the explanation is to be found in the motives that actuate the leadership echelon. . . ."[28] The question, then, is not whether decision-makers are, or can be, responsive; the question is to which articulate minorities do they respond?

THE
ORGANIZATION
OF THIS BOOK

DESPITE ITS prominence as both an analytical concept and popular slogan, surprisingly little systematic assessment of the responsiveness of state and local government has been undertaken in textbooks. Our notion of responsiveness refers to a relationship between the rulers and the ruled, defined in terms of government response to articulated preferences (demands) or unarticulated preferences (attitudes and expectations) of its citizens.

Chapter 2 discusses how citizens participate in state and local politics. Our focus will be on the linkage, or the lack of linkage, between the few who govern and the many who do not. We begin with a description of how people view state and community governments. It is a commonplace observation that state and local governments perform different functions. It is less widely noted that there are important differences in citizen perceptions, participation, and confidence among the three levels of government. Polls show that although Americans see federal government as the most appropriate level to solve major contemporary problems, they have more confidence in the integrity of state and local governments.

This paradox is reflected in patterns of participation. Although individuals and groups are more likely to exercise influence at the state and local levels, citizen participation—in terms of voting—is greatest at the federal level. Indeed, the farther one gets from the grass roots, the greater the participation of the masses. This seeming contradiction is explained by the consequences of the reform movement of the early twentieth century on state and local politics and government.

Chapter 2 will also discuss how well-intentioned reformers actually increased the insulation of state and local governments from their constituents. Just as participation varies by level of government, it also varies according to whether individuals or groups are involved, which individuals or groups are involved, and the subject matter at issue. We discuss in chapter 2 identifiable patterns of group activity at the local level. Of course, participation does not guarantee success. Local governments, for example, tend to be more responsive to business interests than to labor and minority groups. Chapter 2 concludes with an example of this selective responsiveness. Racial minorities have experienced continuous frustration in their attempts to compete with established interests at the local level. Unless they can build successful coalitions with other urban interests, the balance of power will not shift in their favor.

Chapter 3 continues our examination of sustained group activity. The chapter focuses exclusively on interest groups in state politics. Not only is there more group activity at the state level, but group activity is a prerequisite for influence in state politics. The actions of state governments have wider impact than those of local governments. The higher stakes of state politics stimulates the formation of interest groups to compete for benefits distributed by state governments. Organized group activity is a virtual necessity to gain access to state government officials. More so than local governments, state governments are highly bureaucratized; the decision-making process is continuous. Thus, the sustained communications necessary for achieving the desired impact on policy can only be supported by organized group activity.

We consider five patterns of interest group behavior in chapter 3. Although there are differences in the distribution of influence across states, once again we find greater responsiveness to business and professional interests than to other organized groups. Of course, conflict exists among business and professional groups, as well as between such groups and labor, environmental, educational, and other interests. As a result, state capitals are populated by professional lobbyists who work full time at the job of influencing state policy. There is no comparable institutionalization of lobbying in local politics. Chapter 3 discusses lobbying as the dominant mode of communication between organizational elites and legally constituted decision-makers in state government.

Chapter 4 examines the process of decision-making in state and local governments. A six-step model is developed that describes the normal pattern of policy-making at all levels of government. At each step there are different potential governmental and nongovernmental actors. The themes of a cycle of constituent demands and government responses and of a struggle for authority between representatives and experts are developed further in chapter 4. Contrasting degrees of insularity of decision-making and in different levels of government are discussed.

We conclude that there are opportunities for public input, but internal communications are more important than external communications for a number of reasons. As a result, state and local governments tend to be responsive to internal elites, especially professional administrators in executive departments.

Chapter 5 considers the decision-making process in the substantive area of educational policy. We focus on school government because its policy is made by a variety of participants at all levels of government. Indeed, perhaps the most important question for the politics of educational governance in the 1970s is how influence should be distributed among the three levels of government. Should local schools be run in accordance with the preferences of the local communities they serve, or should they be responsive to norms established by state or federal government?

Chapter 5 begins with a discussion of the various levels, actors, and issue areas relevant to educational policy. The current conflict between professional experts and lay people for influence is developed through an investigation of the background and recruitment of school district officials. The six-step model of decision-making of chapter 4 is applied to the policy-making process in school districts. We find that educational governance is quite insulated from constituents at the local level. School districts are responsive primarily to their own professional experts and secondarily to educational professionals at other levels of government.

Educational governance has not always been dominated by experts. The history of educational governance can be characterized as a struggle between lay people and professionals. Chapter 5 concludes with an analysis of how the focus of response of local school boards has shifted from constituents to experts.

Chapter 6 considers our central theme, responsiveness of state and local governments to their citizens, in the broadest context. Generally, state and local governments are not responsive to the preferences of the masses they nominally serve. Chapter 6 discusses barriers to responsiveness in two categories: noninstitutional and institutional. Noninstitutional barriers make responsiveness difficult no matter how strongly governing elites desire to do what the people want. Barriers such as complexity, uncertainty, organizational behavior, heterogeneity of preference, and public apathy exist in all forms of state and local government. There are also barriers to responsiveness in the common institutions of state and local government. These institutions have been evolving, but that evolution has not always enhanced responsiveness to constituents.

Ironically, some procedures designed to increase responsiveness have had the opposite effect. Textbook discussions of American federalism commonly point out that multiple units and levels of government promote responsiveness by allowing governments to pursue different policies according to different needs. These discussions typically neglect the impact of intergovernmental relations on the ability of each unit to act independently. Our interpretation is that intergovernmental relations actually exacerbate noninstitutional and institutional barriers and also create unique barriers to responsiveness.

Chapter 7 concludes this book with a consideration of three interrelated questions: First, how responsive are state and local governments and how responsive should they be? And what structural and political changes would be necessary if the responsiveness of governments to their constituents were to be maximized? Second, are such changes worth it in terms of costs and benefits? Would governments acting in accordance with mass preferences reach policy decisions substantially unlike the ones they now reach? Third, have political decisions become so technically complex, demands so polarized, and solutions so fragile that the concept of responsive government is obsolete? Do we need a new perspective on the classic political question—who should make, at what levels of government, what kinds of decisions, for how large a social unit?

NOTES

1.

This study was conducted by Louis Harris and Associates, Inc. It is found in *Confidence and Concern: Citizens View American Government, A Survey of Public Attitudes* by The Subcommittee on Intergovernmental Relations of The Committee on Government Operations, United States Senate, 93d Congress, 1st session (Washington, D.C.: U.S. Government Printing Office, 1973).

2.

Heinz Eulau and Kenneth Prewitt, *Labyrinths of Democracy: Adaptations, Linkages, Representation and Policies in Urban Politics* (Indianapolis: Bobbs-Merrill, 1973), p. 24.

3.

Sidney Verba and Norman H. Nie, *Participation in America: Political Democracy and Social Equality* (New York: Harper & Row, 1972), p. 300.

4.

Eulau and Prewitt, *Labyrinths of Democracy,* pp. 426–27.

5.

Norman R. Luttbeg and Richard W. Griffin, "Public Reactions to Misrepresentation: The Case of Educational Politics," in Norman R. Luttbeg (ed.), *Public Opinion and Public Policy: Models of Political Linkage* (Homewood, Ill.: Dorsey, 1974), p. 440.

6.

Thomas Payne, "Under the Copper Dome: Politics in Montana," in Frank H. Jonas (ed.), *Western Politics* (Salt Lake City: University of Utah Press, 1961), pp. 197–98.

7.

Eulau and Prewitt, *Labyrinths of Democracy,* p. 427.

8.

See, for example, Philip E. Converse, Aage R. Clausen, and Warren E. Miller, "Electoral Myth and Reality: The 1964 Election," *The American Political Science Review* 59 (June 1965): 332–35.

9.

John W. Kingdon, *Candidates for Office: Beliefs and Strategies* (New York: Random House, 1968), p. 31.

10.

Ibid.

11.

For a further discussion of the 1962 Wisconsin gubernatorial campaign see Leon D. Epstein, "Electoral Decisions and Policy Mandate: An Empirical Example," *The Public Opinion Quarterly* 28 (Winter 1964): 564–72.

12.

William H. Flanigan, *Political Behavior of the American Electorate* (Boston: Allyn and Bacon, 1968), p. 115.

13.

John W. Kingdon, "Politicians' Beliefs About Voters," *The American Political Science Review* 61 (March 1967): 139–40.

14.

E. E. Schattschneider, *The Semi-Sovereign People: A Realist's View of Democracy in America* (New York: Holt, Rinehart and Winston, 1960), p. 68.

15.

V. O. Key, Jr., *Public Opinion and American Democracy* (New York: Knopf, 1961), p. 423.

16.

For a discussion of "doorstep answers" see Robert S. Erikson and Norman R. Luttbeg, *American Public Opinion: Its Origins, Content and Impact* (New York: Wiley, 1973), pp. 35–40.

17.

Philip E. Converse, "Attitudes and Non-Attitudes: Continuation of a Dialogue," in Edward R. Tufte (ed.), *The Quantitative Analysis of Social Problems* (Reading, Mass.: Addison-Wesley, 1970), pp. 168–89.

18.

Erikson and Luttbeg, *American Public Opinion,* p. 35.

19.

Ibid., p. 38.

20.

Hannah Pitkin, *The Concept of Representation* (Berkeley: University of California Press, 1967), p. 209.

21.

Heinz Eulau, *Micro-Macro Political Analysis: Accents of Inquiry* (Chicago: Aldine, 1969), p. 99.

22.

This formulation draws upon Ronald D. Hedlund and H. Paul Friesema, "Representatives' Perceptions of Constituency Opinion," *The Journal of Politics* 34 (August 1972): 730–52.

23.

Ibid., pp. 741–52.

24.

Ibid., p. 750.

25.

For a discussion of the relation between a congressman's vote and his constituency's opinion see Warren E. Miller and Donald E. Stokes, "Constituency Influence in Congress," *The American Political Science Review* 57 (March 1963): 45–56.

26.

Ronald E. Weber and William R. Shaffer, "Public Opinion and American State Policy-Making," *The Midwest Journal of Political Science* 16 (November 1972): 683–99.

27.

Frank Munger, "Opinions, Elections, Parties, and Policies: A Cross-State Analysis" (Paper presented to the 1969 meeting of the American Political Science Association, New York).

28.

Key, *Public Opinion and American Democracy,* p. 537.

2

PARTICIPATION
IN STATE
AND LOCAL POLITICS

WE BEGIN our consideration of the responsiveness of state and local governments to their citizens by examining the processes through which demands, attitudes, and expectations are communicated. Political participation is the means by which the demands assumed by the representational model of responsiveness are transmitted to government officials. Additionally, decision-makers can and do make inferences about broader public opinion from participation according to the congruence model of responsiveness. Our discussion starts with the most basic of political activities, voting, and proceeds to more complex and sustained activities. For each type of participation we will focus on three concerns: descriptions of the overall level of participation, explanation of various factors that stimulate and inhibit participation, and consideration of the impact of participation on responsiveness.

PATTERNS
OF CONFIDENCE
AND CONCERN
IN GOVERNMENT

IN ADDITION to one national government and fifty state governments, there were about 78,000 local governments (65,000 with taxing power) operating in 1972.[1] Such units are quite stable, with the conspicuous exceptions of school districts, whose number has been reduced in the past twenty years by approximately 85 percent.

Do we really need so many governments? Would we not gain considerably in efficiency if there were a single—central—authority? And what about the burden of red tape to the citizen? The average state contains approximately 1,600 separate local governments. The range is from 19 (Hawaii, which has no local school districts) to 3,819 (California).[2] In some cases (Park Forest, Illinois), the citizen pays taxes to 11 governments. More typically, the average citizen is governed by about 4 local governments, exclusive of any state and national ones.

Does the existence of multiple levels of government mean a total separation of function by level of government? A casual examination of the layered nature of American federalism might lead one to assume that policy responsibilities are neatly categorized according to level of government. Such is not the case. Rather, to a greater or lesser degree, each level of government is involved in virtually all policy areas. Obviously, a federal government is more concerned with national defense than garbage collection, but the relative concentration of resources is one of degree. For example, although tax-supported public education is widely regarded as a responsibility of local school districts, the role of both states and the federal government is increasing. Thus, in 1960, 3 percent of the financial burden of education was borne by the federal government; by 1972, the percentage had increased to 9.[3]

To a considerable degree, the public's expectations of government reflect the notion of shared responsibilities. In a 1973 study of elite and mass perceptions of the role of the government, the following functions were viewed as appropriate to all levels of government: drug abuse, air and water pollution, welfare operations, racial demonstrations and racial integration in education, and the provision of low-cost housing (table 2.1).

Table 2.1.   Government Level That Can Best Handle Specific Problems (in percentages)

	Public					Leaders				
	Federal	State	Local	None	Not sure	Federal	State	Local	None	Not sure
World peace	93	4	4	2	2	X	X	X	X	X
Inflation	89	8	4	1	4	X	X	X	X	X
Income taxes	86	24	6	1	2	87	49	16	*	3
Fair taxes for everyone	77	33	20	1	5	72	62	48	2	3
Consumer protests against high prices	64	20	16	3	9	71	18	13	11	5
Low-cost housing	57	35	14	2	5	61	30	32	2	4
Corrupt politician removal	55	32	30	9	14	59	53	54	9	8
Drug abuse	55	43	38	1	3	49	58	66	*	2
Air and water pollution control	54	41	24	1	5	61	62	30	—	—
Gun control	53	28	17	7	6	58	30	25	12	3
Adequate health services	52	38	18	3	6	X	X	X	X	X
Racial integration in education	39	36	32	3	8	41	42	56	4	2
Welfare payments	39	48	26	3	4	51	56	35	1	1
Integrated housing	38	35	31	4	8	X	X	X	X	X
Racial demonstrations	37	34	36	3	10	29	28	71	2	4
Middle-income housing	35	45	20	4	9	48	34	31	12	4
College improvements	29	67	8	2	7	X	X	X	X	X
Highway building	22	85	6	*	2	50	86	15	1	*
Public school improvements	14	50	51	1	3	21	69	58	—	*
Big rock concerts	9	32	53	4	11	5	31	78	3	5
Zoning for housing	8	25	68	1	6	X	X	X	X	X
Traffic congestion	5	37	69	1	3	15	46	85	*	*
Accidents on highways	4	82	18	1	1	11	77	46	—	1
Police protection	3	15	91	*	1	7	23	94	—	1
Garbage collection	*	3	95	1	1	X	X	X	X	X
Street cleaning	*	5	95	*	*	X	X	X	X	X
Street crime	X	X	X	X	X	35	43	87	—	1

Source: *Confidence and Concern: Citizens View American Government, A Survey of Public Attitudes* by the Subcommittee on Intergovernmental Relations of the Committee on Government Operations, United States Senate, 93d Cong., 1st sess., 1973, p. 124.

* Issue areas where both officials and the public endorse the concept of shared governmental responsibility.
— No responses.
X No data on this issue.

On the other hand, there is little doubt—even when there is sentiment for sharing functions—that the federal government is viewed as the more appropriate problem solver by the public. As table 2.1 indicates, of 26 possible functions, the federal government was assigned major responsibility in 14, state government 5, and local government 7. The federal government led by substantial margins in achieving peace, inflation, income taxes, making taxes fair, handling consumer products, providing low-cost housing, getting rid of corrupt politicians, gun control, and providing adequate health services. State government is viewed as being largely responsible for highways and higher education; local government is seen as responsible for police protection, zoning, garbage collection, and public education.

It seems fairly clear that the problems which Americans regard as most urgent are viewed as the appropriate domain of the federal government. There is very little, if anything, that state and local governments can do about inflation or world peace. Such a growing reliance on the federal government is probably reflective of increased complexity in public policy, and perhaps even a developing inability of units as large as nations to offer workable solutions. Perhaps there are no solutions. At any rate, Americans—even as they lose confidence in all levels of government—find state and local government the least relevant levels. A survey published in the 1960s indicated that people who believed that local government had some or a great effect on their lives exceeded those who thought the federal government did so.[4] Although more people thought the federal government had a great effect, more also thought local government had some effect. By the 1970s, there was little doubt that public perception of the influence of state and local governments had receded considerably. Although the phrasing of the question is somewhat different, 63 percent felt the federal government had a great

Table 2.2.   How Government Affects People's Lives (in percentages)

	Federal	State	Local
A great deal	63	39	38
Only somewhat	21	38	33
Hardly at all	13	19	26
Not sure	3	4	3

Source: *Confidence and Concern: Citizens View American Government, A Survey of Public Attitudes* by the Subcommittee on Intergovernmental Relations of the Committee on Government Operations, United States Senate, 93d Cong., 1st sess., 1973, p. 104.

deal of effect on their personal lives compared to vastly fewer who felt the same about state and local government (table 2.2).

However, as the perceived impact of federal government has increased at the expense of subnational governments, confidence in the federal government has receded at a rate more radical than has confidence in state and local government. Indeed, a majority hold state and local government in the same esteem that they did five years ago, while an equally high majority have less confidence in the federal government (table 2.3). Thus, the level of government viewed as least able to cope with pressing problems is viewed with more confidence. Further, substantial numbers, even while looking to the federal government to solve their problems, want to reduce the power of the federal government and strengthen the power of state and local government.

Table 2.3.   Confidence in Local, State, and Federal Government Today Compared to Five Years Ago (in percentages)

	More confidence	Less confidence	About the same	Not sure
Local government				
Total public	13	30	50	7
State officials	25	6	69	—
Local officials	48	18	34	—
State government				
Total public	14	26	53	7
State officials	61	10	29	—
Local officials	20	36	43	1
Federal government				
Total public	11	57	28	4
State officials	9	61	30	—
Local officials	7	62	28	3

Source: *Confidence and Concern: Citizens View American Government, A Survey of Public Attitudes* by the Subcommittee on Intergovernmental Relations of the Committee on Government Operations, United States Senate, 93d Cong., 1st sess., 1973, pp. 42–3.

Although governmental institutions have been undergoing a crisis in confidence, state and local governments have held up rather well. Even though most people do not think state and local governments can solve their most pressing problems, they still believe, in comparison to the federal government, that such subnational governments have, at least, not made life more difficult for them (table 2.4).

The relative immunity of state and local governments from the crisis

Table 2.4.   Confidence in Federal, State, and Local Government, Compared to Five Years Ago

	More confidence			Less confidence			About the same			Not sure		
	Federal	State	Local	Federal	State	Local	Federal	State	Local	Federal	State	Local
Total	11	14	13	57	26	30	28	53	50	4	7	7
Cities	X	13	12	X	30	37	X	48	45	X	9	6
Suburbs	X	13	16	X	30	29	X	49	46	X	8	9
Towns	X	15	15	X	21	26	X	61	54	X	3	5
Rural	X	14	12	X	21	23	X	60	58	X	5	7
White Protestant	10	15	12	55	23	27	31	56	55	4	6	6
White Catholic	11	14	17	61	27	30	24	53	48	4	6	5
White Jewish	—	9	5	75	34	33	19	46	54	6	11	8
Men	11	16	15	56	27	28	29	51	51	4	6	6
Women	10	11	12	58	26	31	27	55	49	5	8	8
Eighth grade	10	9	9	45	24	34	41	61	52	4	6	5
High school	10	11	13	60	27	32	25	55	49	5	7	6
College	11	19	16	60	26	25	25	48	50	4	7	9
White	10	15	13	59	25	28	27	54	53	4	6	6
Black	12	11	14	52	34	36	27	41	36	9	14	14
Republican	17	14	11	45	23	26	35	58	57	3	5	6
Democrat	8	13	14	64	28	30	24	51	50	4	8	6
Independent	9	15	16	61	28	31	26	50	46	4	7	7
Positive toward:												
Local government	14	18	26	50	20	18	33	56	51	3	6	5
State government	15	26	22	51	16	21	30	52	51	4	6	6
Federal government	24	18	21	40	19	21	33	56	49	3	7	9

Active citizenship	9	16	14	60	25	25	28	53	57	3	6	4
Total leaders	8	30	42	61	40	15	29	39	43	2	1	—
East	13	31	48	60	28	14	25	39	38	2	2	—
Midwest	5	37	38	65	24	14	27	39	48	3	—	—
South	6	28	44	64	28	13	27	44	43	3	—	—
West	9	22	39	53	42	20	36	34	41	2	2	—
Total state officials	9	61	25	61	10	6	30	29	69	—	—	—
Executive	—	74	16	67	5	11	33	21	73	—	—	—
Legislative	12	55	29	59	12	4	29	33	67	—	—	—
Total local officials	7	20	48	62	36	18	28	43	34	3	1	—
County	7	15	46	58	44	28	31	41	26	4	—	—
City	4	15	46	63	34	15	30	50	39	3	1	—
Town/village	13	33	52	63	31	15	22	34	33	2	2	—
Republican	15	33	41	43	26	16	41	41	43	1	—	—
Democrat	4	33	42	75	30	17	18	37	41	3	—	—
Independent	3	15	46	59	37	10	35	43	44	3	5	—

Source: Derived from *Confidence and Concern: Citizen's View American Government, A Survey of Public Attitudes* by the Subcommittee on Intergovernmental Relations of the Committee on Government Operations, United States Senate, 93d Cong., 1st sess., 1973, pp. 217, 219, 221.

— No responses.
X No data.

in confidence can possibly be attributed to the fact that such governments have less immediate perceived impact on the daily lives of citizens. Though this is true, it does not necessarily follow that citizens concern themselves less with the affairs of state and local governments. About as many people pay attention to local affairs as to national affairs. Thirty percent say they follow local affairs more closely than national or international affairs. States, however, rank a poor fourth. However, 50 percent rank state affairs either first or second. Though local government does attract a more intense following, both subnational units compete rather favorably for the attention of the public (table 2.5).

Table 2.5.   Rank-Order Distributions for Salience of Governmental Affairs

Government level	First	Second	Third	Fourth
International	20	16	22	42
National	32	31	26	10
State	17	33	27	22
Local	30	20	25	25

Source: M. Kent Jennings and Harmon Zeigler, "The Salience of American State Politics," *The American Political Science Review* 64 (June 1970): 525.

PARTICIPATION AND LEVEL OF GOVERNMENT

SO FAR, then, at least one justification of federalism seems to make some sense: smaller units of government attract a reasonable amount of attention and a reasonable amount of support in comparison to the federal government. Further, if there is a distinction to be made, the advantage rests with local, as compared to state, government.

Somehow, however, the rationale for small units of government goes astray. Even though participation in all forms of elections has been declining, participation in local elections is very low, averaging between 25 and 50 percent. Participation in state elections (such as for governor)

is slightly higher (between 35 and 50 percent), and participation in presidential elections is higher than either. In other words, the levels of government that attract the greatest level of support and at least a reasonable portion of attention also attract the least participation.

There are a variety of explanations for the confounding fact that the smallest units of government—and those whose level of support remains relatively high—attract the fewest number of participants. On one hand, we might make the obvious inference that greater levels of satisfaction produce less need to participate. That is, if most problems are best seen as handled by the federal government, and if the decline of faith in local government has been less radical, why participate? A nonparticipatory population is a happy population, so runs the argument. On the other hand, the cities and the country were torn asunder in the 1960s by a series of riots that, whatever else they indicated, certainly implied a level of disquiet inconsistent with the "happy nonparticipant" theory. Of course, those who rioted were not those who normally voted. Nevertheless, the belief that people avoid local elections because all is well leaves one with a vague sense of unease.

The Impact of Reform

To get a more definitive grasp of why people avoid voting in local elections, we need to know that local elections differ structurally, in most cases, from state and national elections. The operative word is *reform*. Though waves of reform have occasionally been felt at the state and national level, the reformists have enjoyed their greatest victories in local politics.

In the nineteenth century, government in major urban areas became informally organized by "machines"—for example, such local partisan organizations as the Tammany Hall organization in New York City—which, with varying degrees of success or corruption, managed the affairs of cities. The reform movement, from its beginnings shortly after the Civil War, to its peak in the early years of the twentieth century, was dominated by the middle and upper classes. Indeed, the reform movement originated in partial response to the ethnic strength of urban machines. Although some of the early reformist thinking was linked to the more radical progressive movement in American politics, it gradually evolved so as to serve best the business interests of the community. The political goals of the reform movement were to make local government more responsive to the upper classes. "The reform movement is best understood as itself a political strategy, designed to wrest control from the hands of 'bosses' and 'machines' with lower-class clienteles and to invest power instead in the white, middle class."[5]

The goals of the reform movement—to be described below—are typical of the world view of the middle and upper classes who see "politics as a means of moralizing life and which attach great importance to the individual's obligation to 'serve' the public."[6] The emphasis on service—improving the community—is heavily concentrated in the upper and middle classes, and tends to manifest itself in "apolitical politics." That is, the goal is service for the sake of service, as opposed to service for the achievement of personal political ambitions. A strong sense of identity with the community and a corresponding willingness to commit time and money accompany the reform ethos. Structurally, a sense of identity with the community resulted in an internal system that, in reality, reduced incentives to participate. The essential structural reforms introduced were at-large and nonpartisan elections, referenda, and the separation of local politics from state and national politics by holding elections when no other elections were scheduled.

AT-LARGE ELECTIONS   In at-large elections, as distinguished from ward or district elections, contestants do not represent such metropolitan subunits as neighborhoods, but contest the election with the entire city as the constituency. The reformist theory was that city councilmen or school board members would take a community-wide rather than neighborhood view of problems. Thus neighborhood and hence ethnic bloc voting, which was the strength of political machines, was to be consciously circumvented: "The reformers assumed that there existed an interest ('the public interest') that pertained to the city 'as a whole' and that should always prevail over competing, partial (and usually private) interests."[7]

In our framework of responsiveness, the notion of constituents was given a highly significant interpretation. If there is a larger community, and if the interests of such a community are best reflected by those without links to smaller communities, then the interests and expectations of constituents are best served by the suppression of private needs. The constituent must learn community identification.

As we shall see, such an expectation is unrealistic. In any case, most local officeholders are now elected at large. Two-thirds of the nation's city councils and three-fourths of its school boards have at-large elections. Reliance upon at-large elections varies to some extent with size: larger cities are considerably more likely to provide for wards or districts. However, as table 2.6 indicates, reliance on at-large elections is

Table 2.6.   At-Large Election System for City Council, By City Size

City size (in thousands)	Cities with at-large elections
Over 500	52%
250–500	64
100–250	70
50–100	70
25–50	66
10–25	68
5–10	64

Source: *The Municipal Year Book, 1972* (Washington, D.C.: International City Management Association, 1972), p. 25.

pervasive in all but the very largest of cities, and even in these, the division by type of election is in favor of the at-large variety.

NONPARTISAN BALLOT   Clearly linked to at-large elections is the nonpartisan ballot—that is, elections in which candidates are not identified by party affiliation. The rationale for nonpartisan elections bears close resemblance to the rationale for at-large elections: to create a system in which the performance of public service would be unimpeded by political considerations. Hence, the "best" people would be recruited. Less than one-third of the elections for city council and a comparable number for school boards are partisan. Here again, there is a slight relationship to size of city, with the largest ones being somewhat more partisan (table 2.7). The Northeast, where three-fourths of the cities

Table 2.7.   Nonpartisan Elections by Size of City

City size (in thousands)	Nonpartisan elections
Over 500	79%
250–500	79
100–250	75
50–100	75
25–50	77
10–25	70
5–10	72

Source: *The Municipal Year Book, 1976* (Washington, D.C.: International City Management Association, 1976), p. 69.

have partisan elections is a noteworthy exception to this pattern.

Holding local elections at different times from state and national elections was another key plank in the platform of municipal reform, one closely linked to nonpartisan elections. During the early stages of reform it was said that, in order to be efficient, city government must be emancipated from the tyranny of national and state political parties. Only 14 percent of the nation's cities have failed to follow the advice of this suggestion. In this case, however, the trend holds true for the largest as well as the smallest cities.

In examining these various reforms, two keynotes emerge: reformers wanted efficiency and they wanted, apparently, democracy. They wanted to make local government accessible to the people by eliminating political organizations. Yet in eliminating political organizations, they also destroyed a linkage mechanism between constituents and officeholders. The result is simple and predictable: although interest in local politics is relatively high, voting turnout is appreciably lower than in state and national elections. Further (although data for the effect of ward versus at-large elections is lacking), "reformed" cities have significantly lower rates of turnout than "unreformed" cities. In partisan elections, the average turnout is about 50 percent; in nonpartisan ones, the turnout is about 30 percent. In elections held concurrently with state and national elections, the turnout is again about 50 percent. When local elections are held independently, the turnout drops to about 29 percent.

COUNCIL-MANAGER PLAN   The impact of another reform, the council-manager plan, is illustrative of the degree to which another reform institution depressed participation. Under this scheme, citizens elect a council, but not a mayor. The ceremonial duties commonly assigned to mayors are typically shared by council members. Administrative responsibilities are vested in a professional city manager who is hired by the council. Election turnout is roughly twice as high in cities that do not use this plan. If the aim of the reformers was to democratize local government, they demonstrably failed. Most significantly, from the point of view of responsiveness, the reform movement shifted the focus of the response.

LOWER-CLASS DROPOUT   The urban machine was responsive to ethnic minorities and was sustained, partially, by their participation. Reformed governments respond to, and are sustained by, a smaller core of middle- to upper-class voters, whose participation is enhanced by the structure of local elections. Because middle- and upper-class voters tend to be Republican, and lower-class voters tend to be Democratic, we can draw some inferences about the class biases of local elections. Nonpartisan, at-large elections, and those held at different times from state or national elections, are usually not very interesting. People whose community concerns override their purely personal concerns, for example, middle- and upper-class Republicans, vote out of a sense of civic obligation. Those lacking such a sense of obligation, whose motives are private, do not vote. Thus, typical local electoral systems produce an electorate that is overrepresentative of the wealthier strata.

In California, for example, the decline in participation between partisan and nonpartisan municipal elections is greatest in the low-income, Democratic areas: "Precincts which are relatively more Republican exercise greater influence in elections, because of their relatively higher participation, than predominately Democratic precincts."[8] The drop is disproportionately accounted for by the failure of lower classes to participate in reformed local elections.

The reasons for the lower-class dropout are myriad. There is, first of all, the compelling logic of class orientations. According to Banfield, the working-class individual's "participation in politics is motivated not by political principles but by ethnic and party loyalties, the appeal of personalities, or the hope of favors from the precinct captain."[9] It is precisely for such reasons that reformers sought (whether deliberately or not) to change the shape of the local electorate by biasing it in favor of the more community-conscious voters.

Additionally, the issues of local politics are less interesting than national issues, especially to the lower strata. The key issues around which citizen concern centers are economic, and economic issues are especially and personally salient to the less affluent. During a depression, the upper-class, community-conscious citizen generally worries about the state of the economy. His investments may not show their usual profit. For the working- or lower-class individual, depression means unemployment. States and the federal government deal with economic policy, welfare, and the like. The issues of local politics—property tax rates, the quality of education, land use planning—are of more interest to the well-to-do.

Our general discussion of the participation process emphasizes the overactive behavior of the middle and upper classes. However, party identification is a major, indeed, *the* major, voting cue for less well-educated voters. Lacking an issue orientation, less well-educated voters respond more automatically to partisan appeals than do more highly educated people, who have varieties of sources of information about elections (such as newspapers, civic organizations, or personal knowledge of candidates). Clearly, then, "of the various groups which affect political man, the most important is the political party itself."[10] Of course, partisanship, although stable, is not without change. There has been a growing trend toward independence in national voting. However, the decline in partisanship is greatest among the more educated voters. For the common man, the party is the activator.

Referenda

The shape of the local electorate is well illustrated by referenda, another major aspect of the reform package. Here again, the reformers' goal was to democratize, this time by providing a direct opportunity for the expression of preference about *policies* rather than personnel. Referenda were introduced to provide a mechanism to guarantee policy will be responsive to a majority of voters. They are found only at the state and local level, providing an additional comparative opportunity. During a single year, about 16,000 issues are probably voted on by voters at the local level.[11]

As might be expected, the turnout for referenda, the instrument of direct democracy, is consistently lower than the total vote for candidates for major offices. Referenda also disproportionately attract voters from the upper strata. Significantly, referenda voters differ on these characteristics not only from nonvoters, but also from voters in elections for personnel (table 2.8), "Taken in total they suggest that decisions on public policy made through statewide referenda in 1968 disproportionately reflected the views of residents of the suburbs and small cities, of the highly educated, and of those of relatively high incomes and of higher social class in terms of their own self-classification. To put the matter somewhat differently, in 1968, statewide referenda constituted an even less effective means to communicate with, and receive communications from, the poor and the poorly educated, blacks, and residents of large cities and rural areas than did other electoral mechanisms."[12]

Given these characteristics, it is hardly surprising to learn that those who vote in referenda are much more carefully informed about local, state, and national affairs. Indeed, they actively seek information. For example, they read newspapers more than they watch television. The active elite that normally participates in referenda does so with considerable belief in its ability to influence policies; it is efficacious. Mem-

Table 2.8. Socioeconomic Characteristics of Referenda and Nonreferenda
Voters (in percentages)

	Nonvoters	Offices only	Referenda
Race			
White	85	87	92
Negro	13	12	7
Other	2	1	1
N	(286)	(409)	(469)
Education			
Eighth grade or less	37	23	13
High school	44	51	52
Some college or more	19	27	35
N	(285)	(409)	(469)
Income			
Less than $6,000	57	41	22
$6,000–$9,999	26	29	36
$10,000 or more	16	30	42
N	(278)	(399)	(462)
Subjective social class			
Working class	67	55	48
Middle class	28	36	36
Upper-middle class	5	9	16
N	(278)	(400)	(449)
Residence			
Large cities	23	26	25
Suburbs and small cities	30	29	40
Rural and outlying areas	47	45	35
N	(286)	(409)	(469)

Source: Jerome M. Clubb and Michael W. Traugott, "National Patterns of Referenda
Voting: The 1968 Election," in Harlan Hahn (ed.), *People and Politics in Urban
Society* (Beverly Hills, Calif.: Sage Publications, 1972), p. 145.

bers of the elite believe government responds to their needs, and they are
Republicans.

Banfield and Wilson call such participants "public-regarding"; that
is, they participate out of a sense of civic obligation rather than with the
expectation of personal gain.[13] Banfield and Wilson start with the argument that voters should behave rationally in terms of their perceived
self-interests. In local bond referenda, such rational voters estimate the
benefits that would accrue to them if a public expenditure were approved, balance the benefits against the increase in taxes, and vote ac-

cordingly. The authors do not pretend, fortunately, that such an abstract model is necessarily realistic. Referenda are normally phrased in such a way as to make precise calculation impossible even if the potential voter sought to make them. Nevertheless, it is reasonable to assume some rudimentary estimate of costs and benefits. Thus, the knowledge that taxes will go up may be sufficient information for the voter.

Because most local expenditures are financed by the property tax, Banfield and Wilson wonder if those who do not own property, and therefore have nothing to lose, are more inclined to support public expenditure. They found convincing evidence to support this case. In all elections analyzed (in Cleveland and Chicago, including a broad variety of issues such as parks, zoos, welfare buildings, and urban renewal bonds), renters were appreciably more likely to support public expenditures than homeowners. So far their theory holds up well: those who believe they have nothing to lose will support public expenditures (whether property tax increases are passed on from landlord to tenant apparently does not enter into voters' judgments).

However, when the test is carried further, the results become quite different. When the voting preferences of homeowners are examined, the same logic leads to the conclusion that the more property voters own, the less inclined they would be to support public expenditures. After all, the benefits of public expenditures are distributed more evenly than the costs. However, the greatest support for public expenditures comes from the very largest income property owners: "the higher the income of a ward or town, the most taste it has for public expenditures of various kinds. That the ratio of benefits to costs declines as income goes up seems to make no difference."[14] The very wealthy are consistently more supportive than middle- and low-income property owners.

Banfield and Wilson build an additional argument from their data. Not only is wealth strongly associated with voting behavior inconsistent with self-interest (public-regarding), but so is ethnicity. In every income category, voters of foreign origin are more negative than are Anglo-Saxons. The coalition of positive voters then, is one of high-income Anglo-Saxon Protestants and the poor (mostly black) nonhomeowners. Arrayed against this coalition are the middle- and lower-income home-owners and voters of foreign stock.

Whether or not one chooses to regard those who vote against their own economic self-interest as public-regarding it is reasonable to conclude that the two halves of the positive voting coalition have different motives. For the blacks, community identification or public regard would make little sense as an explanatory device, but in simple economic terms, their voting is rational. For the whites, however, the notion of public regard rings true: "voters in some income and ethnic groups are more likely than voters in others to take a public-regarding rather than a narrowly self-interested view of things, i.e., to take the welfare of others, especially that of 'the community' into account as an aspect of their own welfare."[15]

An illustration of the differing motivation of the two partners in the coalition can be provided by a study of a rapid transit referendum in the Atlanta, Georgia, metropolitan area. In November 1968, the voters of Atlanta rejected a proposal to finance the construction of a rail rapid transit system for the metropolitan area. Previously, the dominant voting coalition in Atlanta had been composed of upper-class whites and blacks, but in this particular election, the coalition collapsed.

A survey conducted shortly after the election provides insight into the reliability of the public-regarding thesis. Three authors sought to make explicit the notion of public-regarding behavior.[16] The rapid transit proposal was to be financed by increased property taxes. Voters could, as was the case in the Banfield-Wilson study, gain a rough estimate of expense. Further, they could, probably quite realistically, estimate how much use they would make of a rapid transit system. Thus, those persons who anticipated an increased cost but did not intend to use the system can be said to be "public-regarding." Other categories of voters do not fit the definition. Those who anticipated no tax increase could support the system, whether or not they intended to use it, while those who anticipated a tax increase but also intended to use the system were also operating in their own self-interest.

Table 2.9.   Percentage Favoring Rapid Transit by Self-Interest, Race, and Education

	Whites	Blacks
High education		
Public-regarding	41%	14%
Private-regarding	73	33
Low education		
Public-regarding	20	5
Private-regarding	52	43

Source: Derived from Lewis Bowman, Dennis S. Ippolito, and Martin L. Levin, "Self-Interest and Referendum Support: The Case of a Rapid Transit Vote in Atlanta," in Harlan Hahn (ed.), *People and Politics in Urban Society* (Beverly Hills, Calif.: Sage Publications, 1972), p. 132.

Only a minority of the sample was public-regarding; nearly two-thirds voted according to their own perceived self-interest (table 2.9). However, public-regarding behavior varied considerably by class and race. At least in one category, public-regarding behavior cannot be so closely linked to class as Banfield and Wilson suggested. Only a minority of educated whites displayed public-regarding behavior. On the other hand, private-regarding behavior is heavily concentrated in this category. Whites with less education are only half as public-regarding, and blacks (regardless of education), are even less so. Thus, to the extent that there is a public-regarding culture, it is concentrated in the upper strata of the local electorate.

The Role of
Partisanship

The major purposes of political parties are to contest and win elections and to organize governments to achieve policy goals. Parties serve as intermediaries between voters and officeholders. The role of intermediary is performed by trying to develop a program that they believe will meet the preferences of a majority of voters. Since there are generally two competing parties, only one of which can win, there is an incentive to reflect these preferences accurately and to convince the voters of this fact. Such competition prods reluctant voters to the polls. Once in office, the party seeks to implement its program in response to its electoral mandate. Competition in future elections provides incentive for officeholders to continue to be responsive. However, reformers judged that the evils of partisan politics outweighed the benefits of partisan participation.

If, as we have argued, the working classes need the most prodding, political parties should reduce the disparity in participation between classes. As Verba and Nie explain, if party identification increases political participation, and in turn reduces the disparity in class voting patterns, "then the parties will be playing an important democratizing and equalizing role."[17] In fact, exactly this equalizing process occurs. In the first place, lower-status citizens are more likely to have strong party identifications. Further, this stronger party identification reduces the participation gap between the classes: the lower-status groups receive more of a participatory boost—that is, they gain more from partisan identification.

Again according to Verba and Nie, upper-class citizens are influenced by "general interest in politics, norms about voting, peer pressures"[18] to vote even though their party identification may be weak. Lower-class citizens, on the other hand, are far less likely to vote unless they have strong party identifications. Thus, partisanship is a strong force in motivating lower-class citizens to make the demands on officeholders we cited in chapter 1 as necessary for responsive government.

RACE RELATIONS AND LOCAL COALITIONS

WHILE THE patterns of participation in local elections outlined so far apply to most issue areas, there are a few exceptions. By far the most significant exception is the issue of race relations. Unlike many issues in local politics, race relations is unusually salient to all classes of the population. Consequently, voter turnout for racial questions is apt to be appreciably higher than in normal elections. Additionally, the shape of the public-regarding and private-regarding coalitions in the local electorate changes considerably for racial issues. Because race relations occupies so prominent a place on the policy agenda of local government, its impact on participation will be explored in greater detail.

Typical of the way the race relations issue surfaces are various propositions dealing with fair housing; that is, outlawing racial discrimination in the sale or rental of housing. Two cases illustrate how the white electorate balances freedom of choice (for example, the right to dispose of one's property as one sees fit) against the right of blacks to have equal access to housing. In the summer of 1963, the California legislature passed the Rumford Act, prohibiting racial discrimination by realtors and the owners of apartment houses and homes built with public assistance. In November 1964, an initiative provision was placed on the ballot amending the state constitution to repeal the Rumford Act and to prevent the state or any local community from adopting fair housing legislation. A vote for the proposition was a vote against fair housing legislation. The measure passed by a two-to-one ratio.

A similar proposal was also submitted to the electorate of Detroit, Michigan in 1964. Both proposals were phrased to place maximum emphasis on freedom of choice, as illustrated in the Detroit proposal:

> The purpose and substance of the proposed Ordinance is as follows: to define certain rights of Detroit residents and owners of residential property to privacy, and to the free use, enjoyment and disposition of residential property: including the right of selection or rejection of any persons as tenants or purchasers: the free choice of real estate brokers and to require such brokers to follow the instructions of the owner; and to fix penalties for violations of the provisions of the ordinance.[19]

In Detroit, as in California, the fair housing proposal was defeated. A comparison of the two referenda reveals strikingly similar results. The relation of class to voting in favor of fair housing (as measured by education and income), indicates that it is not until one reaches the absolute top of the ladder that one encounters a predominantly pro-fair housing attitude. Harlan Hahn's detailed study of the Detroit referendum amplifies this point.[20] By dividing his sample of voters into class categories, he obtained the following results (table 2.10):

Table 2.10.   Percentage Favoring Homeowner's Ordinance

Social class	
Lower and lower middle	73%
Middle	77
Upper middle	71
Upper	50

Source: Derived from Harlan Hahn, "Northern Referenda on Fair Housing: The Response of White Voters," *The Western Political Quarterly* 21 (September 1968): 491

Overwhelming majorities of all social classes, except the upper, placed property rights over fair housing. The point is that the base of "liberal" coalitions is extremely narrow—indeed it may be that race relations has strained the coalition to the breaking point, leaving only blacks (most of whom do not vote), and upper-class whites (most of whom do vote). Gone are the upper-middle class white voters who, if the past record is any indication, generally tend to support local referenda (when expenditures are involved). The behavior of the upper middle-class whites in Detroit is especially revealing. A majority agreed with the idea, phrased generally, that "Negroes have a right to live where they wish." However, among those upper middle-class whites who agreed with this statement, 72 percent voted for the homeowners' ordinance, which had the effect of making the implementation of the abstract idea impossible![21] Hahn concludes:

> Upper class whites probably were relatively protected from the possibility of Negro immigration into their neighborhoods, but upper middle class voters may have reacted to the greater vulnerability of their social and residential locations in the city. Although a large proportion of upper middle class whites agreed with the general proposition that Negroes should be allowed to live where they wish, they also expressed strong approval of the Homeowner's Ordinance.[22]

The upper middle classes are normally progressive in local elections (or more so than the lower classes), but not with regard to race. Many studies have observed the peculiarity of local, in contrast to state and national, voting patterns. In state and national elections, there is a strong positive correlation between social class and Republicans. That is, the higher one's social class becomes, the greater the probability of a Republican vote. Because the Republican party is generally (rightly or wrongly) regarded as conservative, these same Republicans might be expected to prefer fiscally conservative local policies, but they generally do not. Conversely, the lower-class Democratic voters might be expected to prefer financially liberal local policies, but they do not. As we have seen, the core of the public-regarding voting population (those most consistently in support of local expenditures) is the upper class. Generally, then, we expect to find consistent relationships between class and local progressive voting (when race is not perceived as salient).

The defeat of black candidate Thomas Bradley in Los Angeles in 1969 (Bradley was subsequently successful in his bid to become mayor) is a good illustration. Accompanying the contest between Bradley and successful candidate Samuel Yorty were a variety of issues requiring either increased taxes or school bonds. There were strong positive associations between social class and support for such expenditures. The higher the social class of the voter, the greater the probability of support for school bonds, school tax increases, and the like. Yet, there were strong negative associations between social class and support for black candidate Bradley. Opposition to Bradley was stronger in relatively high-status areas than in working-class neighborhoods. Hahn and Almy offer an interesting speculation about white voting patterns: "Since black candidates frequently have been the major proponents of redistributive policies concerning education and other issues, they may attract increasing support from working-class voters who might benefit most from those proposals rather than from middle or upper middle-class residents."[23]

The authors are suggesting a substantial revision in the notion of public-regarding behavior. On one hand, there are local controversies involving the simple expenditure of money, such as building parks or schools. On the other hand, there is the question of the redistribution of monies. Redistribution apparently reduces the traditional coalition to its core, alienating middle-income whites, who perceive themselves most directly affected by redistribution, and leaving only the highest status white voters still liberal. In the 1969 Los Angeles election, those with the highest social status supported Bradley.[24]

Similar patterns emerge whenever blacks challenge whites, as in Cleveland, where Carl Stokes was elected in 1967; Gary, Indiana, where Richard Hatcher was elected in 1968; and, Newark, N.J., where Kenneth Gibson was elected in 1970. In these elections, the blacks were running as Democrats, whereas in Los Angeles the election of Bradley was by nonpartisan ballot (both Bradley and Yorty were Democrats, although Yorty's open breaks with his party were widely known). Normally Democratic areas deserted their party in massive numbers to oppose a black candidate. Stokes, for instance, received only 20 percent of the white vote in an area that usually goes Democratic by a margin of about six to one.[25]

A study of these elections revealed similar patterns of support and opposition, which bear directly upon the notion of redistribution of resources. Voters supporting blacks, according to Pettigrew, are to be found in concentrations of Jewish voters and among young urban well-educated whites. Blacks' opponents are mainly lower-middle class whites.[26]

THE POLITICS OF REDISTRIBUTION

THE PREVIOUS discussion shows that the lower-middle class is likely to be the most threatened by the redistributive policies advocated by black candidates. The very poor and the very rich stand in stark contrast. The poor, regardless of race, can be expected to gain from efforts toward a more equal distribution of income (two lower status white precincts in Cleveland that had given Stokes only minimal support in 1967 supported him in 1969 when he opened a playground in the area). The well-to-do really do not suffer from redistribution policies (unless they are extreme, which is highly unlikely). Between these two groups are those who perceive themselves threatened and vote accordingly.

Pettigrew developed a scheme to test this notion, known generally as "relative deprivation." Voters were divided into four groups according to how they viewed their economic situation in relation to their own class or race, and the relevant out-group (blacks versus whites, blue collar versus white collar, and so on). Four categories were developed: (1) those who believe they are doing well within their group and in comparison to the out-group (doubly gratified); (2) those who feel they are doing well within their own group but have lost ground to their out-group (fraternally deprived); (3) those who have slipped behind within their group but have kept pace with the out-group (egotistically deprived); and (4) those who have lost ground to both their in-group and out-group (doubly deprived).[27]

The fraternally deprived group shows the greatest hostility. Fraternally deprived persons are disproportionately concentrated among those of medium income and education and among members of labor unions. Their fears are amply illustrated by the elections we have been discussing (table 2.11).

Table 2.11. Racial Deprivation and White Votes for Black Candidates (in percentages)

	Doubly gratified	Fraternally deprived	Egotistically deprived	Doubly deprived
Stokes (Cleveland, 1969)	31%	12%	49%	29%
Bradley (Los Angeles, 1969)	35	21	52	42
Gibson (Newark, 1970)	19	14	29	20
Hatcher (Gary, 1971)	17	7	30	15

Source: Derived from Thomas F. Pettigrew, "When A Black Candidate Runs for Mayor: Race and Voting Behavior," in Harlan Hahn (ed.), *People and Politics in Urban Society* (Beverly Hills, Calif.: Sage Publications, 1972), p. 116.

Racial conflict increases turnout in a normally bland electoral setting. Such conflict also increases the participation of the fraternally deprived. To the extent that black candidates and various racially linked referenda awaken the local electorate, we can expect to find a continuation and solidification of the coalition against the middle class. However, most local issues do not involve racial conflict, and in such cases the turnout is low. Indeed, there is some evidence that, given what we know about the normal electorate, turnout is related to the success or

failure of local financial referenda. In a normal local election that involves neither party nor race, turnout is concentrated among the upper-
class public-regarding segment of the population.

When local elections generate a substantial increase in turnout, one
can infer that the election is a symptom of a deeply felt community conflict. Coleman's study of fluoridation referenda first noted this
phenomenon.[28] Coleman found a consistent relationship between high
turnout and the defeat of fluoridation. He argued that, because of the
unusually high emotional content of fluoridation referenda, the increase
in turnout reflected a sharp increase in community conflict. Such conflict aroused a desire to vote among voters who normally abstain from
local politics because of the absence of perceived benefits. Recall that
nonpartisan elections leave out the basic ingredient of lower-class
political participation. However, highly charged referenda, such as those
dealing with fluoridation or race, become an adequate substitute for partisan identification. People who are not regular participants in local
elections, and whose identification with the community is low, are suddenly motivated to vote. These added voters generally are disposed to
vote No on fluoridation. Hence, the larger the turnout the greater the
probability of fluoridation's defeat.

Variations in Turnout

EMOTIONALITY AND TURNOUT   Although the content of local
referenda is clearly a variable in reaching a generalization, it is probably
true that referenda that are subject to attachment to vague, emotion-
laden symbols are highly vulnerable to sudden fluctuations in turnout.
Elections associated with education apparently have a similar potential,
and the relationship between turnout and negative voting holds true.
School budgets, bonds, and park development are generally less likely to
become entwined with community conflict than such issues as fluoridation or race relations. Wirt and Kirst, using the frequency of closely contested elections as an indication of community stress, estimate that
three out of four California school tax elections are of the nonconflict
variety.[29] Nevertheless, educational issues do occasionally generate controversy, even when the race issue is not immediately apparent (which,
in large cities is becoming less so every year).

When school budget and bond elections generate controversy, turnout
increases and rate of approval declines. It should be clear that the turnout–negative voting relationship is not perfect. In some cases, for in-

stance, repeated submissions of the same budget finally result in a positive relationship between turnout and a yes-vote.[30] The preponderance of the evidence, nevertheless, supports the original Coleman hypothesis: controversy leads to higher turnout among the least public-regarding whose inclination generally is to vote no.

As Piele and Hall assert, "The likely explanation for the strong relationship between high turnout and negative voting is school-related conflict that in turn leads to a politicized electorate. Theory and research from different kinds of community studies, together with evidence from studies that assessed the relationship between levels of community conflict interest group activity, and school financial election outcome provide strong grounds for adopting the interpretation that the turnout factor simply intervenes between conflict . . . and election outcome. . . ."[31] The point can be illustrated by California referenda held at three separate periods (table 2.12). At least two-thirds of the referenda with less than 20 percent turnout were successful. The success rate was lower in elections which attracted more participation.

Table 2.12. Turnout and Referenda Success in California (percentage successful referenda)

Turnout percentage	1966–67 (N)	1967–68 (N)	1969–70 (N)
0–19.9	(26) 62	(8) 87	(13) 69
20–39.9	(71) 58	(53) 70	(91) 42
40–59.9	(67) 45	(30) 73	(113) 50
60–79.9	(26) 38	(25) 52	(41) 46
80 and over	(9) 44	(6) 67	(1) 100

Source: Frederick M. Wirt and Michael W. Kirst, *The Political Web of American Schools* (Boston: Little, Brown, 1972), p. 106.

The turnout–negative voting syndrome varies also to some extent with size of community. Although individual turnout is normally concentrated in the upper strata, aggregate turnout is highest in cities with large proportions of poorly educated populations. In those cities political cleavages based on economic interests are more visible. Thus, the suburbs, where high-status groups are concentrated, do not achieve higher turnout than central cities. The turnout–negative voting relationship works most clearly when class cleavages are readily apparent and when the lower classes do not perceive a personal gain to be achieved by a positive vote.

Stone has summarized the dynamics of turnout:

1. Most citizens are little concerned with political and governmental matters, particularly those connected with local government. Several factors, however, serve to draw business and professional men, the civic club set, into a direct and continuing involvement with local government.

2. A low turnout referendum is likely to consist primarily of votes cast by individuals who are active in civic activities, business and professional men. These individuals often have participated in the formulation of the proposal to be voted upon, and almost certainly their support has been sought early and strenuously. They are also the individuals most likely to take a long-range view and to think of potential community-wide benefits. Referendum proposals thus tend to be received favorably by these civic activists, so that the outcome of low participation elections is positive in most cases.

3. A high turnout referendum necessarily involves participation by those who are inactive and almost always poorly informed. For these civic inactivists the local political scene is largely unstructured, that is, there is no coherent view, no standing interpretation of what is involved in local government. Consequently, their attitudes are malleable and their voting preferences are volatile.

4. Because the high turnout electorate consists predominately of civic inactivists and because the attitudes and voting inclinations of these inactivists are unstable, election outcomes are unpredictable on the basis of size of turnout. Though less likely than the more predictable low turnout referendum to yield a favorable result, a high turnout may yield anything from a crushing defeat to a comfortable victory for referendum proposals.[32]

The point Stone makes is that high turnout elections may be vehicles of protest if the issue is phrased in such a way as to trigger an emotional response among occasional voters. For whatever reasons, fluoridation and school elections appear to be emotional issues quite likely to result in the turnout–negative voting syndrome.

The implications of the upper-class bias of the local electorate are summarized by Lineberry and Sharkansky:

as far as urban decision-makers represent accurately the preferences of their constituents in policy choices (a point which neither they nor we concede), they are representing a more generous proportion of well-to-do people than is present in a Presidential constituency. Not, of course, that upper-class interests are represented to the exclusion of all others. First, lower-class voters still retain significant potential power through their numbers alone. Officials must anticipate the reaction even of regularly non-participant groups, because nonparticipants can be activated. Second, upper-status groups are more likely than others to be "public-regarding" and thus to take account of underrepresented interests. And third, *state and federal programs, designed by decision-makers who are more directly accountable to working-class constituencies,* determine many policy options of local officials.[33]

PARTISANSHIP AND TURNOUT Whether state decision-makers are more accountable to the less affluent than local decision-makers is an intriguing question. In fact, the state electorate is different in socioeconomic status from the local electorate: it is regularly populated by larger proportions of the lower classes. The normal relationship between socioeconomic status and participation (the higher the status, the higher the participation) is not, of course, reversed. What occurs is quite simple: state elections are normally partisan, thus providing a major source of participation that is absent in local politics. Consequently, turnout in state elections is higher and lower-class participation is greater.

The significance of partisan elections becomes apparent when we think of the obstacles to participation, as are well expressed by Dahl:

> states do not stand out as important institutions of democratic self-government. They are too big to allow much in the way of civic participation . . . an American state is infinitely less important to citizens of that state than any democratic nation-state is to its citizens. Consequently, the average American is bound to be much less concerned about the affairs of his state than of his city or country. Too remote to stimulate much participation by their citizens, and too big to make extensive participation possible anyway, these limits intermediate between city and nation are probably destined for a kind of limbo of quasi-democracy. . . . It cannot even be said that the states, on the whole, can tap any strong sentiments of loyalty or likemindedness among their citizens. . . .[34]

In fact, the salience or importance of state politics is not quite as low as Dahl suggested, but his main premise is correct. A national sample ranked the kinds of public affairs they followed most closely—international, national, state or local (see table 2.5). As Dahl predicted, states fare rather poorly, though local and national politics do quite well. If the first and second ranks are combined, however, state affairs assume an equal place with local affairs. Still, it is safe to say that, at least in terms of highest salience, state politics is the least interesting, to the average citizen, of the four levels.

Yet turnout in state elections is higher than in local elections, mainly because state elections are partisan. The attentive public for state politics differs from the attentive public for other levels of government: "those from the working class and lower educational strata are more likely to form a portion of the attentive public for state politics."[35]

As we have seen, these voters are the people who, lacking individual incentives to participate, are motivated by feelings of partisan identification. Numerous studies have found the effect of partisanship in state elections to be virtually identical with the effects of partisanship in local elections: turnout is improved. The result in table 2.13 is typical.

Table 2.13.   Correlation Between Competition and Turnout

Time period	Correlation
1930–1940	.82
1942–1950	.72
1956–1966	.58

In all time periods, the correlations are positive (that is, the greater the competition between parties for the office of governor, the higher the turnout). The decline of the correlations (that is, the less strong the relationship) over time bears further examination when we consider linkage mechanisms. For now, it is sufficient to note the mobilization function of political parties. As explained by Milbrath: "People tend to follow a close contest with more interest. Furthermore, in a close contest they are more likely to perceive that their votes count and, thus, they are more likely to cast them. An additional factor is that, when parties are fighting in a close contest, their workers tend to spend more time and energy campaigning and getting out the vote."[36]

A possible confounding element is that participation is, as we know, also related to socioeconomic variables. It is thus necessary to assess the independent impact of partisan competition. Thomas R. Dye examined the correlation between party competition and turnout, holding constant income and education. Like Milbrath, Dye found that increased partisan competition increases voter turnout.[37]

Naturally, the extent of partisan competition varies widely across states. Some states have a stable competitive pattern between parties; others do not. In those states without party competition, turnout will be low, indeed just about as low as it is in the normal local election. On the other hand, when states are characterized by vigorous competition, vast increases in turnout are experienced. Consider, as an example, primary versus general elections. In primary elections (those elections held prior to the general elections to determine the nominee of the party) turnout is typically very low, and the shape of the electorate quite similar to the local active electorate. Voters in primary elections are typically better educated, hold more prestigious jobs, enjoy higher incomes, and are more knowledgeable about public affairs. They vote out of a sense of citizen duty.

Ranney has convincingly demonstrated how partisan competition changes the shape of the electorate.[38] By considering a variety of state elections over a fourteen-year period, states are classified as (1) one-party Democratic, (2) modified one-party Democratic, (3) two-party, and (4) modified one-party Republican. Ranney examined turnout in primary nonpartisan elections and general partisan elections within each of these categories (table 2.14).

Table 2.14.   Mean Voting Turnout in Primary and General Elections for Governor, 1962–1968

| | Percentage voting | | |
State groups	Primary elections	General elections	Difference
One-party Democratic	36.7	37.7	1.0
Modified one-party Democratic	29.9	52.0	22.1
Two-party	25.8	57.1	31.3
Modified one-party Republican	27.0	63.4	36.4

Source: Austin Ranney, "Parties in State Politics," in Herbert Jacob and Kenneth N. Vines (eds.), *Politics in the American States,* 3rd ed. (Boston: Little, Brown, 1976), p. 71.

Primary elections are the state counterpart to the local nonpartisan ballot. They were devised by the reformers of the progressive era to take control of nominations away from the party bosses and restore nominations to the people. As Ranney's data demonstrate, just the opposite result was achieved. Not only is turnout higher in general elections in competitive states, but the increase in turnout between primary and general elections is greater.

FORMS AND EXTENT OF POLITICAL ACTIVITY

OUR DISCUSSION of electoral behavior in state and local governments has shown that elections are insufficient modes of communication either to fulfill the demands required by the representational model or to assess the popular attitudes and expectations required by the congruence model of responsiveness. At best, voting is a blunt instrument with little effect on actual public policy. Elections rarely provide office holders with information of sufficient quality to guide them in policy-making. Far more important for providing specific demands and expectations are sustained political activities, those activities which place the citizen, either individually or as part of a group, in a regularized (in some cases, institutionalized) interaction with policy-makers. We now shift our focus to that portion of the state and local population which does more than vote.

Sustained and Occasional Activity

Because most people do not even bother to vote, we can reasonably assume that more sustained activity is even more class-linked and rare. In fact, other than voting, there is relatively little political activity in American states and communities. The more time, energy, and emotional commitment an activity requires, the fewer people participate (see table 2.15). Other than voting in presidential and local elections (even these statistics are inflated by a percentage who say they voted

Table 2.15. Participants in the Political Process (in percentages)

Act	Participation
Regular voting in presidential elections	72
Always voting in local elections	47
Active in one organization involved in community problems	32
Worked with others in trying to solve community problems	30
Attempted to persuade others to vote as they will	28
Actively worked for a party or candidate	26
Ever contacted a local government official about some issue or problem	20
Attended at least one political meeting or rally in last three years	19
Ever contacted a state or national government official about some issue or problem	18
Formed a group or organization to attempt to solve some local community problem	14
Given money to a party or candidate during an election campaign	13
Presently a member of a political club or organization	8

Source: From *Participation in America: Political Democracy and Social Equality* by Sidney Verba and Norman H. Nie: Table 2-1 (p. 31). Copyright © 1972 by Sidney Verba and Norman H. Nie. Reprinted by permission of Harper & Row, Publishers, Inc.

when in fact they did not), less than one-third of the population is even moderately active in their communities. From the percentages in table 2.15, Verba and Nie were able to categorize the population into six quite distinct groups according to the mode of activity in which an individual specializes. Simplified, the groups are:

1. The inactives (22%): Inactives take virtually no part in political life.

2. The voting specialists (21%): Voting specialists limit their activity to regular voting, making no attempt to influence government action in any other way (such as writing letters, joining groups, etc.).

3. The parochial participants (4%): Parochial participants do not engage in community or organizational activity; they do vote, however. Additionally, they make particularized contacts. That is, their activity is limited to responding to an immediate problem which directly affects their personal lives.

4. The communalist (20%): Communalists have a high level of communal activity (such as organizational memberships), but a low level of campaign activity. Such persons prefer to be active in com-

munity affairs in ways which are less conflict-laden than in campaigning.

5. The campaigners (15%): Campaigners, in sharp contrast to communalists, prefer the conflict of campaigns, while remaining aloof from community organizations.

6. The complete activists (11%): As implied by the label, this small group is characterized by sustained participation in all forms of activity.[39]

The Verba-Nie categorization of kinds of activity bears close attention because, unlike prior studies, it draws careful distinctions among the various kinds of sustained activity. We already know the close association between social status and participation; their findings support this notion. Inactives and voting specialists, for example, are disproportionately of lower status groups and blacks. However, lower socioeconomic groups (but not blacks), also constitute the bulk of the parochial participants.

It is when we turn to voters who engage in sustained activities that the dominance of the upper classes becomes apparent. Starting with the communalists, the overrepresentation of upper-status groups emerges: those with high education and high income are found disproportionately here. Blacks are conspicuously underrepresented. Communal activity is also more likely to be found in suburbs and rural areas than in large cities. This is a somewhat surprising finding in light of the fact that much has been written about the extent to which urbanization encourages group activity. Wirth, for instance, concludes that: "Being reduced to a stage of virtual impotence as an individual, the urbanite is bound to exert himself by joining with others of similar interests into organized groups to obtain his ends."[40] Nearly all empirical evidence supports Wirth's conclusion, if not his explanation. Recall, however, that communal activity is relatively nonconflictual, "aimed at the attainment of broad community goals."[41] Communalists prefer to avoid conflict, a preference that cannot be accomplished in an urban setting where conflict is a way of life. In a homogeneous suburb, however, avoiding conflict is considerably less difficult.

On the other hand, one should not carry the argument too far; a fine line separates political and nonpolitical activity. True, communalists eschew partisan activity, but because so much of the political life of the local community is nonpartisan, perhaps the communalists' activity is political in the sense that it is supportive of broadly conceived goals, much in the way that the public-regarding citizen would view the support of, say, a community mental health center, as above politics. In the broader sense, of course, there are no nonpolitical decisions. Nevertheless, it comes as no surprise to learn that communalists are exceptionally strong on measures of civic-mindedness (public regard). They want to do good.

Partisan or campaign activists, though similar to communalists in their high education and income, are fundamentally different both in where they are located and why they are active. They are disproportionately located in urban areas, disproportionately non-Protestant, and distinctly not civic-minded. They view their activity in terms of conflict, what is to be gained or lost, rather than in terms of community identification. Additionally, there is a slight black overrepresentation in this group (which is also true of electoral specialists).

Finally, complete activists engage in every possible type of activity from voting to campaigning. Here, the dominance of the upper classes is striking; they are even more civic-minded than communalists. Complete activists are considerably more likely to be found in small towns than in large cities.

These careful distinctions should not blur the basic conclusion: the more sustained community involvement, that which has the greatest payoff as we shall argue, is the virtually exclusive domain of the upper classes. Assuming that sustained activity is organizationally stimulated (a safe assumption), membership in organizations is strongly relative to class and race (30 percent of the blacks are organizationally active, compared to 41 percent of the whites; 27 percent of those who did not graduate from high school are active compared to 59 percent of those who went to college).[42]

Group Activity

Activity in organizations contributes greatly to political activity, and because upper-status groups are so much more organizationally active, the net result is to create a community group life that greatly overrepresents the upper classes, and greatly underrepresents the lower classes, the poor, and the black: "Upper-status groups are, to begin with, more politically active. They are also more active in organizations. And, because the latter type of activity has an independent effect in increasing political activity—over and above the effects of socio-economic status—their advantage in political activity over a lower group is increased."[43]

From the point of view of a responsive local government, such as a school board or a city council, the demands to which they are expected to respond are phrased with a distinctly upper-class accent. City councilmen listed the kinds of organizations that were active in their cities (see table 2.16).

Table 2.16.   Relationships Between Group Activity Levels and City Size (in percentages)

Councils reporting moderate to high activity	City size			
	Large N=17	Medium N=33	Small N=34	Total N=82
Chamber of Commerce, Jaycees	94	67	41	62
Homeowner, neighborhood groups	76	50	41	51
Civic affairs groups	88	42	31	48
Merchant associations	65	54	31	48
Service clubs	41	45	41	43
Garden clubs, library association	35	33	28	32
Reform/protest groups	47	12	3	16
Political party clubs	18	15	6	12
Trade unions	23	12	3	11

Source: From *Labyrinths of Democracy: Adaptations, Linkages, Representation, and Policies in Urban Politics* by Heinz Eulau and Kenneth Prewitt, copyright © 1973 by The Bobbs-Merrill Company, Inc.

N=Number of cities.

Groups of all kinds are more active in a metropolitan environment; nevertheless, it is clear that the organizational proclivities of the upper classes are translated into actual behavior with regard to city councils. The group life of cities is pluralistic only to the degree that a conflict between the merchants' association and the Chamber of Commerce is regarded as representative of diverse interests. However, in large cities, protest and reform groups, trade unions, and political parties are more active, which suggests again the more conflictual nature of large-city political systems. Additionally, such groups are considerably more active when the large city is also economically impoverished.

Roughly comparable results were reported by Zeigler and Jennings in a study of school boards: the more complex the environment, the more diverse the group life.[44] Even so, both with regard to city councils and school boards, the range of group representation is limited.

Because organizations are linkages—albeit limited or biased—between the governors and the governed, we should expect that a city's group activity would vary, not only with size of place (the more complex the more group activity), but also with the nature of the times. In tranquil times, which are, of course, becoming increasingly rarer, the city council, school board, or planning commission might be left virtually alone. In times of stress, the same council might be under a veritable state of siege.

The Zeigler-Jennings study found a strong association between the degree of general community support for schools and the extent of group activity. The happier the population, the less active the group activity. Of course, demonstrations about schools are more likely to occur in conflict-prone, heterogeneous, urban environments. However, the inverse relation between citizen satisfaction and group activity is not weakened when the size of the community is taken into account. When the population becomes unhappy, groups become active. However, the structure of both city councils and school boards is not designed to maximize the ability of organizations to translate dissatisfaction into action. When school elections are held on a partisan basis (which is not usually the case), the translation of mass unrest into organizational activity is accelerated. The demands are given clearer and more rapid articulation by interest groups: "Partisan elections place the school board squarely within the general political process, thus making the school board the target of the pressures which exist within the general political process."[45]

BUSINESS-LABOR CONFLICTS   Partisanship, then, has consequences for organizational activity similar to its consequences for electoral activity: it maximizes the influence of those organizations whose motives are constrained by a commitment to the public good. Because, as we shall see later in this chapter, business and professional associations provide the main conduit for recruitment to positions of local political leadership, outlooks of local officials and business associations are expected to be compatible. In drawing a contrast between business and labor in local politics, Banfield and Wilson note that

> there appears to be a crucial difference between business and union membership on such bodies [boards of education, the Community Chest, and various public commissions that are appointed rather than elected]. Organized labor—even if it includes in its ranks the majority of all the adult citizens in the community—is generally regarded as a "special interest" which must be represented; businessmen, on the other hand, are often regarded, not as "representing business" as a "special interest,"

but as serving the community as a whole. Businessmen . . . are
viewed as "symbols of civic legitimacy." Labor leaders rarely
have the symbolic quality, but must contend with whatever
stigma attaches to being from a lower class background and
associated with a special-interest group.[46]

We had previously cited the kinds of groups perceived as active. If we
also ask what kinds of groups are perceived as influential, we can see the
accuracy of Banfield and Wilson's argument (table 2.17). The most frequently named choice is the Chamber of Commerce, which is perceived
as influential by two-thirds of the councilmen. General civic organizations comprise one-third of the groups named. However, special interests
(even when they include businessmen) are less frequently mentioned.
Among the special interests, nevertheless, unions do very poorly. It
seems that those organizations which are perceived as legitimate—which serve the community as a whole—have easier access to
local decision-makers.

A similar circumstance exists at the state level, where labor (as we
shall see) is considerably more active. Influence (as distinguished from
activity) requires more subtle indicators. Zeigler and Baer's study of lobbying in four states revealed that labor organizations were regularly
regarded as among the most active groups and were also regarded as
those who routinely applied pressure. In reality, the authors concluded
that labor was no more likely to engage in strong-arm tactics than other
groups. Why, then, did they earn the reputation? The authors found
that even the most innocent comments were likely to be misperceived. If
we assume that Democratic legislators are more sympathetic to
organized labor than are Republicans, we can get a clearer idea of the
perceptual basis of pressure (as well as some clues as to why labor is so
inactive in local politics). It was anticipated that Republicans would
perceive labor with more hostility and hence perceive more pressure.
Such was indeed the case: 60 percent of the Republican legislators, compared to 34 percent of the Democratic legislators, regarded labor as using pressure tactics.[47]

In cities where the rules of the game are considerably more oriented
toward community, as opposed to narrow interests, labor's role as defender of a clearly identified special class is undoubtedly damaged. The
point will be amplified when we discuss the recruitment and
organizational affiliations of local decision-makers, few of whom have
had any sustained occupational or organizational identification with
labor.

In contrasting the relative strengths of business and labor, however,

Table 2.17.   Organizations Named as Influential by City Councilmen

Organization	Times mentioned	Total responses
General economic groups		
Chamber of Commerce, Jaycees	273	
Neighborhood groups, homeowners		
associations, taxpayers groups	172	
Total	445	43%
General Civic Groups		
Service clubs	121	
Women's organizations	101	
(League of Women Voters,		
American Association of		
University Women, PTA)		
Church groups	16	
Press	12	
Miscellaneous (youth-oriented, cultural)	60	
Total	310	31%
Special interests		
Merchants associations	82	
Conservation groups	30	
Realtors associations	27	
Civil rights groups	19	
Builders and developers	14	
Veterans groups	14	
Unions	13	
Political clubs and organizations	10	
Senior citizens	8	
Farmers organizations	5	
"Right-wing" groups	4	
Total	226	23%
Semiofficial and official bodies		
Planning commission, citizens		
advisory committees, school		
committee, county commissioners	25	2%
Total	1.006	100%

Source: From *Local Interest Politics: A One-Way Street,* by Betty H. Zisk, copyright ©
1973, by The Bobbs-Merrill Company, Inc.

one should not be given the impression either that business always is
more influential or that business is monolithic in its demands. Terry N.
Clark's study of fifty-one communities (ranging in population from
50,000 to 750,000) indicates that certain cultural and structural
variables are associated with business dominance. Two distinct patterns

emerged. The first leadership pattern was the business factor, with active participation by the Chamber of Commerce, newspapers, industrial leaders, retail merchants, bankers, and other businessmen. The second factor represented predominantly political leaders: the Democratic party, Republican party, labor unions, and heads of local government agencies.[48]

These patterns of activity were distinctly associated with the structural and socioeconomic character of the city. Terry Clark divides cities into business (in the West) and political (Midwest and East) categories.

> In legal-political structure, the business cities include more reform characteristics, the political cities the opposite. The patterns of decision-making are more decentralized in political cities. The mayor is more likely to be a Republican in the business cities, and the citizens to vote Republican in presidential elections. . . . The political cities, on the other hand, are disproportionately middle income cities, and include fewer upper income residents. The business cities tend to include more Protestants, the political cities (especially the Democratic cities) Roman Catholics. The business cities have a smaller number of citizens who are immigrants or one of whose parents immigrated to the United States. The political cities have more immigrants from Central and Southern Europe.[49] (See table 2.18.)

Clark finds that business influence is greatest when cities are reformed (nonpartisan, at-large elections, etc.) and when the population is more homogeneously middle- to upper-class.

Under these conditions business associations control the basic resources of political influence, making it difficult, if not impossible, for politicians to act without business support. Reform governments are especially important in "business cities" because they minimize the likelihood of the development of independent political organizations.

INTRABUSINESS CONFLICTS   There is, however, the additional, and crucial factor of business unity. Adrian and Press have observed: "So many business groups exert pressure upon government that they would probably overshadow and overpower all of the others if it were not that they spend so much of their time opposing one another."[50] Certainly, business associations are unified in their support for policies supporting economic growth, but even here, the vagaries of growth are considerable, especially as the urban community becomes physically fragmented.

As central cities become economically stagnant, downtown merchants support mass transit and urban renewal, while developers of shopping

Table 2.18.   Correlations of Business and Political Leadership Measures with Community Characteristics

	Business factor	Political factor
Northeast	−.360	.124
Midwest	−.016	.418
South	.100	−.146
West	.280	−.418
SMSA (Standard Metropolitan Statistic Area) population	−.208	−.365
City population	−.147	.201
Density	−.308	.019
Percentage population change, 1950–1960	−.307	−.113
Owner-occupied housing	.289	−.034
Industrial activity (percentage in manufacturing establishments with 20+ employees)	−.098	.275
Economic diversification	.109	−.023
Index of reform government	.217	−.527
Index of decentralization	.031	.319
Last mayor Democrat	−.440	.009
Percentage Democratic vote in 1960 presidential elections	−.315	.350
Civic voluntary activity	.012	−.047
Median education	.297	−.310
Percentage low income (under $3,000 annual family income)	.204	−.072
Percentage middle income ($3,000 to $10,000 annual family income)	−.137	.366
Percentage upper income (over $15,000 annual family income)	.111	−.320
Percentage Protestants	.310	−.062
Percentage Jews	−.201	.077
Percentage Roman Catholics	−.427	.207
Percentage Irish	−.283	.147
Percentage Germans (square root)	−.166	.109
Percentage Polish	−.409	.209
Percentage Mexican (log)	.175	−.214
Percentage Italian (log)	−.208	.134
Percentage Northern European (U.K., Ireland, Norway, Sweden, Denmark, Netherlands, Switzerland, France)	.045	.055
Percentage Central European (Germany, Poland, Czechoslovakia, Austria, Hungary, Yugoslavia)	−.259	.229
Percentage Southern European (Greece, Italy, Yugoslavia)	−.201	.263
Percentage rural and farmers in state	.059	.296

Source: Terry N. Clark, "The Structure of Community Influence," in Harlan Hahn (ed.), *People and Politics in Urban Society* (Beverly Hills, Calif.: Sage Publications, 1972), p. 298.

centers oppose such efforts. Developers, viewing the deterioration of the central city with equanimity, are more concerned with influencing zoning regulations that will maximize the retail and industrial development of the peripheral areas. When such diverse interests are formally organized, as they usually are, under the umbrella of the Chamber of Commerce, the lobbying effectiveness of the Chamber is diminished by its difficulty in reconciling internal differences and presenting a united front. Naturally, the presenting of a united front is made more feasible when intrabusiness conflicts are kept to a minimum. This situation is most likely to occur in small towns, but, especially in the South and Southwest, business unity can be found in larger areas.

Although generalizations about business associations are obviously difficult, business—whether monolithic or divided—is a significant element in virtually all local political systems in terms of responsiveness. The subject will come up again in chapter 5 when we discuss recruitment and power structure, for it is here that the influence, subtle or overt, of business emerges: "Business interests are virtually guaranteed a hearing by local policy-makers, and businessmen tend to be well-educated, to have the social and verbal skills necessary to communicate effectively with bureaucrats and politicians and to perceive higher than average stakes in community decision."[51]

THE BUSINESS-CIVIC ASSOCIATION CONNECTION   Business activity is most efficient when it is shielded by the protective cloak of the civic association. City councils accord legitimacy to an interest group in direct proportion to the degree to which it is perceived as being community-oriented. Thus, civic associations are viewed as influential by city councils, and citizens' advisory committees are viewed as influential by school boards.[52] Roughly one-third of city council members, for instance, named civic associations as influential.[53] However, civic associations are often fronts for business interests or, at least, the interest of middle and upper classes. In Kansas City, Missouri, for instance, civic associations were founded in reaction to the Pendergast machine and succeeded in dominating the recruitment process to the city council. By phrasing their demands in terms of the "welfare of the community," civic associations allow such business and middle-class values as municipal reform to acquire the legitimacy that lower-class values cannot achieve. Because civic associations are public-regarding they attract the middle- and upper-class professionals and businessmen who are also active in business associations. Often, then, governmental reform, urban renewal, mass transit, and other agenda of good government merge with the interests of businessmen through the mechanism of the civic association.

LABOR AND LOCAL POLITICS   The business–civic association nexus, which finds the subject matter of local politics dear to its economic and ideological interests, stands in sharp contrast to organized labor, which both from an economic point of view and from the bias against special interests on the part of local officials, usually finds state politics more to its liking. In the Bay Area City Council Study, for example, only 13 councilmen (out of 435 interviewed) mentioned unions as influential.[54] Labor appears even less active in other arenas of local decision-making, such as school boards. The Zeigler-Jennings study found that only 3 percent of the respondents mentioned labor as being interested in education.[55]

Given the attention afforded organized labor as a national interest group, and (as we shall see in chapter 3) given its relatively intense activity in state politics, why should local politics prove so unwelcome? First, let us repeat the previous point: the accepted mode of group presentation is one that speaks for "the good of the community." Labor clearly does not enjoy such an image, as shown by examining its role in civic associations, which cloak interest group activities under the mantle of good government. Labor leaders do not appear as frequently as do business leaders in such organizations. Further, even when labor leaders do appear among their leadership, they are normally regarded as speaking for a "special interest" while businessmen enjoy the status of speaking for "the community": "Labor leaders rarely have this symbolic quality, but must be content with whatever stigma attaches to being from a lower-class background and associated with a special interest group."[56] In cities, as compared to states, this stigma can be considerable.

Again, the structure of local government, especially in nonpartisan elections, operates to the disadvantage of labor, which is widely (and correctly) identified as partisan. To an important degree: "nonpartisanship makes it difficult to conduct partisan campaigns acceptable to middle-status groups . . . the mass media of communication, which are conservative, are quick to stigmatize labor's political interest as partisan."[57] Additionally, nonpartisan elections weaken the influence of union leaders over union members. The rank-and-file union members tend to be somewhat more conservative than their leaders, especially on questions that bear directly or indirectly on racial issues.

In national elections, welfare and economic issues often obliterate or at least make less salient the racial biases of the working class. However, without party labels, union leaders have a difficult time influencing voting behavior of union members. Thus, in primary elections, despite the strong opposition of organized labor leadership, George Wallace has received a substantial portion of the working class, trade union members' votes. For example, in the 1964 primary elections in the North, considering only manual laborers, Wallace received 57 percent of the union members' vote compared to 39 percent of the nonunion labor vote. However, these same union members did not vote for Goldwater in the general election. "The Democrats and the trade unions raised the specter that a Goldwater victory would undermine all the economic gains made through the growth of unions and the extension of the welfare state. And when faced between a choice of voting their social anxieties or their economic concerns, many workers . . . opted for their economic concerns and voted for Johnson."[58] Without the psychological cue-providing mechanism of the political party, leaders are, at the local level, unable to "deliver."

A particularly apt example is Detroit, where, given the dominance of the automobile industry, the United Automobile Workers of America should be expected to play a major role in delivering votes. In effect, UAW's Committee on Political Education (COPE) functions as a political party by drafting platforms, endorsing candidates, and providing an exceptionally strong precinct organization. In alliance with the Democratic party, COPE has enjoyed extraordinary success in state politics, both electorally and in its lobbying efforts at the state capitol. In Detroit, however, COPE does not benefit from its alliance with the Democratic party, since elections are nonpartisan: there is no automatic voting cue provided. Thus, though well-trained and exhaustively organized COPE precinct workers have generated huge Democratic majorities in partisan national elections, they have conspicuously failed to achieve comparable success in Detroit local politics. The interplay of partisan attitudes and precinct organizational efforts is illustrated by Gray and Greenstone:

> Despite its power, COPE has had relatively little success in local politics. It has never elected a mayor despite repeated attempts, and it has never won a secure majority on the Common Council. There are two major reasons for its difficulties. In the first place, COPE is neither a political party nor a good government group—it is a labor union, on its face, a special interest. When COPE has tried to elect a Mayor, it has been vulnerable to charges of "labor domination" and of being a limited (therefore, presumably, selfish) interest trying to run the government of all

the people. In the second place, non-partisanship in local politics disrupts the complex of loyalties and issues that has led to Democratic victories in state and national elections. Many white union members, particularly the large groups of Poles and the growing groups of Southerners, are loyal Democrats who support the party's national social welfare programs. But they are also homeowners burdened with Detroit's heavy property tax. They are concerned about maintaining the economic level of their neighborhoods and keeping Negroes out. Because they are Democrats they might vote for liberal, pro-Negro candidates if city elections were partisan. But in non-partisan elections they are free to desert the liberal alliance to support conservative, pro-white candidates . . . without having to desert the Democratic party, for which they have great emotional loyalty.[59]

In addition to the ideological and structural bias against labor's participation in local politics, there is the additional factor of the scope of local decision-making. Labor's political goals are dealt with more readily at the state and national level: right to work laws, wage and hour legislation, regulation and enforcement of industrial safety standards. On such issues—as distinguished from the divisive question of race relations—labor can appear relatively united. As explained by labor leaders in Toledo: "City government just isn't as crucial to labor as state and national politics. Labor-management questions and welfare policies are handled in national and state government . . . city government is not as important for us. . . . The state in many ways is the most important . . . since it handles workmen's compensation, unemployment, and such things."[60]

The general rule of labor's lack of interest and lack of impact on local politics is not, of course, without exception. One distinction which can be made is between types of unions. In Los Angeles, for example, Industrial Unions, composed of semiskilled workers, are more concerned with local efforts of state and national governments. Craft Unions, with more highly paid workers, are more concerned with local bureaucracies. Craft Unions, in contrast with Industrial Unions, find sympathetic local bureaucracies helpful in the distribution of municipal contracts for building and construction. In St. Louis, however, a radically different picture emerges. As usual, most of organized labor is unconcerned about local politics. However, the Teamsters have traditionally been much more locally oriented. In the 1950s, Teamsters Local 688 emerged as an articulate local interest group, with its goals heavily loaded toward redistribution of local resources, especially with regard to low-income blacks. The Teamsters lobbied heavily (and successfully) for the enforcement of a rat control ordinance, advocated a graduated city income tax, supported a metropolitan government plan, and threatened legal action if the city did not enforce its air pollution ordinance. A particularly crucial source of support for St. Louis Teamsters was its close relationship to the black community. However, the Teamsters (perhaps to avoid rank-and-file protest), avoided direct involvement in civil rights. Though avoiding civil rights issues was acceptable to moderate black leaders in the fifties, the greater militancy of civil rights demands in the sixties appreciably weakened the labor-black alliance.

In every community, business will be active and effective. In most communities, labor will be neither. The occasional exceptions should not detract from this conclusion. Additionally, as race relations become more locally explosive, existing labor-black alliances (as in St. Louis) will become increasingly hard to sustain.

THE FRUSTRATION OF MINORITIES

AS WE noted in chapter 1, representational models of responsiveness concede a bias in the focus of response. The most consistently active groups are those to whom a response is most frequently made. But what of those who are systematically excluded from participation? Local governments need not be responsive, either representationally or in terms of congruence, if no sanction against nonresponsive behavior exists. The black experience is a case study of such a situation.

Black organizations in cities should be understood within two frameworks, one environmental and the other motivational. Although blacks constitute only about 11 percent of the national population, they are heavily concentrated in central cities, and there is every indication that the trend will continue in the direction of two separate communities within metropolitan areas: the blacks will occupy the central cities and the whites will occupy the suburbs and surrounding towns.

"White flight" can best be demonstrated by the percentages of white and black population shifts in the forty largest cities in the country. In twenty-five cities, the white population has declined. In fourteen, the white population has increased at a slower rate than the black population. In only one case (Indianapolis) has the white percentage of the population increased faster than the black, because of annexation of white suburbs. Blacks currently make up a majority of the central city population of Washington, Atlanta, and Newark. They are approaching a majority in Detroit, Baltimore, New Orleans, Oakland, Birmingham, and Gary.[61]

More importantly, blacks comprise a high percentage of voting age population, from which the active strata will be drawn. Patterson has recently noted that, in cities of 500,000 or more, blacks form perhaps the largest and most cohesive block, ranging between 28 percent (Chicago) to 67 percent (Washington).[62]

Though these population shifts and voting percentages will have conspicuous effects on both elections and recruitment, our immediate concern is with black political organizations. If central cities are becoming black ghettoes, then black organizations can be expected to be somewhat more active than one would estimate on the basis of blacks' lower socioeconomic status.

BLACKS AND POLITICAL ACTIVITY   Blacks participate in organizational politics less than whites, but there are some confounding elements. Racial differences in participation are, normally and correctly, attributed to the tendency of white persons to have higher socioeconomic status than blacks. Here, the argument is made that if *blacks* were to rise in status, their participation would increase. Other major differences between black and white organizational behavior have been discussed. Myrdal, in the 1940s, found blacks unusually active in voluntary (however, nonpolitical) organizations and viewed the situation as pathological: "Negroes are active in associations because they are not allowed to be active in much of the other organized life of American society. . . . Negroes are largely kept out, not only of politics proper, but of most purposive and creative work in trade unions, businessmen's groups, pressure groups, large-scale civic improvement and charity associations, and the like."[63]

Myrdal's thesis is that blacks join organizations for psychic relief rather than political activity. In a similar vein, Floyd Hunter found the Atlanta black community highly organized, with the organizational structure providing a framework for a "subcommunity." However, the subcommunity "stands alone in its isolation from the sources of power as no other unit within the metropolitan area. Its channels of communication in most of its power relations with the larger community are partially blocked, if not totally closed."[64]

Such isolation, far more extreme than that of organized labor, for example, provided the foundations for group consciousness, which in turn offered a basis for urban political organization more assertive than that of lower-class whites. The problem, of course, is that such organizational activity, if isolated, did not bring blacks into the struggle for community influence. Rather than bringing blacks into closer contact with the larger community, their participation would be restricted to the ethnic community. Yet it is also possible that the sense of ethnic identification engendered by organizational participation would spill over once a break in the opportunity structure took place.

Such opportunities began in 1954, with the *Brown* v. *Board of Education* decision[65] outlawing segregation of schools; it was a symbolic victory of major impact. Tangible benefits were minimal. Southern states mounted intense—and effective—efforts to circumvent the decision. However, the decision—in addition to boosting morale—virtually compelled blacks to engage in public disputes with the dominant white power structure. The Supreme Court did intend to have desegregation occur speedily, but it placed primary responsibility for implementation on local school boards. Thus, if blacks wanted to transfer symbolic victory into tangible results, they would have to become active in the larger community. As Kenneth Clark notes: "This [civil rights] movement would probably not have existed at all were it not for the 1954 Supreme Court school-desegregation decision which provided a tremendous boost to the morale of Negroes by its clear affirmation that color is irrelevant to the rights of American citizens. *Until this time, the Southern Negro generally had accommodated himself to the separation of the black from the white society.*"[66]

If Clark was right, then there should be some evidence that blacks, expanding from the comfort of their earlier organizational isolation, engaged in public participation. Such indeed appears to be the case. By 1957, blacks were becoming more public-oriented.[67] By the 1960s, the trend was even more pronounced. The development of racial identity, latent in the black subcommunity of the 1940s and early 1950s, flourished during the civil rights movements of the 1960s, and supports more traditional political efforts in the 1970s.

This development of group consciousness is crucial to the understanding of black urban politics because it may provide a surrogate for the normal stimuli for participation. For the lower-income white, partisan identification serves as such a stimulus. For upper-income whites, social status provides the push. Because most blacks are of lower status, group consciousness could conceivably counteract the usually depressing impact of poverty. For local politics, largely without partisan information, group consciousness could be doubly crucial.

The 1967 Verba-Nie study provides ideal data for testing these notions. Table 2.19 clearly portrays the overall pattern of black involvement, using the modes of participation presented earlier.

Table 2.19.   Over- or Underrepresentation of Blacks in Participation Types (in percentages)

Inactive	+.21
Voting specialist	+.05
Parochial participant	−.19
Communalist	−.24
Partisan	+.03
Complete activist	−.06

Source: From *Participation in America: Political Democracy and Social Equality* by Sidney Verba and Norman H. Nie: Table 10-1 (p. 152). Copyright © 1972 by Sidney Verba and Norman H. Nie. Reprinted by permission of Harper & Row, Publishers, Inc.

Initially, the preceding discussion seems to include some disparities. First, blacks are severely overrepresented in the inactive category. Such is to be expected, given their lower socioeconomic status. Second, there is a surprising underrepresentation in the communalist category. However, communal activity is less conflictual than other modes of participation. It is conceivable (though not, unfortunately, completely verifiable) that, had the same measure been employed prior to the black awakening, communal activity would have been much higher. We suggest, then, that a shift from communal, nonconflictual, to more conflict-laden modes (partisan and complete activists) may have occurred. Such a notion is supported to some extent by table 2.19.

By the 1960s, blacks, despite their comparatively low socioeconomic status, were more active than comparably impoverished whites. Further, and most significantly, the higher the socioeconomic ladder, the greater the overparticipation of blacks. To put it another way, the difference in participation between lower socioeconomic status blacks and upper socioeconomic status blacks is greater than the difference between the lower socioeconomic status whites and upper socioeconomic whites. As Verba and Nie put it: "when blacks break through the barrier that separates the totally inactive from those who engage in at least some activity, they are likely to move to quite high levels of such activity."[68] On one hand, blacks at all levels were activated, but on the other hand, the greatest activation occurred at the higher levels of black society (which contains, of course, fewer people).

An additional factor can be brought into play to explain why blacks are more active than one would predict: group consciousness, a crucial characteristic not shared by the white community. The more blacks are conscious of their group identity—measured by the number of times blacks referred to race in being interviewed—the more likely they are to engage in political activity. But we have already seen that upper status blacks are more active than their white counterparts. That is to say, blacks, regardless of socioeconomic status, participate equally with whites if they have a sense of group identity. If one takes the final step, and looks both at socioeconomic status *and* group consciousness simultaneously, we find an additional boost: upper-status blacks, with a strong feeling of group consciousness, exceed whites in their level of participation.[69]

Organizationally, the implications of the hyperactivity of group-conscious relatively well-off blacks is somewhat ironic. Though blacks at all levels were more active than expected purely on the basis of the standard relationship between class and participation, the organizational activity of blacks tended to cluster among those of higher status, as is also true for whites.

The role of black organizations in local politics is illustrated by James Q. Wilson's statement: "At no time during the 1960's did lower-class or street corner blacks become effectively mobilized or permanently organized as part of the civil rights movement. Such persons from time to time did engage in dramatic confrontations with public officials: any such encounter, for a while, could be made to appear the result of an important organizational effort, when in fact, most were *ad hoc* and short-lived. But these events gave to such groups as CORE and SNCC a distinctive posture—*though composed of middle class members,* they cultivated a lower-class style."[70]

Sustained organizational activity, an essential, if not sufficient, condition for achieving one's political goals, is thus helped and hampered by the bias in black activism. The hostile outbursts of the 1960s did not generate such organizational permanence. Additionally, they reduced the probability of coalitional activities, which had characterized black urban organizations. The riots—and the rioters—came and went, but the urban organizations were left with the problem of negotiation and bargaining with white elites.

In preriot days, most black organizations were dominated by traditional leaders of substantially higher social status than the black masses. Such organizational activists set their sights primarily upon ameliorating the status of blacks without substantially modifying the existing distribution of political influence. In coalition with liberal or public-regarding whites, depending on the racial conflict composition of the city, such organizations as the NAACP and the Urban League sought, for example, higher wages, better housing, and more equitable welfare treatment for *individual blacks.* The political and economic advancement of blacks *as a group* was generally avoided. Nonideological leadership at the local level, while hardly maximizing group consciousness, fit well with the political realities of the day: to achieve even modest individual gains, black organizations had to cooperate with those whites willing to listen.

To some degree, whites listened more attentively when local elections were held on a partisan, ward basis. In such cases, black organizations appeared remarkably similar to the traditional urban machine. Concentrated in black wards, the black electorate was able to achieve some representation on city councils. These representatives, however, could not adopt a black point of view. Chicago is the classic case of the black submachine; its legendary black boss, William L. Dawson, whose power in five all-black wards was surely equal (although more geographically limited) to that of the real boss, Mayor Richard Daley. Indeed, Dawson became a Democratic committeeman in 1939 and developed his style of bargaining with white machine bosses well before Richard Daley was elected in the 1950s. The relationship was mutually beneficial. Dawson himself enjoyed a safe seat in the U.S. House of Representatives, and was able to control the selection of local officials and state representatives from his area of Chicago. He was also able to deliver to the Daley organization a solid black vote. In return, Daley provided Dawson with demonstrable evidence of authority, thus enabling Dawson to hold his machine together. Individual black complaints could be handled efficiently, according to Banfield and Wilson: "Where the direct, material interests of his constituents are at stake, he and his organization are ready to help; they will get a sick man into the county hospital, find out why an old lady's welfare check has not arrived, defend a beleaguered homeowner against the urban renewal authority, and go to the police commissioner and if necessary, the mayor, to see to it that a case of alleged police brutality is properly investigated. Matters involving negro rights in the abstract do not interest them, however."[71]

Dawson's machine agreed not only to avoid abstract issues of race relations and to deliver a large black vote, but also to combat militant opposition to the Daley organization within the black community. Banfield and Wilson report, for instance, that the Dawson machine once packed a membership meeting of the NAACP to unseat a militant officer.[72] "Realistically, the power structure of Chicago is hardly less white than that of Mississippi."[73]

The rise of black consciousness and the consequent development of more ideologically oriented organizations posed a threat to traditional black leadership. In Chicago, the black machine was additionally threatened by Dawson's death in 1970. He was succeeded by Ralph Metcalfe, a former alderman and long-time supporter of the black machine.

The transformation of Chicago's black machine after Dawson's death illustrates the plight of traditional black leadership. An alderman for sixteen years, Metcalfe had never wavered in his support for the Daley machine. His loyalty was rewarded with the opportunity to become a U.S. representative. With heavy machine support, he defeated an insurgent black in the 1970 primary with an astonishing 71 percent of the vote. However, in 1972 Metcalfe broke with the Daley machine because of an act of police brutality. Two black men were beaten up by police, an event that certainly had occurred before. In this case, however, the two black men were middle-class professionals, prominent in the black community. Metcalfe, who had been growing somewhat impatient with the Daley machine, was outraged at the beatings: "He knew that such abuses were common, though their victims were ordinarily of less repute in the community."[74] He demanded and was refused a meeting with Mayor Daley. Thus the break between the black submachine and the larger Daley machine was formalized.

Henceforth, Daley could no longer count on the endorsement of traditional black leadership. Additionally, more organizations of the moderate to militant variety, especially Jesse Jackson's People United to Save Humanity (PUSH), had been urging blacks to be less obedient to the white machine. For instance, operation PUSH conducted massive campaigns to convince black voters to split their tickets on a much more discriminatory basis than they had in the past.

The battle lines were drawn clearly in 1975, when Daley sought reelection. Jesse Jackson, a major leader of the black movement (it successfully replaced Daley's slate at the 1972 Democratic convention), first considered endorsing a white liberal challenger to the Daley machine, then settled on another challenger, a black state senator. Metcalfe supported the white liberal. Thus, a great step in the black revolt against the Daley machine had been taken.

The consequence, however, reveals a basic weakness in black leadership built on cooperative relations with white elites. Though Daley's vote in black precincts declined about 10 percent, he still carried black wards with comfortable majorities and was reelected. At the precinct level, Daley accomplished an extraordinary organizational achievement. He was able to convert black precinct captains, formerly loyal to Dawson and then to Metcalfe, to his own organization. In effect, he seized, for himself the guts of the black machine and left Metcalfe stripped of power. Thus, although his black support was reduced, the Daley machine met—and defeated—the black machine.

Even in defeat (indeed, cooptation), however, the black machine in Chicago provides some hints of the future of black organizations. Certainly the "traditional" black machine politicians have seen their last days. Although Chicago may be unique in that it remains as the last of the urban machines even after Daley's death, it is not unique in its population trends. In addition to the increase in black population within central cities, the 1970 census reveals that Chicago's black ghettoes, like most ghettoes throughout the country, lost population! There is somewhat less concentration of blacks now than ten years ago, a fact that will probably strengthen the hand of moderate, coalitional groups, which, ironically, moderated the intensity of black consciousness.

The Effects of Protest

Obviously, black consciousness was strengthened by the riots of the 1960s. Organizationally, however, the effects of the riots is less obvious. The rise and fall of violent protest is an oft-told tale, one that will forever leave social scientists puzzled about why they occurred and why they ceased (at least for the moment). A few generalizations, however, seem to be accurate. First, a set of rising expectations was clearly generated by national legal victories, for which the NAACP can assume the rightful role of leader. Additionally, a considerable amount of rhetoric surrounded national legislation in the area of civil rights—for example, the "War on Poverty" mandated maximum feasible participation; presidents spoke of the urgent need to correct income discrepancies immediately. This created the impression that the black problem was amenable to quick solution. According to one widely accepted hypothesis, two conditions increase the possibility of violence: (1) persons with a long history of unequal treatment perceive the possibility of an improvement of their conditions; (2) these same persons perceive that they are being thwarted.[75]

The irony of the riots of the 1960s was, of course, that the rising expectations of blacks were created largely, if not solely, as a consequence of national policy. Yet the most available target of black hostility was local government, which, unresponsive though it may have been, had not promised what it could not deliver.

As the disparity between what was promised and what could realistically be accomplished became more evident, the black movement entered a more militant phase. Traditional leaders, such as Dawson and Metcalfe in Chicago, were largely outside the movement. In their stead, nonviolent, organized protests were led by Martin Luther King. He, in turn, was eclipsed even before his death by more militant blacks in the middle of the 1960s. King, confronted (although appalled) by advocates of black power, sought, to maintain control over the movement, to embrace some of the tenets implied in the phrase "black power." He failed, as did his more radical challengers. In reality, however, as the basis of black protest broadened and became more violent, the ability of any organization to guide the protest diminished. The riots spelled the end of both traditional and radical political organizations. This is not to suggest that rioters were riffraff. Whereas whites often perceived rioters as undereducated criminals, they were not. Rioters were, in fact, slightly better educated than the average black, were no more likely to have engaged in previous criminal behavior, and had an income roughly equal to the average black. In Newark and Detroit, for example, "The rioters are not the poorest of the poor. They are not the hard-core unemployed. They are not the least educated."[76]

One would be surprised, given the theory of rising expectations explained earlier, if such were not the case. The rioters were exactly those whose expectations were raised by the promise of a national government responsive, at last, to their needs. Traditional black organizations—even those with the most radical rhetoric and goals—could do nothing. Hence, between 1963 and 1969, more than 300 outbursts of racial violence occurred in central cities. Rarely, however, were they collective acts (in the sense of organizational leadership and planning). Banfield, for instance, has classified the outbreaks as either "rampages," "forays for pillage," "outbursts," or "demonstrations."[77] Though most riots contained at least two of these elements, they were all characterized by the inability of black organizations to gain control of the violence and thus use it as a political weapon. Conceivably, if an organization had been able to promise peace in exchange for, say, an end to police brutality, some political and organizational gains could have been accomplished: "The collective racial violence from 1963 through 1968 was relatively spontaneous and unorganized."[78]

Unfortunately, these spontaneous outbursts destroyed more than property. A far more serious consequence was a polarization of attitudes between blacks and whites and a growing determination of white local, state, and federal authorities to repress violence. Law and order, a crudely phrased synonym for repression, played a major role in the election of Richard Nixon in 1968. It was clear, from 1968 on, that the posture of the national government had shifted.

Additionally, supported by generous grants from the newly created Law Enforcement Administration Association, local police were developing sophisticated riot control techniques. The development of effective counterriot techniques brought yet another, even less structured, phase to black violence.

Violence became exotic and underground, with no claim to mass support. Contrary to popular assumptions by whites, the violence in the 1963–1968 period received the support, if not the active participation, of at least one-third of the black population. Guerrilla warfare, although somewhat more highly organized, could claim only a smattering of support. As Downes has explained, the 1963–1968 period was one of property-oriented outbursts.[79] In response, white authorities developed remarkably efficient techniques to deal with fairly widespread riots. The rhetoric from Washington—and the money for helicopters, mace, and other riot control measures—made it clear that the future of the hostile outbursts was limited.

Thus, the Black Panthers engaged in guerrilla warfare, which was more difficult to confront. Instead of massive assaults against property, this form of violence was manifested by killing policemen and other human symbols of white authority. Predictably, white authorities escalated their efforts to combat such underground organizations. Many black leaders were forced out of the country. Others, like Bobby Seale of the Black Panthers in Oakland, exchanged bullets for ballots (Seale ran unsuccessfully for mayor). Other Panthers seeking local office have received the endorsement of the local AFL-CIO and Democratic party.

Perhaps the last gasp of this phase of urban violence is the bizarre history of the Symbionese Liberation Army. As civil disturbances began to respond to efficient riot control techniques, violent crime, directed against individuals, increased (for example, the number of police killed by felons was 55 in 1963, and 126 in 1971). Hostile outbursts turned into political terror, common to other countries, became a reality with the organization and destruction of the Symbionese Liberation Army. The murder of black Oakland School Superintendent Marcus Foster and the kidnapping of Patricia Hearst were the first examples of the conversion of person-oriented violence into political terror. The SLA appeared to be an outgrowth of black and student protests of the 1960s, but was actually organized by inmates at California's Soledad Prison. At most, the SLA was composed of twenty-five members. Yet, its extraordinary violence produced a threat potentially more dangerous than the riots of the 1960s. Mass political violence can be readily contained; systematic sabotage cannot. A complex society with advanced and centralized public communications can become the target of a small group of ideologically motivated individuals with an impact far out of proportion to their size. Consequently, the extreme brutality with which the SLA was eliminated can be viewed as an inevitable response of white elites to a threat to their survival.

As the violence ran its course, the organizational structure of the black community became fragmented. As it became apparent that nobody was in charge and that no group of black leaders could bargain with their white local counterparts, violence clearly became counterproductive. In any case, the main bargaining agent was not local government, but rather the massive federal bureaucracy that had been assembled to "eliminate poverty." As these programs, originally created to circumvent a hostile local power structure, were dismantled, another opportunity for organization was eliminated. Especially crucial was Nixon's dismantling of the Office of Economic Opportunity, which had—within its limited resources—attempted to be responsive.

Most civil rights organizations of the 1960s, proved ineffective by the violence, have passed from the scene, with the exception of the National Association for the Advancement of Colored People. The NAACP existed before the riots, and it has withstood the challenges of more militant, albeit temporary leaders. It continues to emphasize litigation as a basic resource and has been active in seeking political support for busing, a position which has moved the formerly conservative organization more into the mainstream of black ideology. Additionally, Jesse Jackson, in Chicago, no longer guides the PUSH organization into protest, but rather into "civil economics"—that is, working directly with employers to increase the number of black employees. With regard to responsiveness, such efforts of the past can be understood as a reaction to the fact that blacks could not achieve sufficient response. Inflammatory statements and violent crime were targeted not to officeholders, but toward the mass media. They did not seek to increase responsiveness, but rather to change the rules of the game. Rather than seeking a response from government, they sought a substantial (but unspecified) alteration in the structure of government.

The survival of such organizations as the NAACP and PUSH coincides with the black mood of frustration and, paradoxically, pride. From a power perspective, however, the next decade of black leaders will probably seek to expand black electoral power and the recruitment of black officials. Thus we run full circle: for the immediate future, the black movement will depend on coalition with liberal whites, a coalition made more tenuous both by white backlash and the development of black pride.

CONCLUSION

ALL FORMS of activity in state and local politics—especially local politics—attract a disproportionate share of individuals and groups from the middle and upper social strata. This bias can be accounted for in three ways. First, the relatively well-to-do are more knowledgeable and skillful in politics than their working-class counterparts. Not only do they display a more sustained individual interest by voting, they are linked organizationally to the infrastructure of government. Second, because of the historical importance of the upper classes in the reform movement, state and local governmental institutions are designed to be responsive to the articulate few. Third, the articulate few, however civic-minded they appear, rarely ask governments to engage in redistributive policies. Thus, state and local governments find it easier to be responsive to the upper classes because their demands are for incremental change.

Incremental change also is becoming typical of other minorities. Initially, there was no incentive for congruent responsiveness to racial minorities because their participation rate was low. However, changing demographic or residence patterns are introducing incentives. In many urban areas former minorities are now electoral majorities. Voting and more sustained activity increases the probability of a congruent response.

Such participation also increases the probability of a representative response. As social and ethnic minorities become electoral majorities, they can also reduce the upper-class white bias of elected officeholders.

Prior to the hostile outburst, the limited nature of minority demands could be accommodated by the limited representation provided by white elites. When the scope of demands escalated, response declined. Hence, violence erupted. Violence was both a frustrated reaction and an unsuccessful attempt to change the political structure. The failure required a return to more acceptable patterns of constituent demand and governmental response.

In state politics, mass participation is facilitated by the presence of partisan elections. However, sustained activity is still the province of the few, those who seek to defend the status quo. Chapter 3 considers sustained activity in state politics in greater detail.

NOTES

1.
For an examination of the distribution of local governments between the states see *The U.S. Fact Book: The American Almanac 1977* (New York: Grosset and Dunlap, 1977), p. 257.

2.
Ibid.

3.
Thomas R. Dye, *Understanding Public Policy* (Englewood Cliffs, N.J.: Prentice-Hall, Inc., 1972), pp. 132–133.

4.
Gabriel A. Almond and Sidney Verba, *The Civic Culture* (Princeton, N.J.: Princeton University Press, 1963), pp. 80–81.

5.
William A. Schultze, *Urban and Community Politics* (North Scituate, Mass.: Duxbury Press, 1974), p. 223.

6.
Edward C. Banfield and James Q. Wilson, *City Politics* (Cambridge, Mass.: Harvard University Press and the MIT Press, 1963), p. 139.

7.
Ibid.

8.
Eugene C. Lee, *The Politics of Nonpartisanship: A Study of California City Elections* (Berkeley: The University of California Press, 1960), pp. 139–40.

9.
Edward C. Banfield, *The Unheavenly City* (Boston: Little, Brown, 1970), p. 53.

10.
Gerald M. Pomper, *Elections in America: Control and Influence in Democratic Politics* (New York: Dodd, Mead, 1968), p. 71.

11.
Jerome M. Clubb and Michael W. Traugott, "National Patterns of Referenda Voting: The 1968 Election," in Harlan Hahn (ed.), *People and Politics in Urban Society* (Beverly Hills, Calif.: Sage Publications, 1972), p. 137. Much of the data on referenda voting is adapted from the same article, pp. 137–69.

12.
Ibid., p. 146.

13.

The discussion that follows by Edward C. Banfield and James Q. Wilson on "public-regarding" in local bond referenda is based on "Public-Regardingness as a Value Premise in Voting Behavior," *The American Political Science Review* 58 (December 1964): 876–87.

14.

Ibid., p. 879.

15.

Ibid., p. 885.

16.

This survey, by Lewis Bowman, Dennis S. Ippolito, and Martin L. Levin, is found in "Self-Interest and Referendum Support: The Case of a Rapid Transit Vote in Atlanta," in Harlan Hahn (ed.), *People and Politics in Urban Society* (Beverly Hills, Calif.: Sage Publications, 1972), pp. 119–36.

17.

Sidney Verba and Norman H. Nie, *Participation in America: Political Democracy and Social Equality* (New York: Harper & Row, 1972), p. 210.

18.

Ibid., pp. 218–19.

19.

An item on the 1964 Detroit ballot as quoted in Harlan Hahn, "Northern Referenda on Fair Housing: The Response of White Voters," *The Western Political Quarterly* 21 (September 1968): 485.

20.

Ibid., pp. 483–95.

21.

Ibid., p. 493.

22.

Ibid., p. 493.

23.

Harlan Hahn and Timothy Almy, "Ethnic Politics and Racial Issues; Voting in Los Angeles," *The Western Political Quarterly* 24 (December 1971): 728–29.

24.

Thomas F. Pettigrew, "When a Black Candidate Runs for Mayor: Race and Voting Behavior," in Harlan Hahn (ed.), *People and Politics in Urban Society* (Beverly Hills, Calif.: Sage Publications, 1972), p. 103.

25.
Jeffrey K. Hadden, Louis H. Masotti, and Victor Thiessen, "The Making of the Negro Mayors, 1967," *Transaction* 5 (February 1968): 21–30.

26.
Pettigrew, "When a Black Candidate Runs for Mayor," p. 109.

27.
This discussion of "relative deprivation" comes from Pettigrew, ibid., pp. 113–14.

28.
James S. Coleman, *Community Conflict* (New York: Free Press, 1967), p. 119.

29.
Frederick M. Wirt and Michael W. Kirst, *The Political Web of American Schools* (Boston: Little, Brown, 1972), p. 108.

30.
Howard Hamilton and Sylvan Cohen, *Policy-Making by Plebiscite* (Lexington, Mass.: D. C. Heath, 1974), p. 79.

31.
Philip K. Piele and John Stuart Hall, *Budgets, Bonds, and Ballots* (Lexington, Mass.: D. C. Heath, 1973), p. 149.

32.
Clarence N. Stone, "Local Referendums: An Alternative to the Alienated-Voter Model," *The Public Opinion Quarterly* 29 (Summer 1965): 220–21.

33.
Robert L. Lineberry and Ira Sharkansky, *Urban Politics and Public Policy* (New York: Harper & Row, 1971), pp. 91–92. Italics added.

34.
Robert A. Dahl, "The City in the Future of Democracy," *The American Political Science Review* 61 (December 1967), p. 968.

35.
M. Kent Jennings and L. Harmon Zeigler, "The Salience of American State Politics," *The American Political Science Review* 64 (June 1970): 532.

36.
Lester W. Milbrath, "Political Participation in the States," in Herbert Jacob and Kenneth N. Vines (eds.), *Politics in the American States,* 1st ed., (Boston: Little, Brown, 1965), p. 50.

37.
Thomas R. Dye, *Politics, Economics, and the Public: Policy Outcomes in the American States* (Chicago: Rand-McNally, 1966), p. 71.

38.

Austin Ranney, "Parties in State Politics," in Herbert Jacob and Kenneth N. Vines (eds.), *Politics in the American States,* 3rd ed., (Boston: Little, Brown, 1976), pp. 51–91.

39.

Verba and Nie, *Participation in America,* pp. 79–80. The following discussion on three categories of participation is also from *Participation in America.*

40.

Louis Wirth, "Urbanism as a Way of Life," *The American Journal of Sociology* 44 (July 1938): 22.

41.

Verba and Nie, *Participation in America,* p. 91.

42.

Ibid., p. 181.

43.

Ibid., p. 208.

44.

L. Harmon Zeigler, M. Kent Jennings, with G. Wayne Peak, *Governing American Schools: Political Interaction in Local School Districts* (North Scituate, Mass.: Duxbury Press, 1974), pp. 100–101.

45.

Ibid., p. 105.

46.

Edward C. Banfield and James Q. Wilson, "Organized Labor in City Politics," in Edward C. Banfield (ed.), *Urban Government: A Reader in Administration and Politics* (New York: Free Press, 1969), p. 492.

47.

Harmon Zeigler and Michael Baer, *Lobbying: Interaction and Influence in American State Legislatures* (Belmont, Calif.: Wadsworth, 1969), pp. 113–14.

48.

Terry N. Clark, "The Structure of Community Influence," in Harlan Hahn (ed.), *People and Politics in Urban Society* (Beverly Hills, Calif.: Sage Publications, 1972), p. 296.

49.

Ibid., pp. 296–97, 299. Italics added.

50.

Charles R. Adrian and Charles Press, *Governing Urban America* (New York: McGraw-Hill, 1968), p. 125.

51.
Lineberry and Sharkansky, *Urban Politics,* pp. 66–67.

52.
For city councilmen responses on the influence of civic associations, see, Betty H. Zisk, *Local Interest Politics: A One-Way Street* (Indianapolis: Bobbs-Merrill, 1973), p. 23. For school board responses to the influence of citizens and advisory committees, see Zeigler, Jennings, with Peak, *Governing American Schools,* pp. 99, 114.

53.
Zisk, *Local Interest Politics,* p. 23.

54.
Ibid.

55.
Zeigler, Jennings, with Peak, *Governing American Schools,* p. 99.

56.
Banfield and Wilson, *City Politics,* pp. 282–83.

57.
William H. Form, "Organized Labor's Place in the Community Power Structure," *Industrial and Labor Relations Review* 12 (July 1959): 539.

58.
Seymour Martin Lipset, *Revolution and Counterrevolution: Change and Persistence in Social Structures* (New York: Basic Books, 1968), p. 326.

59.
Kenneth E. Gray and David Greenstone, "Organized Labor in City Politics," in Edward C. Banfield (ed.), *Urban Government: A Reader in Administration and Politics,* 1st ed. (New York: Free Press, 1961), p. 372.

60.
Quoted in Jean L. Stinchcombe, *Reform and Reaction: City Politics in Toledo* (Belmont, Calif.: Wadsworth, 1968), p. 156.

61.
See *1970 Census of the Population* (Washington, D.C.: Department of Commerce, Bureau of the Census, 1972).

62.
Ernest Patterson, *Black City Politics* (New York: Dodd, Mead, 1974), p. 254.

63.
Gunnar Myrdal, *An American Dilemma: The Negro Problem and Modern Democracy* (New York: Harper, 1944), pp. 952–53.

64.

Floyd Hunter, *Community Power Structure: A Study of Decision Makers* (Chapel Hill: University of North Carolina Press, 1953), p. 148.

65.

Brown v. *Board of Education,* 347 U.S. 483, 74 S. Ct., 686, 98L. Ed. 873 (1954).

66.

Kenneth B. Clark, "The Civil Rights Movement: Momentum and Organization," in Talcott Parsons and Kenneth B. Clark (eds.), *The Negro American* (Boston: Beacon Press, 1966), p. 610. Italics added.

67.

Marvin E. Olsen, "Social and Political Participation of Blacks," *American Sociological Review* 35 (August 1970): 694.

68.

Verba and Nie, *Participation in America,* p. 155.

69.

For an excellent discussion of the effect of black group consciousness on black participation see ibid., pp. 149–73.

70.

James Q. Wilson, *Political Organizations* (New York: Basic Books, 1973), p. 189. Italics added.

71.

Banfield and Wilson, *City Politics,* pp. 304–305.

72.

Ibid., p. 305.

73.

Harold M. Baron, "Black Powerlessness in Chicago," *Transaction* 1 (November 1968): 30.

74.

Michael Barone, Grant Ujifusa, and Douglas Matthews, *The Almanac of American Politics, 1974* (Boston: Gambit, 1975), p. 262.

75.

See, for example, James C. Davies, "Towards A Theory of Revolution," *American Sociological Review* 27 (February 1962): 5–19; and Ted Robert Gurr, *Why Men Rebel* (Princeton, N.J.: Princeton University Press, 1970).

76.

Nathan S. Caplan and Jeffrey M. Paige, "A Study of Ghetto Rioters," *Scientific American* 219 (August 1968): 19.

77.
Banfield, *The Unheavenly City,* pp. 187–92.

78.
Downes, *Politics, Change, and the Urban Crisis,* p. 255.

79.
Ibid.

3

INTEREST-GROUP ACTIVITY IN STATE POLITICS

IN THIS chapter we shall examine interest-group activity, particularly lobbyists and their method of interacting with state legislators. Because of the size, complexity, and remoteness of state government, group representation is the most feasible way for individuals' demands to be transmitted to decision-makers. Hence, representational response is the object of our inquiry. Which groups make demands? Which demands are more easily accommodated by decision-makers. As noted in chapter 1, we discuss organized group activity at the state level in detail because it is the most important mode of communication between nongovernmental actors and state officials. We first consider briefly the political-economic setting that influences the strength and behavior of interest groups in the several states. Then we will describe the various patterns of group conflict and accommodation that have emerged in a select category of states. The background of lobbyists and how they communicate demands will complete our analysis.

It is not difficult to establish that the economic and social systems of a society structure its political system, but it is more difficult to establish the manner in which these systems interact. If the socioeconomic structure of a state determines the behavior and importance of interest groups, it probably influences other components of the political system. Furthermore, the strength of the party system itself can inhibit or encourage interest groups. It has long been suggested that strong party cohesion in legislative voting contributes to interest groups. Yet, if we examine the causes of party voting, we find a relationship with great variation between legislative cohesion and party competition. If we probe deeper, we discover that both legislative cohesion and party competition are related to the industrialization and urbanization of a state. Accordingly, it is best to treat economic and political variables as components in a single system, rather than as independent or dependent variables.

Table 3.1 describes the strength of pressure groups in the American states in terms of three variables:[1] strength of party competition, legislative cohesion, and the socioeconomic variables of urban population, including per capita income and the percentage of the population employed in occupations other than agriculture, forestry, and fishing (industrialization index). Taken together, these economic factors indicate the existence or absence of a heterogeneous society with its corresponding increase or decrease in group tensions. A state with a high per capita income, a high percentage of its population employed in industrial occupations, and a high proportion of its population living in urban areas should exhibit a strong and active group life, but not necessarily a strong pressure group system. This becomes clear if we examine table 3.1.

Pressure groups are most successful when political parties and legislative cohesion are weakest and when the socioeconomic variables are lowest. Two patterns emerge: first, strong pressure groups, weak parties (both electorally and legislatively), and low urban population engaged in nonindustrial occupations; and second, moderate or weak pressure groups, competitive parties, and an urban, industrial economy. In short, pressure politics, party politics, and socioeconomic structures are related.

Strong, cohesive political parties could facilitate the responsiveness of governments through the electoral process. In such cases the response would be to a larger group than that normally served by interest groups. However, as we have seen in chapter 2, elections are imperfect instruments for communicating citizens' policy preferences. Strong interest groups, which thrive when parties are weak, are more efficient instru-

Table 3.1. The Strength of Pressure Groups in Varying Political and Economic Situations

| Social conditions | Types of pressure systems[a] | | |
	Strong[b] (24 states)	Moderate[c] (14 states)	Weak[d] (7 states)
Party competition			
One-party	33.3%	0%	0%
Modified one-party	37.5	42.8	0
Two-party	29.1	57.1	100.0
Cohesion of parties in legislature			
Weak cohesion	75.0	14.2	0
Moderate cohesion	12.5	35.7	14.2
Strong cohesion	12.5	50.0	85.7
Socioeconomic variables			
Urban population	58.6	65.1	73.3
Per capita income	$1,900	$2,335	$2,450
Industrialization index	88.8	92.8	94.0

Source: Belle Zeller (ed.), *American State Legislatures,* 2nd ed. (New York: Thomas Y. Crowell, 1954), pp. 190–91; and Austin Ranney, "Parties in State Politics," in *Politics in the American States,* ed. Herbert Jacob and Kenneth R. Vines (Boston: Little, Brown, 1976), p. 61.

[a] Alaska, Hawaii, Idaho, New Hampshire, and North Dakota are not classified or included.

[b] Alabama, Arizona, Arkansas, California, Florida, Georgia, Iowa, Kentucky, Louisiana, Maine, Michigan, Minnesota, Mississippi, Montana, Nebraska, New Mexico, North Carolina, Oklahoma, Oregon, South Carolina, Tennessee, Texas, Washington, Wisconsin.

[c] Delaware, Illinois, Kansas, Maryland, Massachusetts, Nevada, New York, Ohio, Pennsylvania, South Dakota, Utah, Vermont, Virginia, West Virginia.

[d] Colorado, Connecticut, Indiana, Missouri, New Jersey, Rhode Island, Wyoming.

ments of communication. However, they articulate the views of only part of the general population.

Notable exceptions, however, occur in California and Michigan, which are hardly nonindustrial, nonurban states, yet both have strong pressure groups. Nevertheless, the pattern is clear enough that the deviant states do not destroy its applicability. Every state in the South is in the strong pressure group category, because its economy is less developed and organizational memberships are the fewest. What produces a strong pressure group system in these states? The nonindustrial nature of the economy is not a fundamental cause, but rather the lack of diversity in such economies. That is, states with nonindustrial economies tend to be dominated by one type of enterprise, whereas industrial economies are keyed to a larger number of businesses and are less likely to be monopolized.

EMERGING PATTERNS OF GROUP CONFLICT

THE FACT that interest groups thrive in nonindustrial states does not mean that there is a single pattern of group activity. Rather, four distinct patterns emerge from the strong pressure group category of states. First, there is the typical strong pressure group pattern consisting of a nondiversified economy, relatively noncompetitive party politics, and weak legislative cohesion. This pattern describes the southern states and such states as Maine, which have similar economic and political systems. In these states the strength of interest groups is achieved by an alliance of dominant groups.

The next pattern combines an equally nondiversified economy with two-party politics and moderate legislative cohesion, such as in Montana. Here we find that a single dominant interest strengthens the pressure system.

The third pattern consists of a nondiversified industrial economy, two-party politics, and strong legislative cohesion. The best example of this pattern is Michigan, where there is a conflict between two dominant groups.

Finally, California is an example of the fourth pattern, with a diversified economy, two-party politics, and weak legislative cohesion. A classic case of the free play of interest groups in a legislature unencumbered by demands originating from political parties, California illustrates the triumph of many interests. To understand how each system operates, we will explore them in some detail.

Alliance of Dominant Groups

A good example of the first pattern is Maine, of which Lockard writes: "In few American states are the reins of government more openly or completely in the hands of a few leaders of economic interest groups than in Maine."[2] Specifically, electric power, timber, and manufacturing—the "Big Three"—have been the catalysts for much of the political controversy in the state. Other interests occasionally voice demands, but the Big Three clearly outdistance any rivals in political activity and power. The key position of these interests in Maine's economy establishes their crucial position in state decision-making. Over three-fourths of the state is woodland owned by a handful of timber companies and paper manufacturers. These interests, combined with power companies and textile and shoe manufacturers, are often able—insofar as their well-being is directly involved—to control Maine politics.

Maine, like other states with similar economic structures, went through a phase in which the dominant economic interests engaged in rather flamboyant lobbying techniques. Though more restrained today, the Big Three still are able to ensure that public policy is to their liking. Lockard points out that when Edmund Muskie was governor, he secured the passage of most of his legislative program but suffered the largest portion of his defeats on matters opposed by the Big Three. He was unable to establish an intrastate minimum wage, a state labor relations commission, a state income tax, and a corporate franchise tax. Perhaps most indicative of the power of economic interests in Maine was the defeat of a proposed water pollution law in 1955. Despite a determined effort to convince the legislature that prohibiting water pollution would not harm industry, the bill was defeated easily. The passage of strong antipollution legislation in the 1969–1970 session, however, indicates that the situation has changed somewhat.

In Maine, as in most other states, the balance of influence tends to shift away from the established influence structure, as the successful antipollution efforts of 1969–1970 illustrate. As one business lobbyist lamented: "The new legislators tend to be activists. . . . they are consumer- and ecology-minded. While not necessarily anti-business, they are certainly not business oriented. . . . They are prone to view with disfavor proposals from old-style lobbyists representing business."

Whether or not such legislators are not business-oriented is doubtful, because the interest in conservation in Maine is not purely sentimental. Tourism is Maine's second largest and fastest growing industry, bringing in over $500 million annually. The growth of the conservation "business" has provided not only a challenge to the Big Three, but also a new conflict structure to Maine politics: between economic development and conservation. Most governors have generally supported the developers, since Maine's economy has been comparatively stagnant (Maine's population grew only 2.4 percent between 1960 and 1970, compared to a national average of 13.3 percent. It ranked forty-fifth in economic and population growth.).

However, the legislature has proved more receptive to a broad coalition of groups with an interest in slowing growth, especially on the coast. Partners in this new coalition are real estate agents, a large portion of whose sales are second homes, fishermen who fear pollution will limit their catches, and summer residents. Ordinarily, summer residents would not be regarded as a potent force in a state's political influence structure. However, when the summer residents have names like Rockefeller, Cabot, and Du Pont, the picture changes. These families have played a leading role in the antigrowth movement. This coalition successfully supported the 1970 antipollution legislation and ultimately contributed to the development of a strong land use planning commission, placing Maine in the forefront of the movement to restrain growth. Hence, interest groups can serve as the major vehicle between demands and governmental response.

Because nondiversified economies, weak parties, and strong pressure groups are a normal combination, it is not surprising that the political processes of Maine and the southern states—most of which display this combination—are quite similar. V. O. Key, Jr., for example, described the politics of Alabama in 1949:

> The Extension Service–big farmer amalgam, which covers the entire state but is most potent in the black belt, usually teams up with the big money interests. . . . The "big mules" probably exert their strength far more effectively in the politics of legislation than in gubernatorial campaigns. And it is mainly in the legislature that questions of concern for them are settled: measures of taxation and regulation.[3]

At the time Key wrote this, Alabama had an urban population of 30.2 percent. With an urban population of 58.4 percent, according to the 1970 census, Alabama is no longer as noncompetitive a field of combat for the large farmer—"big mule" interests and labor organizations, for example, are becoming more active.

Increasing urbanization and industrialization do seem to countervail against formerly dominant economic power groups. For example, organizations lobbying in favor of state right-to-work laws have generally been successful in southern or midwestern states where union membership is low and union political organization weak. Right-to-work laws have been easily defeated in states with strong and active unions, such as California and Illinois, and have never been a serious issue in other heavily unionized states, such as New York and New Jersey.[4] The pressure for enactment of this kind of legislation is concentrated in such states as Maine, New Hampshire, New Mexico, Vermont, Idaho, Kansas, and Delaware, few of which boast any appreciable union membership.[5] Also, in those states currently having right-to-work laws, there is some evidence of a counterrevolution as urbanization and industrialization increase. In Georgia, for example, labor leaders who remember the days when favoring organized labor on the floor of the General Assembly invited informal but severe censure have seen strong legislative support for improved workmen's compensation laws develop and have adopted the repeal of the state's right-to-work law as a long-range, but feasible, goal. One such leader said, "Things were different at the State Capitol this year. The atmosphere has changed. Labor was treated in a much different manner. Labor was respected. . . . We have our head in the door."[6]

Single Dominant Interest

In Montana, an example of the second system in which a nondiversified economy, two-party politics, and moderate legislative cohesion are combined, the economy has become somewhat more diversified, the urban population has increased, and the dominant role of the Anaconda Company has been diminished by self-restraint and competition. In a state where mining is the major nonagricultural source of personal income, Anaconda is the largest employer. Although "the Company," as it is known in Montana, began its operations in mining for copper, it now owns mills, aluminum companies, railroads, fabricating plants, and forests. The enormity of the Anaconda empire is described by Thomas Payne:

> Its strength rests not only in its wealth and resources, but also in its elaborate network of relationships with key citizens, banks, legal firms, and business organizations throughout the state.

> Rare is that unit of local government—county, city, or school district—that does not have among its official family an associate, in some capacity, of the Anaconda Company.[7]

In addition, until 1959, Anaconda controlled a chain of newspapers with a combined circulation greater than that of all the other daily papers in the state.

In the turbulent frontier atmosphere of the West, Anaconda played the classic role of economic royalist, making frequent and extravagant forays into the electoral process. Politicians like Burton K. Wheeler became legendary as courageous foes of the Company in much the same manner that Senator William E. Borah built a political career on the crusade against Anaconda's monopolistic influence. Much of Montana's political history reflects a basic division of the population: people were either for the Company, or, in the case of the unions and Farmer's Union, against it. In Wheeler's autobiography, the struggle against Anaconda is the major theme of the portions dealing with his career prior to becoming a senator. Conflict in the state seemed to be structured around the Company rather than the political parties. Wheeler wrote that "in the 1911–1912 legislature the Democrats controlled the House, the Republicans controlled the Senate, and the Company controlled the leaders of both."[8]

Montana politics is not completely dominated by Anaconda; although the Company is a major actor that can claim success in many instances, it sometimes has been forced to accept defeat. For instance, its efforts to elect the "right" candidates have met with only moderate success. Wheeler was consistently supported by organized labor and enjoyed electoral success in spite of—indeed, perhaps because of—Anaconda's opposition.

The best example of the strength and weakness of Anaconda in Montana is the struggle to increase the taxation of mines. The mining companies had succeeded in including an extraordinary clause in the state constitution in 1889 when Montana was admitted to the Union. The clause provided that mining claims could be taxed only "at the price paid the United States therefor" and that taxes could be levied on "net proceeds" only. In accordance with this constitutional provision, oil production, which grossed only one-sixth as much as mines, paid twice as much in taxes. Mines contributed less than 9 percent of Montana's revenue while farms contributed 32 percent. As early as 1916 the legislature had become aware of the inequities of this situation, and in 1918 a faculty member of the University of Montana began a study of the tax system, only to be dismissed by the chancellor. A book based on his research was published, however, and Anaconda's role in its suppression became apparent.[9] As a result of the furor over the author's dismissal, the state board of education reinstated him with back pay.

The next step in the taxation episode took place in 1920 when Wheeler—on his reputation as an enemy of the Company—ran as Democratic candidate for governor against Republican Joseph Dixon, who had the Company's support. Although Wheeler promised tax revision, he was defeated by Dixon who promptly urged the legislature to find a way to increase mine taxes. His proposal for a license tax based on each ton of ore produced was defeated in the legislature when Anaconda lobbyists worked vigorously against him. To overcome his lack of influence with the legislature, the governor submitted the tax revision to the voters in the form of a referendum in the 1924 election. Dixon, now the enemy of the Company, lost the gubernatorial election. The taxing proposal was approved, however, even though Anaconda maintained that "the mining industry cannot stand any additional tax load."[10]

Defeats such as this convinced the Company that its wisest course of action lay in more moderate demands. In the 1920s the Company press was vitriolic in its treatment of its opponents; in the 1930s the papers became less venomous and simply did not mention enemies or their activities. By the 1940s and early 1950s the papers began to print hostile speeches and their editorials took on a rather neutral flavor; in the late 1950s the Company disposed of its newspapers. In more recent years Anaconda has remained as quiet as possible, confining itself to blocking adverse legislation and reducing its efforts to influence the electoral process.[11]

Furthermore, Anaconda has encountered resistance similar to that of the Big Three in Maine. The conflict first became apparent in Butte, where Anaconda employs one-third of the work force. In 1955 an open-pit copper mine was opened, creating a tangible threat to the business community (the pit covers about 20 percent of the land area of Butte). Local businessmen, already victims of a declining economy, feared further urban decay. However, since Anaconda actually has the right of eminent domain (that is, the authority normally reserved to governmental bodies to condemn property) and since 1961 the authority to condemn surface land, it could, if it chose, scoop away the entire city.

Awareness of such awesome power had led to a strengthening of the environmental movement in Montana, especially the National Wildlife Federation, the Sierra Club, a new coalition of fishermen's organizations, and other outdoor groups such as the American League of Anglers, the Montana Wildlife Federation, and the Montana Wilderness Association.

The experiences of Montana with the Anaconda Company seem roughly parallel to those of other states with a single dominant economic interest—such as oil in Texas or Du Pont in Delaware. In both these states the reputation for absolute control is widespread. However, a difference between specific and generalized power can be suggested. Anaconda is probably capable of protecting or enhancing its interest in areas of specific concern, but success in a specific area can lead to misleading assumptions about generalized power, especially by those who use power as a symbol to be attacked. Thus, we might ask: do the timber, paper, power, and manufacturing interests control Maine or do they partially control public policy as it impinges upon their interests? Does Anaconda control Montana or is the Company a significant and frequently decisive determinant of policy in its area of involvement? The same question could be asked in other states where policy disputes are bipolarized by the concentration of economic power.

For instance, the chairman of the Texas Democratic State Executive Committee once said: "It may not be a wholesome thing to say, but the oil industry today is in complete control of state politics and state government."[12] No one needs to be reminded of the loyalty of Texas politicians to the oil depletion allowance in the federal tax structure, but this matter directly and vitally affects the oil producers. A recent case study of the Texas legislature suggests that oil producers are indeed influential, but are opposed by equally influential competitors. The study covered the 1961 session of the Texas legislature, which, in attempting to pass a tax bill, had to decide between income and sales taxes. The governor, trying to avoid either tax, presented a program calling for, among other things, an increase in the tax on natural gas production. Manufacturing groups, led by the Texas Mid-Continent Oil and Gas Association, countered with the general sales tax proposal. The opposition to the governor was sufficient to ensure that the sales tax would be the final solution, but the legislature also supported a tax on the natural gas pipeline companies.[13] Neither side enjoyed total victory, and neither group of protagonists controlled the outcome of this issue, much less the sum of the decisions reached by the state government.

The confusion between power and the potential for power occurs most frequently in bipolarized states. It is natural to presume that those with sources of influence will choose to maximize them, but this assumption is not always true. Like Anaconda, many other dominant economic interests have found it prudent to restrict their activities and hence to avoid excessive demands. In their study of American tariff policy, Raymond A. Bauer, Ithiel de Sola Pool, and Lewis A. Dexter found that large corporations were reluctant to speak openly of their views on foreign trade because of sensitivity about their public images. With so much weight to throw around, the giants were afraid of a public display of strength. In Delaware, for example, Du Pont is traditionally protectionist, but none of the elected officials from the state think that they are under pressure to oppose reciprocal trade. The authors explain: "A business can be too big to be politically effective along some lines."[14]

This is not to say that large companies are always the "good guys." Rather, it means that unless such companies can operate within the processes of government that are relatively secure from direct public participation, the fear of public response is sufficient to restrain their actions. Perhaps this provides a partial explanation as to why right-to-work laws are usually approved by legislatures in nonindustrial states. In industrial states most large corporations are reluctant to attack labor unions directly.

The low-keyed approach to influence that is increasingly undertaken by apparently dominant interests of a state and the lack of total victory accompanying their efforts indicate that the increasing diversification of the American economy and the urbanization of society are reducing the power of single dominant interests. This reduction has been accelerated in recent years because diversification and urbanization have brought an expansion of communications and increasing awareness of economic and social interdependence. Issues that in the past have been of local or regional concern now arouse national interest. This dynamic widens the basis of potential support for groups opposing entrenched interests.

Such issues as water and environmental pollution, the treatment of minorities, and auto safety could be successfully manipulated by strong local or regional interests as long as the issue interested only people and organizations within their sphere of influence. Attempts by powerful area-specific interests to control the situation are much less likely to achieve success when they must counter the efforts of individuals such as Ralph Nader and the late Dr. Martin Luther King, who command attention from a broad and active spectrum of the population.

It is even more difficult for powerful interests to engage in low-visibility efforts to influence legislators when spectacular events such as riots, demonstrations, and leaking offshore oil wells bring national attention to the issues in question and turn a spotlight on the actions of legislators at the moment when reaction to the event has unified opposition forces. As a result, the number of states in the single dominant interest pattern of the theoretical classification has been diminished.

Diminution has not been limited to single interests alone. For example, the Big Three in Maine were easily able to defeat legislation aimed at curbing water pollution in 1955, but were themselves defeated in 1969 and 1970.[15] Public opinion across the nation had come to favor such measures, and such events as uncontrolled oil leakage from an offshore platform in the Santa Barbara Channel had alerted voters in Maine to the magnitude of the problems posed by oil exploration.[16] The issues were further dramatized when, almost simultaneously with the passage of the legislation, a large oil tanker ran aground and broke up off the coast of Nova Scotia, endangering the livelihood of fishing and tourist interests in the area.[17] Under these conditions the Big Three were unable to turn the tide running against them.

Conflict Between Two Dominant Groups

The states considered up to this point have had rather underdeveloped economies that contribute to bipolarization of political conflicts. Michigan is an industrial, urban, competitive state with strong cohesion in legislative parties—a combination of factors sharply deviant from the normal strong pressure group pattern. Michigan is the only state in the strong pressure group category that contains no single characteristic in common with the other states in this category, at least insofar as the variables in table 3.1 are concerned. However, Michigan's economy is perhaps less diversified than even that of Montana, since its economic life is strongly keyed to the activities of the automotive industry, a fact that has contributed to periodic crises that probably would not have occurred in a more diversified economy. A progressive diversification of the economy now is taking place. In 1951, automotive workers accounted for 22.7 percent of all wage and salary workers in the state (excluding farm workers, railroad employees, and the self-employed), and 39.3 percent of the manufacturing wage and salary workers; by 1968 these percentages had declined to 13.4 and 28.5 respectively.[18] Still, automobile manufacturers are the largest single employer.

These circumstances promote the conflict between union and management that has been a consistent theme in Michigan politics since industrialization.[19] The presence of many organized interests in Michigan, as in most urban states, prevents a single interest from achieving dominance. However, as in the other states examined so far, when matters of concern to powerful interest groups are raised, these groups become major determinants of public policy. As Joseph

LaPalombara concludes, "No major issues of policy (taxation, social legislation, labor legislation, etc.) is [sic] likely to be decided in Michigan without the intervention, within their respective parties and before agencies of government, of automotive labor and automotive management."[20]

The major difference between Michigan and the other bipolarized states is the degree to which interest-group cleavages have been mirrored and hence institutionalized in the structure of the political parties and the legislature. In Maine, the Big Three functioned to some extent within the Republican party, but the loose and sprawling nature of that organization made efforts at control hardly worth the effort because control of the party would not improve the chances of controlling the legislature. In Montana, Anaconda worked first with one party, then with another, finally showing slightly more interest in the Republicans. However, LaPalombara speaks of the intervention in Michigan of unions and management "within their respective parties."[21] This statement reflects the fact that the Michigan unions, especially the United Automobile Workers, are deeply involved in the affairs of the Democratic party while the automotive managers are equally involved in the Republican party. It would be an exaggeration to maintain that either interest controls its party, but labor and management are surely the most active and influential components of their parties.[22]

Neither management nor labor makes much of an effort to extend its base of operations beyond the parties because the cohesion of the legislative parties is strong and strong cohesion reduces the necessity to respond to interest groups. On matters of labor legislation, the Michigan legislature has revealed parties as cohesive as those of the House of Commons. For example, in the 1954 session of the legislature the indexes of cohesion on partisan roll calls were 77 for the House Democrats and 75 for the Senate Democrats. However, on partisan roll calls involving labor legislation the index of cohesion for House and Senate Democrats was 97.[23]

A recent study of issue conflict in the fifty states based on a questionnaire administered to state legislators in 1963 indicates that the labor-management bifurcation still follows party lines. According to Wayne L. Francis, Michigan ranked sixth among the states in the amount of partisan conflict perceived by a sample of legislators from that state and fourth in amount of pressure group conflict perceived. Ranks on the nonparty (or cross-party) categories of regional and factional conflicts, on the other hand, are considerably lower, 13 and 47, respectively.[24] If interest-group conflict were not primarily related to party conflict, we would expect that the use of other than party channels of influence by opposing interests would raise the rankings of regional or factional conflict to the point where they exceeded or at least came close to the rank held by partisan conflict.

It would seem, then, that the coincidence of cleavage contributes to an intensification of group conflict in Michigan. Rather than serving as moderators of group conflict—as the national parties do—the Michigan parties communicate interest-group values to the electorate and to the governmental officeholders.[25] Still, the vigor of pressure groups does not mean that the Michigan parties function as auxiliaries; if anything, the reverse is true. Neither unions nor management are so cohesive as to avoid the periodic squabbles that allow other interests to compete more effectively. Further, if unions and management are the single largest contributors to their respective parties, it is these parties that maintain the machinery necessary for contesting elections. It would be hard to imagine the United Automobile Workers deciding to withdraw support from the Democratic party.[26] Key's description of the pressure group as a "junior partner" in the alliance with a party holds true even in Michigan.[27] The unions must remain Democratic to maintain a viable bargaining position. If the pressure group has little choice but to support party candidates, the party usually assumes a position of dominance in the relationship.

Triumph of Many Interests

The economic structure of California is more diversified than that of any state considered in this analysis. Raw materials, which were primarily derived from forest land in Maine, for example, are abundant and of considerable variety in California. Manufacturing enterprises range from cement to motion pictures, and agriculture is far from a single-crop activity. Under these circumstances, although the economic basis for strong pressures is apparent, the structure of economic activity leads to a fragmentation of interest-group activity. Indeed, the diversification of the economy and the attendant competitiveness of politics make it difficult to comprehend the strength that interest groups have been able to develop in California.

At one time in California's history, a single interest—the railroads, especially the Southern Pacific—dominated both parties and the legislature.[28] However, the national reaction against the trusts that arose in the early years of the twentieth century contributed to a wave of reformism in California, weakening the parties and, ironically, paving the way for pressure groups that, even when the most lurid and sensational exposés are discounted, were perhaps more powerful than those in any other state legislature. One feature of party-weakening reform was the introduction of cross-filing in elections. From 1917 until 1954 the election laws of California allowed voters to contest both the Democratic and Republican nominations without their party affiliation appearing on either ballot. After 1954 party labels were required, and in 1959 cross-filing was abolished. The system of cross-filing seriously weakened the ability of the party to assume any significance in the consciousness of the legislator. Further, the lack of any effective party organization left candidates for the state legislature on their own as they sought adequate funds for campaigning. As in the southern one-party states, the interest groups of California were willing and anxious to meet this need for capital.

The spectacular nature of California politics and lobbying attracted reporters and resulted in some extravagant statements concerning the nature and source of interest-group strength in California.[29] Recently, California politics has come under the scrutiny of more systematic observers. In his superb study of the California legislature, William Buchanan looks carefully at interest groups in California and concludes that the sensationalism of journalism should not obscure the fact that, especially during the "lobby era" of 1942 to 1953, the initiation of public policy was largely the responsibility of organized groups.[30]

During the administration of Governor Earl Warren in the 1950s, the practice of cross-filing became quite common and the viability of parties diminished. Buchanan notes that "the advantage went to the candidate who best could obscure his party affiliation, attract or pay for attention in the press, and wangle endorsements from editors and the local units for pressure groups."[31] Very few legislators could afford to meet the costs of such requirements and very few could resist the temptation of easy money from interest groups. The interest-dominated environment of California is well illustrated by the perceptions of legislators of their career patterns. Nine percent of the California legislators referred to interest groups as sponsors of their careers as compared to 1 percent in New Jersey and 2 percent in Ohio. Only in Tennessee, where parties are less competitive than those in California, did legislators refer to interest groups as sponsors (16 percent) more frequently.[32]

In one sense, the interest groups in California actually resemble political parties in organization. The most famous lobbyist, Artie Samish, expended a great amount of money and energy in the electoral process. Samish began his career as a lobbyist for bus companies in the

1930s but soon expanded his operations to include a host of other interests, including the California State Brewers' Institute, railroads, horse racing, gambling, and motion pictures.[33] It is not unusual in the state legislatures for lobbyists to represent more than one client. Moreover, Samish was a successful agent for his numerous clients. In most cases legislators see relatively little of multigroup lobbyists because they are frequently responsible for a series of explicit and limited interests that are concerned with a small portion of the legislative output. There is little doubt, however, that Samish's influence with the California legislature was considerable. Buchanan maintains that Samish's influence was developed not from the fact that his clients were affluent but because he welded the diverse interests he represented into an organization that functioned as a political party in the individualized environment of California politics. The common denominator of these interests was that they were all industries new to the state when Samish began to recruit his organization in the 1930s. Samish's main effort was to prevent state taxation of these enterprises.

Other constellations of interest groups functioned simultaneously with the Samish organization but not necessarily in competition with it. For example, a conservative lobby of insurance companies, large farmers, and utilities were interested in preventing any departure from an antitax philosophy and found cooperation with the Samish organization useful. This collection of interest groups, essentially nonideological like a typical American political party, selected candidates to run for office and supplied them with the funds for effective campaigning. When campaign costs were high and parties unwilling to pull their share of the load, the Samish organization was the most significant factor in the life of the legislator. As Buchanan wrote:

> In the absence of adequate party machinery at the local level they [interest groups] took over what is ordinarily the party's function of financing and managing campaigns. Thus they came to restrict the potential candidate's route of access to legislative power. It is not difficult then to snatch from the limp hands of the party the privilege of organizing the legislative chambers. Once influential in legislative organization, lobbyists could make attractive offers of exchange of power inside the legislature.[34]

The California experience is somewhat special because of the unusual previous legal restrictions on partisan activity. However, it affords us an opportunity to speculate on the relationship of parties and pressure groups in a period of flux. The addition of party labels to the ballot in

1954 coincided with structural reforms in the legislature that gave political parties a part in organizing that body. During the same period the
legislature, stung by national publicity surrounding the activities of lobbyists, passed a lobby control act. An embryonic partisanship—expressed first in the form of factional alignments—indicated that the
legislature was moving away from lobby dominance and toward active
participation by parties.

In 1957, the year the California legislators were interviewed in connection with the preparation of Francis's book, partisanship still had not
developed to a degree comparable with other urban, competitive states.
Three out of five legislators believed parties played little or no part in
the legislative process, a proportion nearly as high as that of Tennessee,
a weak minority party state. It is significant, however, that in this unset-
tled situation the Democratic party was judged to be more influential
than the Republican party. Though legislators did not perceive parties
as influential, roll-call analysis indicated that party membership accounted for more divisions in voting than any other characteristic of the
members. Party influence was growing and was more important than the
members themselves believed.

Did emerging partisanship reduce the influence of interest groups? We
should be cautious not to imply a single cause-effect relationship. After
all, legislative salaries had increased to a point where it was possible to
survive in Sacramento without the largess of lobbyists, and the exposés
of Artie Samish had reduced the legitimacy of lobbying to some extent.
Further, lobbying by the Samish organization had developed during the
1930s, a partisan period by California standards. Nevertheless, there
does appear to be some inverse relationship between the strength of parties and interest groups. As the parties began to play some role, however
small, in the legislative process, they also began to meet campaign costs,
which reduced the necessity of interest groups. In terms of legislative
output, the challenge to the interest groups by parties resulted in 1959 in
the first significant increase in beer taxes, despite the prediction of the
brewers, once the heart of the Samish organization, that the tax could be
defeated.

Like Maine and Montana, California's structure of influence has been
somewhat altered by the emergence of active environmentally oriented
lobbies. Such efforts tend to be concentrated upon statewide referenda
as well as the legislature. The Sierra Club was especially active, for instance, in the successful support of a statewide initiative to conserve the
coastline, imposing a complex system of regulations upon developers.
The proposition was approved in 1975 despite the opposition of all major
business and labor groups, and the governor's office.

In an attempt both to moderate the effect of this proposition and to stem the environmentalist tide, the California Council for Environmental and Economic Balance (a coalition of oil companies, utilities, and labor) was created with former Governor Edmund Brown as chairman. This coalition worked successfully in the legislature against the creation of a statewide antipollution agency. However, the next round (again in the electoral arena) was won by the environmentalists, this time joined by the 65,000-member chapter of Common Cause. The goal was the passage of Proposition 9, the Political Reform Act of 1974. Opposed by the traditional alliance of labor and business, it was nevertheless approved. Containing a wide-ranging list of reforms, it had direct impact upon the lobbying process by prohibiting lobbyists from spending more than a total of $10 a month, including campaign contributions, to influence state officials. Proposition 9 was thus (properly) construed as an effort to disrupt the traditional lobbying system.

Contrasting Patterns: States Without a Dominant Pressure System

A strong party system contributes to a balancing of power between parties and interest groups or, in some cases, to a clear dominance of the parties. If the strength of parties produces a more balanced distribution of power, we can expect to find that interest groups are vigorous and active, but clearly rely on parties to help them influence governmental decision-makers. Contributions are channeled to the candidate through the party organization, and the candidate owes fealty to the party. Further, each party tends to develop its own constellation of interests from which support can be expected. These interests rarely attempt to persuade individual legislators to cast a favorable vote on a specific issue but rather devote their attention exclusively to party leaders. In these situations it is clear that the party is in control. In Connecticut, for example, parties are able to punish an interest group if its demands become intolerable by refusing access to decision-makers.

In contrast to this pattern of cooperation, Missouri is an example of a genuinely low pressure system. Salisbury has described the pressure system of Missouri as one of temporary rather than permanent alliances. He found that broad coalitions of groups in conflict with rival combinations do exist, but are a rare phenomenon.[35] The shifting, temporary issue-oriented alliances in Missouri cannot compete with the stable and competitive party system. Lacking a major economic cleavage, interest groups have not developed either the ability to work closely with a party as in Michigan or the power to circumvent and dominate the parties as in Maine or California. In fact, Missouri and California have similarly diverse economies. It is probable that, had California not undergone its unique historical development, its pressure system would have been as weak as Missouri's. Diffusion and fragmentation of power, a pluralistic situation endemic to most industrial urban states, provides parties with the opportunity to function without severe competition from interest groups.

THE BIAS OF THE PRESSURE SYSTEM   Despite what has been outlined above, the structure of all lobbying has fundamental similarities: the overrepresentation of business and professional groups is conspicuous in all settings. As expressed by Presthus:

> In the United States, 44 percent of all members of all types of groups are described as upper middle class by their directors. Less than one-fifth are perceived as being working class, with some 38 percent being defined as a mixture of all classes. Such judgments, reinforced by other research indicates that those who join groups possess disproportionate amounts of such political resources as higher education, occupational status, and the psychopolitical resources that typically accompany such properties, including conceptual and forensic skills, an appreciation of one's stake in society, and the political knowledge and interest inspired by this definition of one's situation.[36]

Much the same process was observed by Verba and Nie. In general, they found that the upper classes receive a participatory boost: for example, "organizations increase the disparity in participation between upper and lower status groups because upper-status individuals are more likely to take advantage of that gain."[37]

Accordingly, we should expect that business and professional groups are most active in the state legislature. The point is amply demonstrated by the fact that roughly 58 percent of the registered lobbyists in the American states represent business, acting for either single corporations or trade associations.[38] Additionally, Francis discovered that such lobbyists were far and away the most likely to be identified as powerful by legislators.[39]

Regardless of the fundamental similarities in the structure of lobbying, the patterns of interest groups' conflict and accommodation still persist. These patterns, which we have described above, are partially linked to the style and techniques of lobbying. In the following section, much of the data that are used to describe the various styles and techniques of lobbying will be drawn from four states: Massachusetts, North Carolina, Oregon, and Utah. It is necessary, therefore, to designate the appropriate pattern for each of these states.

Massachusetts appears most similar in political and economic structure to states characterized by conflict between two dominant groups. Although the prominence of the insurance industry gives Massachusetts somewhat the flavor of a single dominant interest, its actual pattern of group behavior most closely resembles that of Michigan. Like Michigan, it is urban, heterogeneous, industrialized, and its parties are legislatively cohesive. Such an oligarchical political system makes interest groups auxiliaries of political parties.

Utah and Oregon come closest to the single dominant-interest model. In Oregon, the lumber and ancillary wood products industries are the major source of employment and their representatives speak often and with authority in state legislative politics. In Utah, the comparable single dominant interest, as in Montana, is mining. Both states, although electorally competitive, are characterized by extremely low party cohesion in legislative voting.

Finally, North Carolina seems to be a state without a dominant pressure system. Less economically developed, less competitive politically, the North Carolina system does not foster the development of strong representation through interest groups.

Roughly speaking, then, Oregon and Utah are "strong" lobby states, while Massachusetts and North Carolina are "weak" lobby states. As we turn to a discussion of lobbying, the differences will become apparent.

As is the case for the outlined dominant patterns of interest group behavior in the previous section, the types should be regarded as suggestive rather than absolute. Just as the Big Three in Maine and Anaconda in Montana have been challenged by coalitions of environmental groups, so has the dominance of the lumber industry been challenged in Oregon. The Associated Industries of Oregon, heavily representative of the lumber industry, has suffered some major setbacks. In 1971, the Oregon legislature, under strong pressure from Governor Tom McCall, passed a land use planning bill, a coastal preservation bill, and, with a flourish of national publicity, a bottle bill prohibiting the use of nonreturnable bottles. Industry lobbying was intense but unsuccessful in all these cases.

Even in such states as Maine, Montana, and Oregon, which have a relatively concentrated economic and hence political influence structure, interest-group pressure is not monolithic. Challenges by competing organizations can be developed and decision-makers have to respond to more than one group to balance competing demands. Such challenges seem to be more difficult in Massachusetts and North Carolina, where political influence appears more structured or stable.

LOBBYING AS A COMMUNICATIONS PROCESS

TO ACHIEVE success in state politics, that is, to make state government respond to its demands, an interest group must have access to key decision-makers. Up to this point, factors within the political and socioeconomic system over which interest groups have no control have been described in terms of their influence on the performance of groups. Such factors structure and limit the activities of interest groups, and success or failure is probably more dependent on the nature of the society than on the skills or techniques of lobbyists. Nevertheless, it is within the power of interest groups to maximize whatever advantages accrue to them through their place in a social system.

A high-status manufacturers' organization might sacrifice its initial advantage by using lobbying techniques that offend the sensibilities of legislators or make it difficult for them to vote the way the organizations would prefer. If, for example, such an organization publicly threatens to defeat all legislators who vote the "wrong" way, it may be necessary for these legislators to establish their independence by voting against the wishes of the organization. In Massachusetts, for example, 66 percent of those legislators who believed they were pressured by education lobbyists favored an increased education budget as opposed to 90 percent who felt no pressure. Access, then, does depend to some extent upon skills. In lobbying, as in any other profession, such skills are acquired by experience and practice. A pertinent question is, how experienced are state lobbyists?

The Characteristics
of State Lobbying

The experience of lobbyists in relation to legislators varies widely. Although Patterson found that about 47 percent of his sample of forty-three Oklahoma lobbyists were registered for their first term at the time of the interview,[40] Massachusetts, North Carolina, and Utah "had more 'freshmen' among legislators than lobbyists and more lobbyists than legislators who have been around for 25 years or more."[41] The lobbyists had also chalked up more mean years of experience than legislators, the differences ranging from 1.1 in Oregon to 7.3 in Utah.

To lament the amateurism of the legislators, however, is to forget that the lobbyist is often not any more of a professional. DeVries's study of lobbying in Michigan, for example, points out that most lobbyists are not very frequent visitors to Lansing; only a core of regulars are really familiar with the vagaries of the legislative process. Of equal significance is the fact that not very many lobbyists spend their full time lobbying during the session. Patterson found that over 60 percent of the Oklahoma lobbyists spend half their time or less engaged in lobbying.[42] In Massachusetts, lobbyists spend an average of 2.5 hours a day on the job, in North Carolina 3.9, and in Utah 4.5. Only in Oregon, a weak party–strong lobby state, does the figure approach full-time proportions at 7.7 hours.[43] Like legislative skills, lobbying skills develop with experience and practice; like state legislators, relatively few lobbyists possess such experience.

LOBBYISTS' BACKGROUNDS   What kinds of backgrounds do state lobbyists have? One striking difference between state and national lobbyists is that few state lobbyists are lawyers. Milbrath found that most Washington lobbyists were lawyers, but this is not true in the states for which we have information. In Oklahoma, only four out of a sample of forty-three lobbyists listed law as their occupation. The figures for Michigan, Massachusetts, Oregon, and Utah are 12, 21, 19, and 19 percent, respectively. However, in Virginia and North Carolina the respective percentages were 46 and 51.[44]

Whether the higher proportion of lawyers as lobbyists in southern states is a coincidence or a reflection of the cultural or political structure of the South cannot be ascertained from so few cases. The largest single occupational category in both Oklahoma and North Carolina is that of full-time executive or employee of an association engaged in lobbying. In Virginia, association executives are second to lawyers. In

Massachusetts, Oregon, and Utah professionals and managers, not lawyers, occupy the modal category. Beyond this, the occupational background of lobbyists has little pattern. The absence of lawyer-lobbyists in most states is worthy of attention because of the popularly held assumption that legal experience contributes to political effectiveness.

That legal experience may not always be necessary for effective lobbying is indicated by the relationship between attitudinal similarity and interaction. In Massachusetts, North Carolina, Utah, and Oregon, legislators with high interaction rates are the most likely to perceive lobbyists as "intelligent and knowledgeable"[45]—an attitude conducive to further interaction. Because individuals coming from similar backgrounds are likely to share similar attitudes and viewpoints, occupation can make a difference in attitude, especially in the crucial first few encounters when the lobbyist may have to break through a legislator's negative view of his purpose and function. Shared attitudes also contribute to lobbying effectiveness; the greater the congruence in communicating, the less ambiguity is likely to be involved in the transaction. In a situation of greater congruence, the lobbyist is able to make his point clearly and the legislator finds out what he wants to know. As a result of the communication, neither is likely to be surprised by the actions of the other, and mutual faith is reinforced. The same cannot be said of transactions involving considerable ambiguity.[46] In the strong lobby states of Oregon and Utah where "among legislators, professional and managerial personnel without legal training far outnumber lawyers,"[47] the percentage of lobbyists who are lawyers is correspondingly low.

It would seem that interest groups would be anxious to employ people who had an intimate knowledge of the legislature, and that ex-legislators would be eagerly sought after. They may be sought, but relatively few ever become lobbyists. Zeller, Patterson, Epstein, and DeVries have called attention to this absence.[48] This does not mean that ex-legislators are not useful as lobbyists. DeVries's study suggests a significant relationship between any amount of legislative experience and lobbying effectiveness, but because so few ex-legislators become lobbyists, very few groups benefit from their experience.

The scarcity of ex-legislators acting as lobbyists could be partially explained by differences in career motivations and job orientation between legislators and lobbyists. Legislators tend to take an interest in politics fairly early in life. Over half the legislators in the Zeigler-Baer study recalled having an interest in politics before they were twenty years of age, as compared with slightly more than 10 percent of the lobbyists interviewed. Similarly, one-third of the legislators but 85 percent of the lobbyists stated they previously had nonpolitical occupations.[49] The legislator, generally a person moving upward, contrasts greatly with the lobbyist. Though a legislator can enjoy the security of a relatively high-status position, the latter faces considerable status insecurity—a fact reflected in his tendency to drift into the lobbying profession. The highest percentage of legislators in the four-state sample drifting into their position is 22 in North Carolina; the lowest percentage drifting into the job of lobbying is 79 in Oregon, a strong interest-group state that views lobbyists favorably.[50]

On the other hand, quite a few lobbyists have had some form of governmental or political experience. Whereas the previous experience of legislators is likely to involve elected positions on the local level, lobbyists are much more likely to have occupied an appointed position on the state or national level.

DeVries found no significant relationship between nonlegislative experience and lobbying effectiveness, confirming the supposition that legislative service provides the most desirable background for lobbying.[51] Moreover, there is a significant relationship between length of government service and effectiveness: the longer the experience, the greater the effectiveness. The same relationship exists with regard to experience in a political party. Milbrath noted that the Washington lobbyists find it useful to avoid partisan activity and that "the party with which a man identifies appears to be relatively unimportant in lobbying."[52]

The competitive nature of Congress would make open partisanship hazardous, but in states in which one party can be relied upon to control the legislature the risks are fewer and the advantages considerable. Although Patterson found that few Oklahoma lobbyists had held party positions, this condition did not hold for Michigan and North Carolina, where more than half the lobbyists had been active in party affairs.[53]

Membership in the dominant legislative party is an asset to lobbyists, who can use party ties as a means of access to legislators. Thus, in Michigan the lobbyists with a considerable number of years of experience in the Republican party were more effective than those lacking such experience. Certainly this would be true in a state in which the party greatly influenced the determination of public policy. However, a strong party system does not necessarily mean the diminution of the influence of interest groups but may mean that pressure is put upon holders of party office rather than upon the party rank and file. In Michigan and Massachusetts, for example, labor organizations frequently serve as auxiliaries to the parties.

No clear relationship between the governmental experience of lobbyists and the strength of interest groups appears in the four-state study because the state with the largest percentage of lobbyists with such experience is North Carolina, a weak lobby state, and the state with the second highest percentage, Utah, is a strong lobby state.[54] Irregularities peculiar to the states concerned could account for this, however, and until data covering more states can be gathered for this particular variable the precise form of the relationship cannot be discerned. Nevertheless, the data do highlight an area of difference between lobbyist and legislator. Lobbyists are likely to have become directly involved in the activities of interest groups, whereas legislators holding elective positions have developed a different orientation. This adds another reason for the lack of occupational interchange between legislator and lobbyist.[55]

Money and Access

Using money to establish a satisfactory relationship with a group of legislators cannot be ignored, but it can be put in proper perspective. It is relatively easy for journalists to nod knowingly at the magic power of money and to assume that merely by uttering the word they have offered the insider's explanation of how legislation is enacted. But what does money buy? How is money spent? These questions are frequently left unanswered. Consider entertainment, for example. Reports on various states such as Wisconsin, Florida, and Michigan suggest that lobbyists at the state level do more entertaining than lobbyists in Washington.[56] State lobbyists do not rate entertaining as high as other techniques, however, and its role is probably exaggerated by popular accounts. In the four-state sample, committee hearings were the primary method of communication between lobbyist and legislator. The percentages listing "social gatherings" as a method of communication are small: 4 percent in Massachusetts, 2 percent in North Carolina and Oregon, and none in Utah.[57] Although some lobbyists maintain an open bar for legislators, most entertaining falls into the category of lunches for small groups or annual dinners for the entire legislature.

UNSCRUPULOUS LOBBYING   A popular conception of lobbying is that, for the most part, lobbyists provide elaborate entertainment for legislators, offering bribes and, if all else fails, threatening the recalcitrant legislator with defeat in the next election. Insofar as the national legislative process is concerned, recent research has fairly well dispelled this notion.[58] Scandals do occur, but rarely so. However, there does seem to be evidence that at the state level the high-handed methods of the past still persist. Robert Engler, for example, discussed the techniques of oil lobbyists before state legislatures: "The crude and more obvious practices commonly identified with lobbying are still familiar here." Engler referred to a remark by a Standard Oil executive to Rockefeller in the early days of the growth of refining companies that he had "arranged to kill two bills in the Maryland legislature at comparatively small expense."[59] Although he concedes that it is difficult to document such activity today, Engler gives the impression that unscrupulous lobbying is still the order of the day.

The belief in the crude nature of state lobbying techniques is documented further by Lester Milbrath. In interviewing lobbyists and legislators in Washington, D.C., he found that they perceived state lobbying to be considerably more corrupt than national lobbying. Some of the comments of his respondents illustrate this belief:

> Lobbying is very different before state legislatures: it is much more individualistic. Maybe this is the reason they have more bribery in state legislatures than in Congress.

> In the state legislatures, lobbying is definitely on a lower plane. The lobbyists are loose and hand out money and favors quite freely.

> Lobbying at the state level is cruder, more basic, and more obvious.

> Lobbying at the state level is faster and more freewheeling and less visible; that is why it is more open to corruption.[60]

In theory, several characteristics of state legislatures and legislators contribute to more corrupt lobbying techniques. State legislatures meet less often and for shorter periods than does Congress; therefore, an internalized set of formal and informal rules such as those of the U.S. Senate would be more difficult to develop. Such a system of internalized expectations of behavior would, perhaps, impose limits on individual legislative behavior and thus restrict the operating limits of interest groups. Also contributing to the lack of internal systems of authority is the rapid turnover of state legislators. Because about a third of these legislators are first-term members of their respective houses, their unfamiliarity with the legislature improves the general access of lobbyists. State legislators are less likely to be professionals than their counterparts at the federal level and more likely to regard a legislative career as a secondary aspect of their lives. Finally, state legislators make less money than national legislators; because they usually do not reside in the state capital, they incur more expenses in relation to their income than national legislators.

In practice, however, illegal lobbying techniques do not appear to be as widespread or as effective as some believe. Analyzing the responses to an intensive survey of lobbyists and legislators in Massachusetts, North Carolina, Oregon, and Utah, Zeigler and Baer found that "both groups rank bribery as the least effective method" of influence.[61] Entertainment was not ranked much better, although state lobbyists gave entertainment and parties higher scores than Washington lobbyists. In fact, Milbrath states that parties are so numerous in Washington that invitations are a burden. However, "Such a situation is not characteristic of state legislators, who frequently are anxious to burn the candle at both ends. Since legislative sessions do not last very long, and since the social life in state capitals is considerably less developed than social life in Washington, state legislative sessions occasionally acquire the atmosphere of a long and extravagant house party."[62]

Entertainment, however, does not set the stage for a bribe or provide opportunities for applying pressure against a legislator. Rather, it facilitates communication between legislator and lobbyist.[63] A basic rule among lobbyists is that they do not discuss business at these sessions unless a legislator introduces the subject. As one lobbyist put it:

> We don't talk issues unless the legislator brings them up. The basic purpose is to get the legislator to call you by your first name. So much lobbying has to be done in a short span of time. You've got 30 seconds to talk to the guy and I don't want to spend any of this time introducing myself and telling him whom I represent.[64]

These findings should not be surprising, for interest groups function at the legislative level—state and national—by having their representatives communicate with legislators and transmit information to them, not by employing overt pressure and threats. Thus, if the legislator cannot get what he wants in the often hurried environment of the committee hearings[65] and lacks knowledge of, or contacts with, legislators "in the know," the lobbyist is close at hand.[66]

INFORMATION AND ACCESS   The information provided by the lobbyist is likely to be more technical and more precise with regard to the views and problems of a segment of the population than that obtained through channels connected to the political party apparatus.[67] Information supplied by party sources can be expected to contain a political bias geared toward success at forthcoming elections—a bias prone to overlooking the technical aspects of a bill and the areas that need attention but do not appear politically relevant at that time.

As a result, information from political parties tends to lag behind events. Popular issues such as pollution, the preservation of natural ecological relations, and the protection of the environment had to catch the public eye before both political parties jumped on the bandwagon they provided. These issues have been around for years, however, and much technical information already had been disseminated by conservationist organizations such as the Sierra Club and the Audubon Society.

Because people tend to communicate most readily with those who share similar views and backgrounds, it may be difficult for a lobbyist to gain access to a legislator who holds a key vote or can exert influence over the votes of other legislators if the lobbyist possesses opposing beliefs and attitudes.[68] Although legislators do tend to respond to those with whom they agree, if the legislator's need for information is great, he will be more favorably disposed toward communication with lobbyists he differs with.

Where such inertia is high, the lobbyist must initiate the attempt to break through it, for "the legislator has the power to vote; the lobbyist has an interest in that vote. Therefore, the lobbyist must seek to interact. Since the lobbyist has no formal power but is dependent upon one who does, interaction is a matter of necessity for him."[69] Thus, lobbyists keep open the communication channels between active sections of the community and the legislature, decreasing the chances that demands of important groups in the population will be ignored completely.

In sum, the lobbyist gains the ear of the legislator by providing information and assistance the legislator needs to carry out his obligations and responsibilities. The lobbyist may on occasion do research for the legislator and provide information about voting blocs and coalitions taking shape on bills coming before the legislature. Indeed,

> whatever their image of lobbyists, legislators are more likely to look on them as service agents than as opinion manipulators. . . . Typically, legislators utilize lobbyists as sources of influence in three ways: by calling upon lobbyists to influence other legislators, by calling upon lobbyists to help amass public opinion in favor of the legislator's position, and by including lobbyists in planning strategy in an effort to negotiate a bill through the legislature.[70]

In this context, entertainment is a meaningful activity, for it allows the legislator to "peruse the fields" and to become familiar with the area of expertise represented by the lobbyists he encounters.

Several factors create legislators' willingness to interact with lobbyists and to rely on them as sources of assistance and information. Those peculiar to the political environment of state politics already have been mentioned as characteristics traditionally associated with strong interest-group systems: short legislative sessions, frequent turnover, the amateur status of state politics, and the part-time nature of the legislator's job.[71] The strength of interest-group representation and influence varies among the states, however, indicating that the need for lobbyists and the functions they perform is not constant across all states, but depends on economic and social as well as political variables.

CONTRIBUTIONS AND OTHER FORMS OF MONETARY EXCHANGE

We can exclude overt bribery from our consideration of state lobbying techniques because it is either extremely rare or impossible to substantiate. In addition, it is ineffective: in the four-state sample, both legislators and lobbyists rank bribery as the least effective of all methods of communication.[72] On the other hand, contributions to political campaigns can be an important part of group strategy. Realistically speaking, money does not win elections. If it did, Republicans would win more often than they do. But money can create a relationship of gratitude and trust. Politicians seeking public office have basic campaign costs to meet, and those organizations willing to meet some or all of these costs certainly can be assured of at least formal access to decision-makers.

The Artie Samish organization in California (discussed earlier in this chapter) was perhaps the prototype of the interest group using money for this purpose. More recent examples are equally useful because we can compare the use of campaign contributions in states with competitive and noncompetitive party systems. The basic difference seems to be that in the competitive systems the contributions are channeled to candidates through the party organization, while in one-party systems the contact between candidate and organization is not disturbed by an intermediary. Within the competitive systems, a distinction can be made between groups that contribute with a specific goal in mind and groups that make contributions because of general agreement with a political goal.

Andrew Hacker's study of the conflict between railroads and truckers in Pennsylvania describes interest groups that contribute with a specific goal in mind. The truckers, undertaking a long and arduous campaign to repeal a state law limiting the weight of trucks to 45,000 pounds, contributed heavily to the campaigns of state legislators. The specific goal was the repeal of the law; the partisan sympathies of the trucking companies did not matter. Therefore, the $76,000 collected by the Pennsylvania Motor Truck Association was divided almost equally between the parties. Hacker writes that the organization expected to recoup this expenditure by revenue gained from a more favorable weight law: "Many of the men who voted for S.615 (to increase the permissible weight of trucks) knew they were doing so to repay a campaign debt or in anticipation of future contributions. . . . They consciously made a bargain to limit their freedom in return for a payment."[73]

Such an unequivocal exchange is unlikely to take place in situations where groups with long-range goals are giving money. The best example is, of course, organized labor. Labor contributions usually flow through the offices of the Democratic party on a more or less permanent arrangement. Labor organizations, because of their relatively large membership, are also anxious to offer their services in mobilizing voters for the Democratic party. Alexander Heard points out that the financial resources and potential voting strength of unions are concentrated in seventeen states[74] where the percentage of union members among all persons of voting age equals or exceeds the national percentage and where the percentage of nonagricultural employers was 30 or more.[75]

In such states as Massachusetts and Michigan, the collaboration between the unions and the Democratic party is complete to the point where the unions serve as auxiliary parties and assume many of the responsibilities of the formal party organization. In Massachusetts, Lockard writes, "In some areas the Democratic party . . . will leave to labor almost the whole job of campaigning for state candidates, and in many campaigns the money labor gives is a very crucial factor in the Democratic effort."[76]

In the other states mentioned by Heard, the collaboration is less formal. In Washington, for example, the unions are friendly to the Democratic party but have not infiltrated to the extent that they have in Michigan and Massachusetts. These contributions are probably not accompanied by explicit expectations. Also, it is likely that, at least in Michigan and Massachusetts, less money filters down to candidates for the state legislature than ends up in the coffers of gubernatorial candidates.

In one-party states, the exchange between candidate and interest groups is more explicit because of the absence of a party organization. Joseph Bernd's investigation of contributions in Georgia shows that about 50 percent of the money received by major candidates for governor came from liquor dealers and highway contractors, both of whom have clear and narrowly defined expectations.[77] Here again, the money flows past the legislature to the place where it is expected to do the most good.

Though campaign contributions do form a part of the strategy of those groups in state politics able to afford it, it would be inaccurate to assume that more contributions are made at the state than the national level. The total amount of money spent at the state level is much lower, although a little money goes a longer way at the state level because candidates are personally less well-off and generally of lower social status than candidates to the national legislature.

There is some indication that the extent of campaign contributions varies with the strength of the interest-group system. "In the weak-lobby states, less than a majority of legislators have received financial help in their campaigns from interest groups (32 percent of legislators in Massachusetts and 42 percent of legislators in North Carolina)." In Oregon and Utah the figures are 58 and 62.[78] The most visible result of such contributions appears as an increased rate of interaction, and thus responsiveness, between legislator and lobbyist.

In terms of the strength of the interest-group system, it would appear that a dollar spent supporting legislators in weak lobby states goes farther than one spent in strong lobby states where a favorable environment for communication already exists, although Utah is an exception. In that state the inexperience of the legislators and their consequent need for information rather than any special regard for lobbyists accounts for most of their interaction. Thus, a campaign dollar spent in Utah is probably worth more than one spent in Oregon.

Money may also be used in public relations campaigns, but, with a few notable exceptions, state interest groups are not as concerned with this "new lobby" technique of mass persuasion. Public relations campaigns usually occur when state interest groups have an affiliation with a national organization that provides much of the propaganda. For instance, the struggle over right-to-work laws has attracted national organizations that supply state units or sympathetic but unaffiliated organizations with literature, arrange for public meetings, and the like. The perennial conflict between trucking companies and railroads has understandably interested the representatives of the respective national associations. The relatively slight use of public relations at the state level is not difficult to understand. The indirect communication of the mass media, for example, is not presumed to be as persuasive as personal communication. Because state legislators are generally more accessible than their national counterparts, using indirect methods to create a favorable climate of opinion is not really necessary. Daily atten-

dance at the state capitol, cultivating key legislators, and establishing
feelings of respect and confidence among legislators with authority in
the area of interest to the lobbyist and his organization—these are the
preferred techniques of experienced lobbyists.

This preference is borne out by the lobbyists' perceptions of effectiveness. On a scale ranging from 0 (ineffective) to 8 (effective), lobbyists rated personal presentations of arguments highest, with public
relations campaigns lower, but above the mean in all states (see table
3.2). One factor against extensive use of public relations campaigns is
their cost; it is simply cheaper to work directly with the legislature.
However, public relations tactics remain in the repertory of the lobbyist in case he needs to invoke the actions of a larger public.

Table 3.2. Lobbyists' Perception of the Effectiveness of Two Methods of Communication on a Scale Ranging from 0 (Ineffective) to 8 (Effective)

	Massachusetts	North Carolina	Oregon	Utah
Personal presentation of arguments	6.6	6.7	6.9	6.4
Public relations campaign	3.7	4.6	4.0	4.6
Mean for all techniques of communication used	3.0	3.5	3.5	3.7

Source: L. Harmon Zeigler and Michael A. Baer, *Lobbying: Interaction and Influence in
American State Legislatures* (Belmont, Calif.: Wadsworth, 1969), p. 176.

The Advantage of
the Defense

Groups whose basic goal is defensive, who are satisfied with the status
quo, and who concern themselves primarily with maintaining it have a
better chance of success than those who try to alter the existing distribution of values. In Michigan, high-status groups such as manufacturers or
professional associations have been able to play the role of policeman
with considerable success, whereas such groups as labor unions that are
struggling for social change think they are at a disadvantage. The coexistence of high-status groups and defensive posture is not coincidental,
but it does not necessarily mean that labor unions will usually be attack-
ing state legislatures. In Massachusetts, for example, the unions spend
practically all their time in conscious maneuvers to prevent the opposition from weakening existing labor laws. Of course, labor's most consistent defensive position has been against right-to-work laws. In Heard's

list of states with the greatest concentrations of union membership, the union lobbyists act as policemen while business groups must induce the legislature to change the status quo.

Biemiller gives an excellent description of the policeman's role:

> One morning in late January the four-man legislative team of the Oregon A.F.L.–C.I.O. in Portland was scanning the batch of bills dropped into the hopper of the newly convened legislature the previous day.
>
> This was a daily routine for the labor watchdog committee. An important part of the job was to read every bill introduced in the two branches of the legislature as a safeguard against reactionary attacks on the rights of working people in the states.[79]

Biemiller then described how the labor lobbyists discovered a "backdoor" right-to-work law hidden in legislation that seemed on the surface to be unrelated to labor-management relations. A civil rights bill introduced by a Republican legislator in 1961 would have amended the Oregon Fair Employment Practices Act to provide that no person should be denied a job because of race, religion, color, or "membership or non-membership in any organization of any kind." The quoted words were the extent of the proposed amendment. The discovery of this sleeper by the labor lobbyists and the subsequent death of the amendment in committee illustrate not only the value of the defense but also the necessity for full-time, rather than amateur, lobbyists.

Utah illustrates another dimension of the advantage of the defense. Like independent regulatory commissions that are "captured" by their clientele after associating closely with them and viewing their problems firsthand, legislators and lobbyists tend to come from occupational and educational backgrounds that favor business and other status quo interests more than civil rights, labor, or educational interests. This situation is disadvantageous to lobbyists who represent groups with interests or orientations that differ markedly from those of the legislator they seek to influence.

For example, attempts by education lobbyists to interact with legislators whose views diverge from their own lead to a vicious spiral. The number of interaction attempts is not correlated with the amount of information transmitted or the likelihood of a successful transaction, but rather with an increased probability that the legislator will believe that he has been pressured by the lobbyist. The legislator will become hostile toward the lobbyist, and will be even more unwilling to assist in the pursuit of his goals.

Under these conditions intensive lobbying is dysfunctional. Instead of leading to change, it reinforces the status quo, or even worse, leads to reaction and the introduction of countermeasures against the organization. Thus, Utah has more education lobbyists on the job than any other state in the four-state sample, but legislators, especially Republicans, feel pressured. The result is that Utah ranks fourth in dollars expended per pupil.

This reaction need not be interpreted exclusively in direct causal terms. An initial unwillingness to meet the demands of a segment of the population can produce mobilization and an attempt to change the legislator's priorities. The best tactic is to reduce attitudinal discrepancies by working through intermediaries whose views are more consonant with those of the legislators involved. Campaign contributions might be used in a quiet attempt to build a legislative obligation. Failing this, low-key public relations campaigns, the publication of voting records, and petition drives may be necessary to change attitudes significantly. Because the line between efforts that result in success and efforts that result in reaction can be thin, the skill of the lobbyist counts heavily.

Lobbying Techniques

Once a lobbyist has achieved access to legislators and other government officials, how does he or she work to gain influence? We now turn attention to the techniques lobbyists employ in their attempts to make state government responsive to their demands, preferences, and expectations.

THE COMMUNICATION OF INFORMATION   We cannot assume that because the more experienced lobbyists are more successful, their experience includes knowledge of the ways to manipulate legislators, to guide unpopular legislation through a series of hostile entrapments, and, in general, to utilize pressure. In practice, the duties of skilled lobbyists are far less dramatic. Generally, their jobs are little more than that of agents communicating the position of a group on an issue to someone they believe will have some control over the outcome.[80] Of course, it is also part of the lobbyists' job to communicate the notion of group power, but this is largely determined without the intervention of lobbying skills. Actually, communication—the job of the lobbyist—is quite an assignment, for information cannot automatically be transmitted. To whom should communications be addressed? When is the proper time to approach a legislator? How should the argument be phrased? These questions are not answered the same way for every situation.

As the example of the education lobby in Utah indicates, communication directed at legislators who are unfavorable to the goals of an organization is likely to result in failure. Interaction and communication are more probable with a favorable attitude. In the four-state sample, 11 percent of the legislators with negative attitudes toward lobbyists were high interactors, compared with 27 percent with neutral attitudes, and 61 percent with positive attitudes.[81]

Recent studies of Washington lobbying all have a similar conclusion: lobbying is very rarely directed at legislators who have taken a position in opposition to the desired goals of the group employing the lobbyist. Most contact between lobbyist and legislator occurs between two partisans who are reinforcing agreement.[82] In this context, pressure is not very useful. In the legislature, as with the general public, pressure is a tactic only opponents engage in. If the legislator and lobbyist have similar goals, communication is likely to be perceived as the legitimate expression of a sound point of view. Consequently, if a legislator feels that the legislature is under considerable pressure, either the lobbyists are talking to the wrong people or the legislator "has heard" of great pressure by his opponents. In all four states studied by Zeigler and Baer, for example, legislators "had heard" of education and labor exerting pressure. Because of the background and attitudinal differences between legislators and lobbyists representing such groups, "nothing more than hearsay evidence" was sufficient to make the rumor credible.[83]

A study of the Indiana legislature further illustrates the tendency for a legislator's perceptions of a group to accord with his background and predispositions, a factor militating against forces of change.[84] Once again, the occupation of the legislator was correlated with his attitudes toward specific interest groups. The clearest relationship is that of sympathetic identification between legislators and lobbyists from the same occupational category. Thus, legislators whose occupation is farming agreed with the goals of the Farm Bureau; businessmen agreed with the goals of business groups.

Naturally, the attitudes of the legislator are related to his ranking of the legislative efficiency of various groups. Legislators who agreed generally with the goals of a particular organization ranked that organization somewhat higher in effectiveness than those groups with which they disagreed. Democrats ranked the AFL–CIO higher than the Farm Bureau, whereas Republicans reversed the order. However, the question that elicited this response was phrased so as to equate effectiveness with the group's skill in presenting its case to the legislature, a judgment that would be colored by the values of the legislator. A rural Republican would hardly credit labor with much skill in presentation.

When the question was phrased to include the word "powerful" different responses were obtained. In this case, legislators who disagreed with the policies of the group were more likely to name that group as powerful.

The evidence of occupational sympathies in Indiana demonstrates again the amateur status of state legislators. Because serving in the state legislature is in many cases a part-time job, legislators retain active ties with their businesses or professions. The possibility of built-in access exists because state legislatures are likely to contain more people without the perspective of a career politician and more people engaged in private business on an active basis than the national legislature.

CHOICES OF STRATEGIES   When establishing a contact with friendly legislators to transmit the position of their organizations, lobbyists have a choice of strategies. In most cases they will choose to operate through the official channels of the legislature by giving testimony at committee hearings, because most legislators rely heavily on them. Over three-fourths of the legislators in Massachusetts, North Carolina, and Oregon indicated that committee hearings were their primary source of information. In Utah the figure was 48 percent.[85]

Lobbyists believe that testimony in committee is most effective when it is supplemented by other communication contacts that will lend credibility to the hearing and familiarize the legislator with different points of view. Of course, lobbying to a considerable extent is a process of bringing about opinion change or getting someone to see things in a slightly different light. When these changes are of major proportions because of the attitudes of many legislators, lobbyists may run into trouble. Thus, it is to their advantage and to the advantage of those seeking changes in existing legislative priorities to prepare legislators for what is to take place in the committee hearing, thereby reducing the chances that ambiguity and hostility will obstruct a fair consideration of the issues.

When faced with strong opposition, experienced lobbyists are likely to rely upon indirect methods, most notably working through another legislator who is more favorable toward the legislation championed by the lobbyists and has access to those the lobbyists seek to influence. In this manner lobbyists attempt to reduce gradually the discrepancy between attitudes. Although they prefer an intermediary who is another legislator, "lobbyists will frequently try to buttress the work of other legislators with contacts by influential constituents. When lobbyists are unable to persuade a legislator to lobby for them, constituents become the major agent of mediation."[86]

This kind of activity is especially conducive to change and to involving articulate segments of the community in decision-making. Lobbyists "frequently interpret opposition as a difficulty in communications rather than as a problem of ideology,"[87] which indicates that those seeking representation through the mediation of interest groups are inclined to work within the system and to have faith in its ability to fulfill their demands.

To supplement testimony, lobbyists seek informal meetings with committee members. This alternative was used frequently by Utah lobbyists who must face formal hearings conducted rapidly. Meetings by appointment with individual legislators are also used. Chance meetings and social gatherings are generally not relied on to any great degree.[88]

Contrary to popular belief, a very effective strategy for the lobbyist is building a reputation for knowledgeability and honesty. Because perceptions of pressure are most likely to arise from those who imagine that the lobbyist is out to push a particular viewpoint, credibility and expertise are important lobbying resources. One lobbyist, frequently called on by legislators to provide information, indicated that he would discuss the bad as well as the good points of bills even though he supported them. As he put it: "I am not going to try to fool you. I'm not going to be as persuasive with the other arguments as I am going to be with my own, but I will tell them to the limit of my ability the other side."[89]

Lobbying techniques depend to some extent on the political system in which the lobbying takes place. Interest groups have been able to establish a more permanent web of interaction with administrative agencies than with the legislature because of the inherently monopolistic tendencies of administrative politics. At the state level, each agency is responsible for a narrowly defined set of operations and comes into almost daily contact with a clientele whose interests are affected by the agency's operations. Constantly associated with a specific clientele, administrators see very little of a more general public and gradually tend to identify their values with those of their clientele. The establishment of a set of mutually shared values between agency and clientele can be useful not only in turning legislative defeat into administrative victory but also in the pursuit of group goals through legislation. A combination of private interest group and administrative agency is valuable in the event that a group without access to the agency tries to change the structure of power through the legislature.[90]

Because of the unstructured nature of state legislatures, lobbyists devote much time to cultivating valuable personal relationships. Consequently, full-time experienced lobbyists prefer to operate as what Patterson calls "contact men." In his article on Oklahoma, Patterson

describes the contact man as one who makes and maintains
relationships with legislators:

> The Contact Man provides a direct communications link be-
> tween the interest group and the individual members of the
> legislature. When faced with a legislative problem for his group,
> the lobbyist with a Contact Man orientation is likely to propose
> as the solution the personal contacting of as many members of
> the legislative body as possible, directly presenting the interest
> group's case to them.[91]

Patterson found that more than half the Oklahoma lobbyists were contact men but, more important, a substantially greater portion of the
contact men were on the job more than half the time. Similar findings
appear in DeVries's study of Michigan.[92] The lobbyists at the top of the
effectiveness scale were more likely to rely on personal presentation of
arguments than those at the bottom of the scale and less likely to rely on
formal presentation at committee hearings than those at the bottom of
the scale.

In Massachusetts, North Carolina, Oregon, and Utah, lobbyists who
were high job investors—individuals who devoted most of their time to
the lobbying profession—were more likely to be contact men than administrators who spend most of their time preparing testimony, writing
speeches and letters, or observing the legislative calendar for bills affecting their client organization.[93]

Lobbyists spending a lot of time on the job are also more likely to consider themselves professionals and to be experienced; the chances of
legislators interacting with them increase accordingly.[94] Thus, no significant differences for the high investment category appear between the
states, although North Carolina, a weak lobby state, has fewer high investors who are able to take the contact man approach. When the sample is viewed as a whole without regard to experience or job investment,
however, we see that lobbyists in the weak lobby states are more likely
to be administrators than their counterparts in strong lobby states.
Where access is difficult, as in Massachusetts, where strong party cohesion and many legislators confound the problems of achieving success by
contacting a few key members of important committees, the less direct
administrative technique is preferred. In Oregon, the reverse is true.[95]

THE FLOW OF COMMUNICATION   The question of whom to
contact is answered to some extent by the structure of the legislature
and the role of the political party in determining legislative policy.
Needless to say, lobbyists do not spend much time talking to legislators

they regard as unimportant. They want to communicate with party leaders in states with strong party discipline and cohesion and with the chairmen of standing committees in states with a tradition of committee dominance like that of Congress. In states where the parties and their satellite interest groups exist in a well-defined system of interaction, the problem of access does not exist. Business groups can talk with Republicans and labor unions can talk with Democrats with confidence that their views will be taken seriously.

Only in legislatures without the control of a party organization does the job of locating and impressing the key decision-makers become acute. Jewell has noted that standing committees in state legislatures rarely exercise the independence of congressional committees. Most important bills are guided to a few committees dominated by a few legislators, usually party or faction leaders.[96] To establish and maintain access to these committees becomes a major goal of the state lobbyist. In the frantic atmosphere of a legislature that meets only for a few months every other year, the rush of legislation makes the task of the lobbyist difficult. Competition for access is keenest. Time becomes quite important. Consequently, the patient cultivation of goodwill can make the difference between talking to a legislator or waiting all day: "The harassed member will give his ear to those advocates he knows and likes in preference to persons he knows only distantly."[97]

Lobbyists concentrate their energies on those who are neutral and can swing a vote or those who are already inclined to favor their viewpoint. As indicated earlier, they will use indirect rather than direct means if they think they must reach a legislator strongly opposed to their position. Thus

> the overwhelming majority of lobbyists who spend most of their time talking to supporters do so because they want these supporting legislators to line up further support. . . . When a persuasion-oriented lobbyist is talking to a supportive legislator, much of the conversation is related not to the merits of a bill, but to the role the legislator can play or is willing to play in contributing to the defeat or passage of the bill.[98]

LIMITS ON THE EFFECTIVENESS OF TECHNIQUES   The discussion of the techniques of the lobbyist should not obscure one fundamental point. The techniques of lobbying as practiced by an interest-group representative are less important than the group itself in contributing to any given legislative outcome. In the words of the authors of *The Legislative System*, "reasons connected with a group's claim to be represented or with its general political power appear . . . to be more significant than reasons associated with its lobbying activities in the legislative arena itself."[99]

General political power, of course, is difficult to define and is probably best understood as a subjective definition on the part of the individual legislator. Groups represented by experienced lobbyists rarely will threaten a legislator with electoral defeat and they will rarely flaunt economic power openly. On the other hand, wealth or potential electoral strength are credited by legislators as being critical factors in the effectiveness of groups. One plausible explanation is that frequently legislators perceive political power and representative quality in an organization as synonymous.

For example, the Florida Dairy Products Association, an organization representing practically all the milk distributors in Florida, had a virtual monopoly on access to the house Public Health Committee, which would never report out a bill opposed by the organization. Those who sought alteration in the laws governing the sale of milk in Florida did not go to the legislature or to one of its committees. They went first to the Florida Dairy Products Association. Why was this true? The large milk distributors in the association, such as Sealtest, Borden's, and Foremost, are economically powerful, but it is difficult to believe that control of the legislative committee was caused exclusively by wealth. Nor was the strength of the association due to its voting strength. It is more likely that its representative quality made the legislative committees willing to accord it the role of legitimate spokesman for an economic interest.[100]

CONCLUSION

JUST AS the strength of political parties varies from state to state, the significance of interest groups varies depending on various circumstances, which we have outlined in this chapter. A major variable is the political and social structure of the state. The long-assumed notion that pressure groups do not thrive in states with cohesive political parties has some validity, but in many cases peaceful coexistence and mutually beneficial cooperation are possible. Political parties as cohesive agencies direct pressure away from the individual legislator and perhaps reduce the salience of pressure politics for the rank and file. Within a political-economic structure, the importance of pressure groups varies with the peculiarities of the situation. Groups powerful in some situations are powerless in others. Even states characterized by a few strong and active groups are likely to have a pluralistic rather than a monolithic structure of power. This conclusion is supported both by the decline in the number of states in the single dominant-interest category and the fact that high-pressure lobbying by powerful interests is not a satisfactory technique of persuasion. Interest groups may be conceptualized as one of several actors in the political process with influence that increases or diminishes in relation to other actors.

The importance of lobbying as a technique of persuading and communicating information has increased with the decline in de facto control of the legislative process by single or amalgamated group interests. Faced with increasing industrialization and urbanization, interest groups have changed their tactics. The techniques used to exert influence have become less flamboyant and more closely attuned to the political dynamics of individual state legislatures. Overt pressure has been replaced by the subtleties of the legislator-lobbyist interchange.

As an example of representational responsiveness, the lobbying process provides further evidence for the claim that this model is flawed because of its systematic underrepresentation of certain groups. Interest-group politics is dominated by professional lobbyists representing established business and professional groups. Labor organizations compete at the state level more than they do in local politics, but without consistent success. Ethnic and minority groups rarely are involved. Hence, strong interest-group states, those most likely to be dominated by a single interest, would be judged most responsive, even though their response is limited—the response is to interest groups rather than to the general public.

The inverse relation between party strength and interest-group dominance need not imply that the importance of the interest group in the political process of the American states has declined greatly or that interest groups can be expected to fade from the scene in a short time. Rather, the resulting changes have shifted the analysis from an emphasis upon the specific, presumably invariant attributes of interest-group power to the more complex and often contingent relationships that determine the outcome of interaction between the legislator and the lobbyist. This contingency will be discussed in the next chapter, which shifts attention to the larger process of policy-making. The role of interest groups in both state and local politics is integrated with that of other actors.

NOTES

1.
The classification of states according to strength of interest groups and legislative cohesion is taken from Belle Zeller (ed.), *American State Legislatures,* 2nd ed. (New York: Thomas Y. Crowell, 1954), pp. 190–91. Because of certain methodological problems, the classification is subject to criticism. To decide whether a state is characterized by strong, moderate, or weak interest groups, questionnaires were sent to political scientists in each state. The limitations of this method are apparent. However, there is reason to assume that these evaluations are relatively accurate in view of the consistent patterns that appear in the economic and political factors associated with the three groups of states. The measure of legislative cohesion is taken from the same study but is not subject to the same criticism, since objective evaluations of cohesion do exist. The extent of party competition, taken from Austin Ranney's classification in "Parties in State Politics," in Herbert Jacob and Kenneth R. Vines (eds.), *Politics in the American States* (Boston: Little, Brown, 1976), p. 61, is appropriate since it relies only on state elections. One modification has been made in Ranney's classification. Modified one-party Democratic and modified one-party Republican states are merged into a single category since the direction of the partisanship is of no concern.

2.
Duane Lockard, *New England State Politics* (Princeton, N.J.: Princeton University Press, 1959), p. 79.

3.
V. O. Key, Jr., *Southern Politics in State and Nation* (New York: Knopf, 1949), p. 56.

4.
Hywell Evans, *Governmental Regulation of Industrial Relations* (Ithaca: New York State School of Industrial and Labor Relations at Cornell, 1961), pp. 92–93.

5.
Proceedings of the AFL-CIO, 4th Constitutional Convention 2 (1961): 176–80.

6.
Quoted in Joseph R. Gladden, Jr., "A Modern Revolution in Georgia: Organized Labor and the General Assembly," Senior honors thesis, Emory University, 1963, p. 28.

7.
Thomas Payne, "Under the Copper Dome: Politics in Montana," in Frank H. Jonas (ed.), *Western Politics* (Salt Lake City: University of Utah Press, 1961), pp. 197–98.

8.

Burton K. Wheeler with Paul Healy, *Yankee From the West* (Garden City, N.Y.: Doubleday, 1962), p. 84.

9.

Joseph Kinsey Howard, *Montana: High, Wide, and Handsome* (New Haven, Conn.: Yale University Press, 1943), p. 245.

10.

Ibid., p. 249.

11.

Richard T. Ruetten, "Anaconda Journalism: The End of an Era," *Journalism Quarterly* 37 (1960): 3–12. See also John M. Schiltz, "Montana's Captive Press," *Montana Opinion* (1956): 1–11.

12.

Robert Engler, *The Politics of Oil* (New York: Macmillan, 1961), p. 354.

13.

Clifton McClesky, *The Government and Politics of Texas* (Boston: Little, Brown, 1963), pp. 136–50.

14.

Raymond A. Bauer, Ithiel de Sola Poole, and Lewis Anthony Dexter, *American Business and Public Policy* (New York: Atherton, 1963), p. 266.

15.

See *The New York Times*, November 9, 1969, p. 40, and February 6, 1970, p. 1. Increasing federal support of antipollution measures provided some of the impetus for this legislation.

16.

On national interest in the Maine legislation see *The New York Times*, January 15, 1970, p. 44. On changing voter attitudes on the "oil and timber oligarchy" and the immediate effects of the oil spill in The Santa Barbara Channel on prospective offshore oil developments in Maine, see *The New York Times*, February 7, 1970, p. 1.

17.

Legislation aimed at curbing pollution passed in February 5, 1970. The tanker *Arrow*, grounded a day earlier, did not begin major break-up until after this date. Although not directly affecting the vote, it may be surmised that this event will hamper attempts by oil interests to circumvent the effects of the legislation. On the *Arrow* episode see *The New York Times*, February 8, 1970, p. 82; February 9, 1970, p. 78; February 12, 1970, p. 74; February 13, 1970, p. 1; February 15, 1970, p. 2.

18.

Percentages for 1951 are computed from data contained in U.S. Bureau of the

Census and U.S. Bureau of Old-Age and Survivors Insurance, cooperative report, *County Business Patterns, First Quarter, 1951,* Part 1, United States Summary (Washington, D.C.: Government Printing Office, 1953), p. 107. Percentages from 1968 computed from data contained in U.S. Bureau of the Census, *County Business Patterns, 1968,* Michigan CBP-68-24 (Washington, D.C.: Government Printing Office, 1969), pp. 4–9.

19.
Stephen B. Sarasohn and Vera H. Sarasohn, *Political Party Patterns in Michigan* (Detroit: Wayne State University Press, 1957).

20.
Joseph LaPalombara, *Guide to Michigan Politics* (East Lansing: Michigan State University, Bureau of Social and Political Research, 1960), p. 104.

21.
Ibid.

22.
See John P. White and John R. Owens, *Parties, Group Interests and Campaign: Michigan '56* (Princeton, N.J.: Citizen's Research Foundation, 1960) for a careful analysis of the role of labor unions and automobile manufacturers in party finance.

23.
Robert Lee Sawyer, Jr., *The Democratic State Central Committee in Michigan, The Rise of the New Politics and The New Political Leadership* (Ann Arbor: University of Michigan, Institute of Public Administration, 1960), p. 261.

24.
Wayne L. Francis, *Legislative Issues in the Fifty States: A Comparative Analysis* (Chicago: Rand McNally, 1967), pp. 44–45.

25.
See Austin Ranney and Willmoore Kendall, *Democracy and the American Party System* (New York: Harcourt, Brace and Company, Inc., 1956), pp. 459–533, for a discussion of national parties as moderators of group conflict.

26.
Nicholas A. Masters, "Organized Labor as a Base of Support for the Democratic Party," *Law and Contemporary Problems* 27 (1962): 255.

27.
V. O. Key, Jr., *Public Opinion and American Democracy* (New York: Knopf, 1961), p. 524.

28.
Joseph P. Harris and Leonard Rowe, *California Politics,* 2nd ed. (Stanford, Calif.: Stanford University Press, 1959), p. 20. The dominance of railroads has been noted in other states. See Dayton David McKean, *Pressures on the*

Legislature of New Jersey (New York: Columbia University Press, 1938), and Andrew Hacker, "Pressure Politics in Pennsylvania: The Truckers vs. The Railroads," in Alan F. Westin (ed.), *The Uses of Power* (New York: Harcourt, Brace and World, 1962), p. 326.

29.
See, for example, Lester Velie, "The Secret Boss of California," *Colliers,* August 14 and 20, 1949.

30.
William Buchanan, *Legislative Partisanship: The Deviant Case of California,* University of California Publications in Political Science, Vol. 13 (Berkeley: University of California Press, 1963).

31.
Ibid., p. 22.

32.
John C. Wahlke, Heinz Eulau, William Buchanan, and LeRoy Ferguson, *The Legislative System* (New York: Wiley, 1962), p. 100.

33.
Edwin N. Atherson and Associates, *Legislative Investigative Report* (Sacramento, Calif.: Premier Publications, 1949). This is a reprint of the report prepared by H. R. Philbrick and printed in the *Senate Journal,* April 4, 1939, and subsequently removed from the record.

34.
Buchanan, *Legislative Partisanship,* p. 143.

35.
Nicholas A. Masters, Robert H. Salisbury, and Thomas H. Eliot, *State Politics and the Public Schools* (New York: Knopf, 1964), pp. 37–38.

36.
Robert Presthus, *Elites in the Policy Process* (Cambridge: Cambridge University Press, 1974), p. 110.

37.
Sidney Verba and Norman Nie, *Participation in America* (New York: Harper & Row, 1972), p. 205.

38.
L. Harmon Zeigler and Hendrik Van Dalen, "Interest Groups in the States," in Herbert Jacob and Kenneth Vines (eds.), *Politics in the American States,* 1st ed. (Boston: Little, Brown, 1965), p. 110.

39.
Wayne Francis, "Legislator Perceptions of Interest Group Behavior," *Western Political Quarterly* 14 (December 1971): 705. See also Presthus, *Elites,* p. 235.

40.
Samuel C. Patterson, "The Role of the Lobbyist: The Case of Oklahoma," *Journal of Politics* 25 (1963): 79.

41.
L. Harmon Zeigler and Michael A. Baer, *Lobbying: Interaction and Influence in American State Legislatures* (Belmont, Calif.: Wadsworth, 1969), p. 61.

42.
Walter DeVries, "The Michigan Lobbyist: A Study in the Bases and Perceptions of Effectiveness," Ph.D. dissertation, Michigan State University, 1960, p. 36; John P. Hackett, "Lobbying in Rhode Island," *Providence Sunday Journal,* August 11, 1963; and Patterson, "The Role of the Lobbyist," p. 79.

43.
Zeigler and Baer, *Lobbying,* p. 76.

44.
DeVries, "The Michigan Lobbyist," p. 63; Thomas J. Moore, "An Analytical Study of Lobbying During the 1962 Session of the General Assembly of Virginia" (unpublished), p. 36. The last source was made available through the courtesy of Spencer Albright of The University of Richmond. See also Zeigler and Baer, *Lobbying,* p. 44.

45.
Zeigler and Baer, *Lobbying,* p. 84.

46.
See Harmon Zeigler, "The Effects of Lobbying: A Comparative Assessment," *Western Political Quarterly* 22 (1969): 122–40.

47.
Zeigler and Baer, *Lobbying,* p. 43.

48.
Zeller, *American State Legislatures,* p. 249; Patterson, "The Role of the Lobbyist," p. 76; DeVries, "The Michigan Lobbyist," p. 78; Leon Epstein, *Politics in Wisconsin* (Madison, Wisconsin: University of Wisconsin Press, 1958), pp. 118–19.

49.
Zeigler and Baer, *Lobbying,* pp. 46–49.

50.
Ibid.

51.
DeVries, "Michigan Lobbyist," pp. 65, 78–79, 222–23.

52.
Lester Milbrath, *Washington Lobbyists* (Chicago: Rand McNally, 1963), p. 77.

53.
Patterson, "The Role of the Lobbyist," p. 78.

54.
Zeigler and Baer, *Lobbying,* pp. 46–49.

55.
Ibid., p. 53.

56.
Epstein, *Politics in Wisconsin,* p. 103; DeVries, *Michigan Lobbyist,* p. 177; William C. Havad and Loren P. Beth, *The Politics of Misrepresentation* (Baton Rouge: Louisiana State University Press, 1962), pp. 235–36.

57.
Zeigler and Baer, *Lobbying,* p. 169.

58.
Milbrath, *Washington Lobbyists,* pp. 241–82.

59.
Engler, *The Politics of Oil,* p. 380.

60.
Milbrath, *Washington Lobbyists,* pp. 302–303.

61.
Zeigler and Baer, *Lobbying,* p. 191.

62.
Milbrath, *Washington Lobbyists,* p. 271.

63.
Zeigler and Baer, *Lobbying,* p. 192.

64.
Ibid.

65.
Ibid., p. 165.

66.
Ibid., p. 105.

67.
Ibid., p. 85.

68.
John W. Thibaut and Harold H. Kelley, *The Social Psychology of Groups* (New York: Wiley, 1961), p. 48; and Zeigler and Baer, *Lobbying,* pp. 38–40, 81–82.

69.
Zeigler and Baer, *Lobbying,* p. 82.

70.
Ibid., p. 107.

71.
Ibid., pp. 20–21.

72.
Ibid., pp. 176–77.

73.
Hacker, "Pressure Politics in Pennsylvania," p. 333.

74.
The states are New York, Pennsylvania, California, Illinois, Ohio, Michigan, New Jersey, Indiana, Massachusetts, Missouri, Wisconsin, Washington, Minnesota, West Virginia, Oregon, Montana, and Nevada.

75.
Alexander Heard, *The Costs of Democracy* (Chapel Hill: University of North Carolina Press, 1960), p. 175.

76.
Lockard, *New England State Politics,* p. 163. See also Joseph LeVow Steinberg, "Labor in Massachusetts Politics: The Internal Organization of the C.I.O. and A.F.L. for Political Action, 1948–1955," Senior honors thesis, Harvard University, 1956.

77.
Joseph L. Bernd, *The Role of Campaign Funds in Georgia Primary Elections, 1936–1958* (Macon: The Georgia Journal, 1958), p. 3. Another good example of the explicit expectations that accompany contributions is the case of Ellis Arnall and an oil investor group. The investors agreed to provide strong backing for Arnall in his 1942 gubernatorial race against Eugene Talmadge because Talmadge failed to support statutory authorization for a pipeline project. See Bernd, pp. 4–5.

78.
Zeigler and Baer, *Lobbying,* p. 114.

79.
Andrew J. Biemiller, "R-T-W Forces Try 'Back Door,' " *American Federationist* 68 (1961): 5.

80.
Bauer, de Sola Pool, and Dexter, *American Business and Public Policy,* pp. 422–33. See also Donald R. Matthews, *U.S. Senators and Their World* (Chapel Hill: University of North Carolina Press, 1960), pp. 177–78.

81.
Zeigler and Baer, *Lobbying,* p. 82.

82.
Frank Bonilla, "When Is Petition 'Pressure'?" *Public Opinion Quarterly* 20 (1956): 46–48.

83.
Zeigler and Baer, *Lobbying,* pp. 112–13.

84.
Kenneth Janda, Henry Teune, Melvin Kahn, and Wayne Francis, *Legislative Politics in Indiana* (Bloomington: Bureau of Government Research, Indiana University, n.d.), pp. 18–19. See also Henry Teune, "Occupational Affiliation and Attitudes Towards Interest Groups," paper presented to the 1962 meeting of The American Political Science Association.

85.
Zeigler and Baer, *Lobbying,* p. 163.

86.
Ibid., p. 131.

87.
Ibid., p. 130.

88.
Ibid., p. 169.

89.
Ibid., p. 110.

90.
J. Leiper Freeman, *The Political Process: Executive Bureau–Legislative Committee Relations* (Garden City, N.Y.: Doubleday, 1955). On state administrative politics, see Harmon Zeigler, *The Florida Milk Commission Changes Minimum Prices* (New York: Inter-University Case Program, 1963); Donald G. Balmer, *Interest Groups in Action: A Case Study of Oregon Milk Control, 1933–1954,* Ph.D. dissertation, University of Washington, 1956; William W. Boyer, "Policy Making by Government Agencies," *Midwest Journal of Political Science* 4 (1960): 267–88; James W. Fesler, "Independence of State Regulatory Agencies," *American Political Science Review* 34 (1940): 935–47.

91.
Patterson, "The Role of the Lobbyist," p. 83. See also Patterson, "The Role of the Labor Lobbyist," paper presented to the 1962 meeting of The American Political Science Association, Washington, D.C.

92.
DeVries, "The Michigan Lobbyist," pp. 115–21.

93.
Zeigler and Baer, *Lobbying,* pp. 77–78.

94.
Ibid., pp. 77, 136.

95.
Ibid., p. 148.

96.
Malcolm E. Jewell, *The State Legislature* (New York: Random House, 1962), p. 93.

97.
Buchanan, *Legislative Partisanship,* p. 102.

98.
Zeigler and Baer, *Lobbying,* p. 130.

99.
Wahlke and others, *The Legislative System,* p. 334.

100.
Harmon Zeigler, "The Florida Milk Commission Changes Minimum Prices," reprinted in Edwin A. Bock (ed.), *State and Local Government: A Case Book* (Tuscaloosa: University of Alabama Press, 1963), pp. 395–428.

4

THE POLICY-MAKING PROCESS IN STATE AND LOCAL GOVERNMENT

THIS CHAPTER examines the process by which state and local governments make decisions. We commonly speak of governments making decisions or initiating policies, but actually these activities are undertaken by people. Sometimes the authoritative agents of government are individuals who make individual decisions, such as welfare workers, teachers, and policemen. More often the authoritative agents are collective units that make collective decisions, such as committees, task forces, and legislatures. In all cases government decision-making is a process of people responding to people. In this chapter we will explore who the decision-makers are and to whom they respond.

Our discussion of the representational and congruence models has stressed the variety and complexity of processes by which information about citizen demands, preferences, and expectations is communicated to government officials. We now consider the variety and complexity of the process of policy-making—that is, the activities government officials pursue in their attempts to be responsive. The policy-making process can be thought of in terms of six successive steps: proposal development, executive recommendation, legislative action, supplementary decision, implementation, and review. With some modification, the six-step process can describe the normal decision-making process in all levels of government.[1] Different actors participate at the different steps. As a result, at each step there are different modes of decision-making, and therefore diverse opportunities and incentives for responsiveness. In the following discussion we will pay particular attention to the important actors and the opportunities for responsiveness in state, city, and school district governments. Since the notion of process is relevant only to the representational model of responsiveness, the discussion of responsiveness in this chapter focuses exclusively on that model.

PROPOSAL DEVELOPMENT

PROPOSAL DEVELOPMENT begins when the need for government action is articulated and one or more policy alternative is suggested. Proposal development does not necessarily have to be initiated by government officials. Indeed, as we shall see, those decision-makers generally thought of as most influential and powerful are not the typical policy initiators. Proposal development can originate with either governmental or nongovernmental individuals or groups within the political system, or it can even originate outside the governmental unit. However, as the term "development" implies, this step is more than the mere expression of a desire or preference. In the words of Rakoff and Schaefer, inputs must be translated into demands acceptable to the political system to cross the system boundary.[2] Proposal development involves making a communication that policy-makers can understand and take action on. Thus, proposal development includes participation of some sort by a government official and typically involves preparation of a formal proposal for consideration by other government officials.

Although proposal development has not been the subject of extensive research by students of decision-making, it is an extremely important step in any decision-making scheme. A policy-making process must consist of, at a minimum, proposal development and implementation. Aside from being a necessary element, proposal development is important because it entails the agenda-setting function. It is at this step that issues are defined and acceptable policy alternatives are listed. The end product of the proposal development step is a formal commitment by a governmental unit to address itself to a particular problem. Agreement on the political agenda between the governing elite and constituents has been introduced as a minimal definition of responsiveness. If action at the proposal development step is not responsive, it is nearly impossible for responsive policy to be enacted.

Scholars of the legislative process almost unanimously agree that such bodies as state legislatures, city councils, and school boards rarely initiate policy. As Chamberlain said, they are "law-declaring rather than lawmaking bodies."[3]

> The legislature rarely acts of its own volition. Proposals are made to it by parties interested, and it is for the legislature to afford a forum before which those measures can be debated.[4]

Although most state and local legislative bodies require that resolutions be formally introduced by members, original drafts are most often prepared by one of the interested parties.

Most important measures introduced in the states are suggested by nonofficial groups or administrative departments that have studied the subjects involved and are prepared to present to the legislature the information on which it may base its action.[5] By the time the legislature, council, or school board comes into play, the issue and the policy options are well defined.

Judicial bodies also rarely participate in the proposal development stage of policy-making. Their function is passive; judicial intervention in the policy process must be solicited by some other actor. State and municipal courts most frequently act at the implementation and review steps. However, when state courts review and find policy unacceptable, they engage in the proposal development activities of articulating a need for new policy and setting the policy agenda. On some occasions they take the initiative to propose (or impose) a policy alternative. The most prominent recent examples of judicial proposal development are cases in which courts have imposed integration and busing plans on local school districts. State courts took the policy development initiative only when other actors were unwilling.

Sources of Proposal Development

The major contributors to proposal development within government are employees of the executive branch. Chief executives usually receive the credit for policy initiation when they endorse proposals at the executive review step in the policy process. However, proposal development seldom originates within the office of the governor, mayor, or school superintendent; instead, within government, it comes from bureaucrats—the corps of officials, usually civil servants in states and cities, who make a career of government service. These "line" workers interact on a regular basis with clientele inside and outside of their governmental unit. Their major role in the policy process is implementation of decisions made by legislative, judicial, and senior executive authorities. But they also serve as a major channel of communication from the masses to the governing elite. In addition, administrators in states, cities, and school districts are increasingly asked not only to oversee programs but to evaluate them as well. Thus, lower level officials in executive branches have a dual feedback role. They make proposals in their capacity as policy implementors and they relay suggestions they receive from those they serve outside of government.

The two major sources of proposal development aside from government officials are individuals and groups within the polity, and other governments. Organized interest groups pursue policy goals by making their preferences known to executive and legislative policy-makers and occasionally by instituting judicial proceedings. Studies of interest-group activities in state and local government have documented that policy officials regard lobbyists, letter-writing campaigns, and other activities undertaken by groups to influence policy as valuable sources of information about popular concerns.[6] In a recent survey of city council members, two-thirds replied that groups were more successful at influencing policy than individuals. Among the reasons offered was the observation that groups were more effective because they were seen to represent a large number of constituents and were concerned about issues that affected wide segments of the community.[7] It is clear that major state and local policy-makers perceive organized interest groups as legitimate spokesmen for large segments of the political system. Thus, they are responsive to their communications at the proposal development step.

On the other hand, the typical individual representing only himself or herself does not have great influence on major policy-makers. The first problem is access. Sheer numbers make it impossible for governors, mayors, school superintendents, and their executive staff to interact with every constituent who seeks an audience. Even though they have a smaller and more discrete constituency, legislators, council members, and school board members would also find it impossible to speak with all opinion holders on all issues in their districts.

The second problem is impact. A public official certainly does not give equal weight to the opinion of an individual and the representative of a large group. Aside from sheer numbers, group leaders are presumed to represent organizational resources and expertise. The average man on the street can make no such claims to importance.

Yet the views of individuals do result in proposal development, mainly through the regular interaction of individual clients with the government officials who serve them. In a study of citizen utilization of government agencies, Katz and others point out that almost everyone has regular contact with certain government constraint agencies. For example, such activities as filing an income tax return or getting a driver's license are nearly universal.[8] In a national survey dealing with encounters with government agencies providing services, Katz and his associates found that 58 percent of their sample had utilized agencies in several selected areas. Of those respondents, over 63 percent said their most important experience with a government agency occurred at the state, county, or local level.[9]

The upshot of these frequent face-to-face meetings of service agency officials and clients is an exchange of ideas about desirable changes in programs and procedures. Officials of service agencies generally have favorable perceptions about their clients and hold them in relatively high esteem.[10] It is not uncommon in local governments for organizations to be formed to facilitate cooperation between agency officials and the citizens they serve. Outstanding examples are Chambers of Commerce and parent-teacher associations. Ample opportunity exists for individuals to initiate proposal development by communicating with sympathetic agency personnel.

A growing body of research suggests that a sizable proportion of policy proposals—perhaps a majority—originate outside the adopting unit of government. Directly or indirectly, these proposals originate in other governmental bodies. Jack L. Walker has suggested that it is useful to distinguish between a horizontal mode and a vertical mode of intergovernmental communications on proposal development.[11]

HORIZONTAL MODE OF COMMUNICATIONS   Walker's horizontal mode is a process of decision-making by emulation. He suggests that the rule of thumb employed might be stated as: "look for an analogy between the situation you are dealing with and some other situation, perhaps in some other state [or locality], where the problem has been successfully resolved."[12] Justice Brandeis once observed that a major advantage of the federal system of government was that some governmental units could serve as laboratories by attempting novel social and economic experiments without risk to the rest of the country. Considerations of novelty and risk aside, it is clear that state and local officials follow the activities of their contemporaries with the intention of finding useful policy proposals for their own units of government.

Walker notes that a number of formal organizations facilitate communications among state governmental officials.

> Several organizations now exist, such as the Council of State Governments, the Federal Commission on Intergovernmental Relations, and the recently established Citizen's Conference on State Legislatures, whose primary function is to improve com-

Table 4.1. Professional and Service Organizations Serving Local and State Governments

Organization	Year organized	State or regional chapters	Individual members
American Association of Airport Executives	1928	6	1,050
American Association of School Administrators	1865	—	18,000
American College of Hospital Administrators	1933	—	10,209
American Institute of Architects	1857	179	25,000
American Institute of Planners	1917	35	10,000
American Library Association	1876	58	28,111
American Public Health Association	1872	51	25,106
American Public Power Association	1940	—	86
American Public Transit Association	1882	—	—
American Public Welfare Association	1930	—	8,000
American Public Works Association	1894	59	15,752
American Society of Planning Officials	1934	—	11,500
American Society for Public Administration	1939	84	12,000

Organization	Year organized	State or regional chapters	Individual members
American Water Works Association	1881	38	20,000
Building Officials and Code Administration International	1915	13	3,000
Canadian Federation of Mayors and Municip.	1935	—	290
Council of State Governments	1933	—	—
Governmental Research Association	1914	—	450
Institute of Traffic Engineers	1930	33	6,000
International Association of Assessing Officers	1934	65	9,000
International Association of Chiefs of Police	1893	—	10,400
International Association of Fire Chiefs	1873	8	7,200
International City Management Association	1914	45	5,821
International Institute of Municipal Clerks	1947	—	2,250
International Personnel Management Association	1973	54	4,800
League of Women Voters of the U.S.	1920	1,350	150,000
Municipal Finance Officers Association	1906	51	5,280
National Association of Counties	1957	—	—
National Association of Housing & Redevel. Off'ls.	1934	38	7,000
National Association of Regional Councils	1967	—	250
National Environmental Health Association	1937	47	6,000
National Governors' Conference	1908	—	54
National Institute of Governmental Purchasing	1944	—	—
National Institute of Municipal Law Officers	1935	—	—
National League of Cities	1924	48	521
National Legislative Conference	1948	—	7,600
National Municipal League	1894	—	6,500
National Recreation & Park Association	1965	60	11,176
U.S. Conference of Mayors	1933	—	—
Water Pollution Control Federation	1928	63	23,000

Source: *The Municipal Year Book 1975* (Washington, D.C.: International City Management Association, 1975), pp. 365–6.

munications among the states. Most important of these specialized communications networks are the professional associations of state officials, such as the National Association of State Budget Officers, or the National Association of State Conservation Officers.[13]

There are similar organizations for municipal officials—for example, the National Municipal League, the International City Managers' League, and the Conference of Mayors; and for school district officials—the National School Boards Association, the American Association of School Administrators, and the Association of State School Officials (see table 4.1). Federal, state, and local officials, are often members of these organizations, thus facilitating the spread of policy innovations between and within levels of government.

These organizations provide a second communications function by serving as "occupational contact networks" and facilitating the movement or transfer of professional personnel.[14] By rapidly spreading knowledge of new programs through meetings, seminars, and publications and by contributing to the mobility of high level administrators, these professional associations help to shape consensus in policy areas concerning desirable programs and indirectly set policy agendas in state and local governments.

VERTICAL MODE OF COMMUNICATIONS   The vertical mode of intergovernmental communications transfers policy proposals across levels of government. Examples of federal influence on state and local governments are the most obvious. The federal executive and legislative branches enforce their wills on state and local governments by manipulating the regulation of various grants-in-aid programs—for example, the recent implementation of a nationwide highway speed limit of 55 miles per hour. Highway traffic regulations are part of the legal authority of each state, but the federal government was able to effect a policy change by making the new speed limit a condition for eligibility for highway trust funds. The federal judicial branch enters the policy-making process for state and local governments when it rules on the constitutionality of legislation and legal procedures. The U.S. Supreme Court, in *Reynolds* v. *Sims,* the famous "one man, one vote" decision, set the policy agenda for the states by affirming that equal population districts were required in both houses of all state legislatures.[15] Federal, executive, and judicial authorities also create policy demands for local governments, as witnessed by recent Health, Education and Welfare Department, Justice Department, and federal court interactions with school districts on such topics as civil rights, integration plans for local schools, and distribution of financial resources.

Intergovernmental communications also occur vertically between states, counties, and municipalities. According to the legal principle known as Dillon's Rule, local jurisdictions are the creatures of the state and may exercise only those powers expressly granted them by the state.[16] Thus states, which have the authority to create and dissolve local units of government, can require or influence policy within their borders. States, like the federal government, use the power of the purse to stimulate policy changes in local governments. State governments not only set the rules by which local governments are eligible for state funds, but they also set limits on local taxation, bonding, and expenditures. Few states provide local units of government much flexibility or discretion over revenues, even over those commonly defined as "revenues from own sources."[17] State governments set a substantial proportion of the policy agendas of local government.

We have discussed the vertical mode of intergovernmental policy proposal communications as a movement from central to more local authorities. Occasionally, the opposite pattern occurs—federal governments take policy proposals from local and state sources. A prime example is the recent responsiveness of New York State and, finally, the federal government to policy proposals from New York City arising from its financial crisis. Both state and federal governments responded favorably to New York City's demands for deadline extensions, loans, and other aid. As noted above, the exchange of ideas and personnel facilitated by national organizations of professional governmental administrators makes possible the spread of policy innovations from small to large polities, as well as the reverse.

EXECUTIVE REVIEW

ONCE A formal proposal has been submitted by one of the actors in a political system, it is usually reviewed by the office of the chief executive. The basic legal mandate of governors, mayors, and school superintendents is the administrative oversight function. However, the accepted role of the chief executive has expanded from supervising implementation of decisions to include responsibility for screening policy proposals before they come to the legislative body. The importance of executive review has grown along with the increased centralization of technical and informational resources in the executive branches of governments. Legislative bodies cannot and do not ignore policy proposals that pass the executive review step. On the contrary, most state legislatures, city councils, and school boards solicit and, in some cases, require executive evaluation of proposals across the entire spectrum of policy content.

The executive review step consists of interaction between the source of a proposal and the office of the chief executive, deliberation and consideration of the proposal and alternatives, and recommendation of a policy to the legislative body. When proposal development originates within the executive branch, the interaction consists of negotiation between the executive office and the initiating agency. When proposals originate within government but outside the executive branch with other governments or with nongovernmental individuals and groups, executive agency personnel are included in executive review deliberation as expert consultants. Whatever the origin of a policy proposal, the goal of the executive recommendation step is to eliminate bad proposals and to modify good proposals to make them relevant, effective, and, perhaps most important, acceptable to all parties within and without government.

As noted earlier, the policy-making process at minimum consists of proposal development and implementation. The minimum policy process generally occurs when all participants are within the same department of government. Whenever a policy decision requires the participation of multiple governmental actors or communications with individuals or groups outside of government, the decision-making process will almost certainly include an executive review step. The chief executive is called on to make policy recommendations for six important reasons:

1. LEGAL REQUIREMENT   An increasing number of states, municipalities, and school districts are imposing a legal obligation on their chief executives to present specific policy recommendations to their respective legislative bodies on a regular basis. For example, most state and local governments require the preparation of an executive budget, which is the chief executive's report of anticipated revenues and recommendations for expenditures. Legislative and judicial authorities frequently direct executives to prepare special reports and evaluations of existing programs and potential problem areas, which include discussion and recommendation of policy alternatives.

As student enrollments decline because of the falling birth rate, many school boards have directed their superintendents to recommend the most efficient use of existing staff and physical plants. In the wake of New York City's recent crisis, a number of city councils have charged their mayors and city managers to prepare reports on the status of bonded debt and to recommend policy changes necessary to ensure that financial obligations do not exceed resources. In response to recent mandates for change in systems of distribution of funds, employment opportunities, and student assignment to schools, state and local legislative bodies have routinely turned to their chief executives and passed on the burden of evaluating and recommending policy alternatives. Both legislative and judicial authorities are calling on executive department officials for aid in their own policy deliberations and are increasingly requiring such aid by law.

2.   COMMUNICATIONS CENTER   More than any other branch or department of government, the chief executive's office serves as the center of communications within a polity. Numerous studies have affirmed that, for the vast majority of citizens, chief executives are the most recognized and visible government officials. Governors and mayors are more readily identified by the man in the street than state legislators and city council members. The average citizen can more readily supply the name of the local superintendent of schools than his United States congressman, to say nothing of elected school board members. As a consequence, governors, mayors, and school superintendents receive the lion's share of letters, telephone calls, and personal visits from the public.

By virtue of its position of authority over the vast majority of government employees, the chief executive's office is also the nerve center within a political system, and, as discussed earlier, the chief executive's office is the ultimate recipient of most information and policy recommendations from other units and levels of government. The chief executive's position in the flow of information ensures that a high proportion of decisions will include executive recommendation because this central office is the linking agent between the major sources of proposal development and legislative and judicial authorities.

3.   POLITICAL POWER   Governors and most mayors are chosen by an electoral process; city managers and school superintendents serve at the pleasure of elected bodies. Whether or not the electoral process is direct or partisan, the chief executive stands as the symbolic, if not the actual, head of a ruling party or coalition. Chief executives enjoy—at least at their initiation—the confidence of, at minimum, a plurality of voters or the representatives of voters. Governors, mayors, city managers, and superintendents have a base of popular and elite support that they can use as a resource in the decision-making process. The mass popular identification of government with its chief executive, who has the singular position as the only official chosen directly or indirectly by the entire citizenry, makes the chief executive the tribune of the people. Unlike minor executives, whose loyalty is to their clientele; legislators, whose loyalty is to their individual districts; and judges, whose loyalty is to judicial principle; the chief executive claims all citizens as his constituency. Thus, those who would enact and implement a given policy seek out the consultation and support of governors, mayors, superintendents, and other chief executives through executive recommendation in deference to the political resources they may command.

4. EXPERTISE   The chief executive is often called on to make policy recommendations because of his or her control of the informational and technical resources of the professional executive bureaucracy. Although a growing number of states have established legislative reference services to give legislators a source of information independent of the governor's office, most state legislatures and the vast majority of city councils and school boards do not possess the resources to produce data and analyses on policy options and thus must rely on the chief executive.

The professional elite who constitute the ongoing staff of state and local government contend that they have mastered a general technology of public administration and a specific substantive technology (for example, about education, health, or police services) that qualify them as expert consultants on all policy questions if not the rightful designers of "proper" policy. Leaving aside questions about the state of development of various technologies of public service, there can be no denying that those who administer programs on a day-to-day basis control a valuable wealth of information appropriate for consideration by other policy-makers. Executive review provides an opportunity for those who are most familiar with current programs and conditions in a unit of government to share their knowledge and opinions with others.

5. COMPREHENSIVE PROGRAM   Another reason that chief executives are called on to make policy recommendations is that they are the only actors in the decision-making process who are presumed to be overseeing a totally integrated policy program. Other actors clearly seek actions in limited spheres. For example, individuals and interest groups seek policies in their own self-interest; judicial authorities enter the policy-making process on a piecemeal basis through the stimulus of others; agencies promote the interests of their clientele; legislative bodies, as will be discussed later in this chapter, divide expertise and authority among committees that often act as rivals. Chief executives, in their roles as tribunes of the entire polity and overseers of all policy, are expected to weigh the conflicting input from segments of the population, bureaucracy, and legislature and to present a balanced, comprehensive program of governmental activities. The executive recommendation step thus promotes compatibility of new and existing policies in two ways. First, the chief executive's office will certify that its package of recommendations does not contain elements which are mutually exclusive or in conflict. Second, the chief executive's comprehensive perspective will ensure that elements of the total program are appropriate to and capable of achievement with the resources available to the government.

6.   ENFORCEMENT   Implementation of policy decisions made by legislative and judicial officials is the prime legal mandate of the chief executive. Other policy-makers, therefore, request executive recommendation to involve the ultimate administrator of the chosen policy in the process of evaluating alternatives. One purpose, as discussed earlier in the chapter, is to tap the expertise of those most intimately associated with program implementation—to discover what is possible and reasonable. A second purpose is to test the reaction of executive officials to policy proposals and to estimate how each might be carried out.

This second purpose is extremely important because legislative bodies must, of necessity, grant wide latitude to chief executives in the actual implementation of the programs they pass. Most state and local legislators are underpaid, understaffed, part-time officials. They have neither the resources nor the time to pass such explicit and detailed legislation that administration has only to implement it. On the contrary, both the spirit and the letter of the law are often open to multiple interpretations. Executive review gives an opportunity for those who will be responsible for carrying out a decision to explain how they intend to behave.

Use of the executive review step to consider alternative strategies of implementation is important for at least three reasons:

First, policy discrepancies: Including an executive review step helps reduce the number of cases in which programs are not realized because executives refuse to carry out the instructions of legislatures and courts. This sort of conflict was recently prominent at the federal level when President Nixon refused to spend funds appropriated by Congress in excess of his executive recommendations. Differing policy orientations among senior officials is a major problem in jurisdictions where legislative bodies and top executive posts are controlled by members of opposing parties or factions. It is obviously counterproductive for legislators to impose a program that a chief executive will refuse to implement. Executive review will at least highlight possible conflict and may lead to acceptable compromise or accommodation between contending parties.

Second, selective enforcement: State and local legislatures commonly enact statutes that they intend to be invoked by officials according to their own discretion. Curfew laws are an example of measures intended for selective enforcement. Police have the option of ordering home (or arresting) juveniles they believe to be looking for trouble, while not stopping others attending postcurfew school or church activities. Executive review provides the executor with the opportunity to comment on his proposed use of selective enforcement authority.

Third, decentralized enforcement: State and local authorities are increasingly enacting uniform laws that permit differing enforcement in different areas of the polity. This local enforcement scheme is gaining popularity in the area of regulation of pornography and sexual conduct among adults. States are letting local prosecutors establish guidelines for determining criminal obscenity within their districts. Several major cities have used a similar strategy to establish "flesh districts" where so-called adult theaters and book stores are concentrated. Executive review is useful for gathering reactions to and ideas about the consequences of such schemes of decentralized enforcement.

LEGISLATIVE ACTION

IF PROPOSAL development is characterized in terms of agenda-setting, executive review should be characterized as agenda-refining. Legislative

action, then, is the process of making authoritative decisions concerning
the items on the policy agenda. Legislative bodies lay down rules and
issue orders not only to citizens under their jurisdiction, but also to
courts and administrative officers who must see that legislative decisions are carried out.[18]

Yet, although legislative bodies are very powerful actors, they play a
passive role in the policy-making process. American legislatures have
evolved into bodies that react to the initiatives of chief executives, who
have become the chief legislators. Most state legislatures emulate Congress by hearing a "state of the state" message from the governor that
includes a package of recommended legislation. City councils spend the
greatest amount of time considering proposals initiated by the executive
branch.[19] And 96 percent of American school boards have delegated control of their meeting agendas to their superintendents.[20]

Legislative action takes place at all levels of American government—national, state, county, municipal, and special district.[21]
Legislative bodies engage in investigation, deliberation, and debate to
produce laws, statutes, resolutions, authorizations, and directives. The
types of decisions that require legislative action are generally made explicit in such enabling documents as state constitutions and city or
county charters. Popular opinion supports the view that the principal
mission of state and local legislative bodies is the promulgation of
statutory law—generalized rules of conduct to be followed by ordinary
citizens. However, the preponderances of civil and criminal law remain
unchallenged and unchanged from year to year. The main role of state
and local government is no longer governing in the sense of enforcing
restrictions on the behavior of individuals, but rather is governing in the
sense of providing goods and services for the general welfare. Thus, state
legislatures and city councils spend considerably more time considering
how current traffic laws can best be enforced than they do considering
new traffic laws. The legislators are generally more actively involved
with police budgets and operating procedures than they are with the
statutes and ordinances the police are expected to enforce. As a consequence, state legislatures, city councils, and school boards in the 1970s
are more concerned with establishing rules for the conduct of government officials than with rules to be followed by citizens.

Legislative Authority

American state constitutions and local government charters give the legislative branch various kinds of authority over the executive and judicial branches.[22] One of the most important of these is authority over public finances, the power to levy and collect taxes and to spend public funds. The battle cry of the American Revolution, "No taxation without representation," is manifested to this day in the requirement that elected representatives—legislators—must participate in establishing taxing and spending policies. Legislatures authorize the executive branch to act in several other spheres: to reorganize itself, to select its major officials, and to regulate the economy. Similarly, legislative systems in the United States confer authority upon the courts, authorizing them to assert jurisdiction, create their organizational machinery, and qualify their members.

American legislative bodies are institutions of public policy decision-making that manifest the concept of representative government. With the exception of some school districts whose board members are appointed, members of American legislative bodies—federal, state, and local—are chosen by popular election at regular intervals. And, although some school board and city council members are chosen on an at-large basis or are appointed, the overwhelming majority of American legislators have an explicit constituency to represent.

Amateur Government

Unlike the United States Congress, state and local legislative bodies also continue the American tradition of amateur government. With few exceptions, the titles school board member, city councilman, and state legislator signify a part-time job rather than an occupation. Legislative sessions are short. In thirty-one states the regular session of the legislature is limited either to a maximum number of official days in session—generally less than 90, or a maximum number of calendar days—generally less than 180 days. Only four states have legislatures meeting virtually year-round (Michigan, New York, Pennsylvania, and California), and eight state legislatures hold regular sessions only every other year. City councils and school boards meet year-round but the typical schedule calls for two monthly meetings that last only a few hours.

Remuneration and perquisites for state and local legislators further suggest part-time status. The vast majority receive nominal or no salaries, and office facilities, supplies, and secretarial and research assistance are minimal or nonexistent.

The job of the state and local legislator is also part-time in the sense that few individuals remain in office for long. High turnover in membership is a constant characteristic of state and local legislative bodies. Recent studies suggest that the ratio of new members to the number of positions available is on the order of 30 percent in state legislatures,[23] approximately 50 percent in city councils,[24] and 34 percent in school boards.[25] Most turnover is voluntary—incumbents simply do not seek reelection. As a result, state and local legislatures can be characterized as representative bodies composed largely of amateurs and novices.

With the exception of Nebraska, which has a unicameral legislature, state legislative bodies consist of two chambers that must concur on all acts. All have sizable memberships: upper house memberships range from 20 in Alaska and Nevada to 67 in Minnesota, and lower house memberships range from 40 in Alaska and Nevada to 400 in New Hampshire. As a result of their size and bicameral structure, state legislatures employ formal and informal rules of individual conduct and policy-making procedures similar to those of the United States Congress. The most important element common to these legislative bodies is the committee system.

The Committee System

Congress and the state legislatures implement a division of labor scheme in the form of standing committees. The legislative action step of the policy-making process originates when a bill—a proposal for legislation—is formally introduced by a legislator. (Formal introduction by a member of the legislature is a common parliamentary requirement. However, as we have seen, most bills are not initiated by legislators.) Bills are then referred by the legislative leadership to the appropriate standing committee. In theory, standing committees allow legislatures to make the most efficient use of limited time resources. Committees permit a smaller number of legislators to make preliminary investigations, reports, and recommendations to the larger body. The task of the committee is, first, determining policy, then studying the situation on which it is proposed to legislate, fixing the general lines of the proposed bill, devising administrative machinery to carry out the purpose decided on, and, finally, drafting or approving the draft of a bill.[26]

An important function for responsiveness—holding public hearings on important bills—is delegated to state legislative committees. Chamberlain points out some important differences between hearings in Congress and in the state legislatures.

> An important measure may remain in a congressional committee through the two or more sessions of a Congress, thereby affording a much longer time for the committee to develop the information which it needs to enable it to pass on the facts and on the principle and details of a bill. So hearings are of real importance in building up a mass of information for the benefit of the committee and in bringing to light mistakes which it may be making. State legislatures have but one regular session, generally short, so there is not the same possibility of deliberate consideration in committee. . . . Furthermore, hearings in a committee of Congress are made a permanent record by being printed, while hearings in state legislative committee are usually not.[27]

As a result, public hearings and committees in state legislatures generally have far less impact than those in the U.S. Congress. To a much greater degree measures referred to state legislative committees remain under the control of their introducers.

The deference to subcommittee expertise so prevalent in national and state legislatures has its counterpart in municipal and school district government. Generally speaking, the larger the city or school district, the greater the likelihood that its legislative body will have committees, and the larger the number of committees it will have (see table 4.2). City councils have an average of 8.7 special committees. A recent survey of fifty-one public school districts in the forty-nine largest cities found that 46 percent of the school boards had standing committees, and 82 percent used temporary committees.[28]

Table 4.2.   Population and Use of Committees by City Council

Population (thousands)	Average number of committees
10–25	7.8
25–50	9.6
50–100	11.4
100–250	16.1
250–500	14.9
Over 500	16.7

Source: *The Municipal Yearbook 1972* (Washington, D.C.: International City Management Association, 1972), p. 24.

Even in those councils and school boards which do not employ standing committees, there is a tendency for members to specialize in substantive policy areas. The legislator who declares a special policy interest may establish a liaison with appropriate executive department officials to receive documents and other detailed information beyond that normally supplied to the legislative body. The legislator-specialist may also become a target of input from individuals and groups outside of the government who are also interested in that policy area. For example, a councilman or school board member who declares a special interest in employee relations will be inundated with materials from the executive personnel department, the municipal employees' or teachers' union, and communications from taxpayers' groups, individual citizens, employees, and parents. The legislative body will tend to defer to those with special interest in their area of concentration because they have superior knowledge both of the policy area and of the climate of opinion within the general and professional communities.

The legislative function of standing and special committees is essentially the same in state legislatures, city councils, and school boards: to make a policy recommendation to the larger body based on an inquiry that includes the testimony of experts and interested parties. An important difference between committees of state legislatures and committees of local legislative bodies is that state committees are composed exclusively of state legislators, while local legislative committees frequently include executive officials and members of the public. City councils and school boards seek to increase both representativeness and expertise by including nonlegislators on their committees. Executive personnel are obviously chosen for their expertise, but, to a considerable extent, so are members of the public.

A special committee chosen by the school board in Eugene, Oregon, to study the problem of declining enrollments and the possible need to close some schools in the district illustrates the strategy of increasing representativeness and expertise by including members of the public. The board decided that the committee should consist of six administrators in an *ex officio* capacity, representatives from the eight smallest schools, and six "citizens"—a real estate broker, a professor of architecture, a lawyer, a certified public accountant, a television news director, and an official of the county labor council—individuals who could bring considerable expertise from their professional lives to bear on the school closure issue. Citizens asked to serve on committees for local legislative bodies are by no means selected at random from the constituent population. Their backgrounds and values tend to reflect those of the legislators themselves: leaders of the business and professional communities with specialized knowledge and prestige and a predisposition to defer to experts as opposed to the masses.

Public Attendance at Legislative Sessions

A final major difference in legislative procedure used by state and local legislatures, of particular importance to the question of responsiveness, is the opportunity for public attendance and input at regular sessions of the entire legislative body. The average citizen obviously finds it much easier to attend a local city council or school board meeting than to attend a meeting of the legislature in the state capital. The impediment of geography to mass attendance of state committee and legislative sessions is exacerbated by the fact that most state capitals are not located in major population centers. Most state legislatures are not seated in the New York cities, Philadelphias, and Los Angeleses, but in the Albanys, Harrisburgs, and Sacramentos. Furthermore, because of the smaller size of their constituencies and the smaller size of the legislative bodies themselves—approximately 90 percent of city councils and school boards have fewer than ten members—local legislative bodies can accommodate and solicit public attendance and participation at their regular sessions. Most city councils and school boards have rules of order that permit comments from citizens attending meetings while substantive agenda items are on the floor, and many also have an additional agenda item for comments and concerns from those attending the meeting. State legislatures do not permit public participation in their general meetings.

Perhaps the most important difference between state and local legislative bodies as representative and responsive institutions is not in their different procedures, but in their different proximity of representatives and represented.

> Probably the single most important factor conditioning the distinctiveness of local legislative politics is sheer proximity to the electorate. The local legislator, especially in the smaller and middle-size communities, must indeed operate in what Burke termed "the strictest union with his constituents"—right in the middle of them, in fact, twenty-four hours a day. Although he may be in a formal legislative session only once every couple of weeks, there are endless other meetings: with fellow officials, interest groups, and private citizens. He can scarcely walk down

Main Street or shop in a supermarket without being engaged in conversation by someone concerned with local government actions of one sort or another. His constituents are omnipresent; they can pick up the telephone and talk with their representative at almost any moment, and it is no problem at all to appear at his front door.[29]

However, little evidence suggests that private citizens actually take advantage of the closeness of local government to attend meetings and initiate contact with local officials. Verba and Nie report that approximately 20 percent of the population have *ever* contacted a local government official about an issue or problem.[30] There are approximately 214 million Americans and 500,000 elected local government officials. Thus, on the average, each elected official can expect some communication from about 80 constituents. Verba and Nie did not ask about frequency of citizen contact, but it is interesting to note that if each active constituent limits his or her contacts to elected officials and makes four contacts per year, the average elected official will receive only one communication a day.

The apparent contradiction of legislators reporting contacts with constituents and constituents reporting few contacts with legislators is easily resolved. Most of the 20 percent who contact elected officials want to express an opinion or request that some action be taken as an individual, and do so infrequently. However, some people specialize in maintaining close contact with state and local legislators as well as other governmental officials and seek to influence decision-making to the benefit of groups they represent. These are the lobbyists as discussed in detail in chapter 3.

Lobbyists are at work in the city halls, county courthouses, and state capitols of the United States, as well as in Washington, D.C.[31] State and local legislators view lobbyists as service agents who provide helpful information on constituents' opinions and desires. Lobbyists also provide expert opinion and information, such as technical data, research reports, testimony at hearings, and interpretation and evaluation of executive proposals. Thus, lobbyists present legislators with supplementary information and often an alternative point of view to that of experts within government. To the typical amateur state and local legislator, this is a most helpful service.

Lobbyists can frequently provide political as well as technical resources to the legislator. Zeigler and Baer note that lobbyists can influence other legislators, amass public opinion, and help plan strategy to negotiate a bill through the legislative process.[32] They also found in a study of lobbying in four state legislatures that lobbyists tended to remain in their occupation for longer periods of time than legislators.[33] Thus, it is not surprising that when:

> legislators seek out lobbyists for information, they frequently want, in addition to technical information, estimates of the probable success of a particular piece of legislation. This is a chore which experienced lobbyists are believed to be capable of performing.[34]

Most state lobbyists are professionals employed by business, professional, or interest groups, while most local lobbyists are volunteers. In a study of lobbying in city councils Levitt and Feldbaum found that:

> Spokespersons are usually members of the association and act as lobbyists in a volunteer capacity, rather than being hired as full-time agents or as members of a professional staff. Though some local groups may occasionally hire consultants to speak for them, the spokespersons are usually the presidents of the local associations, or other volunteer members who have the extra time, special skills, communication abilities, or contacts needed to effectively represent the group's position on a matter before the council. The time and effort that those men and women offer generally goes materially unrewarded by the group.[35]

Professional lobbyists are probably necessary at the state level for at least three reasons, as shown in chapter 3. First, state legislatures are so large that the job of contacting individual legislators requires a full-time lobbyist. Second, because most state legislatures are faced with both a huge agenda of bills and a constraint on the maximum length of the legislative session, numerous bills are considered at the same time. Interests that use lobbyists at the state level must have active spokespersons during the entire session to compete for the legislators' attention.

Local interests, on the other hand, have the comparative luxury of the slower legislative pace of city councils and school boards. They can marshall their voluntary resources when items of special importance arise; for state interests, virtually all items are under consideration at once. Finally, since state capitals are often physically isolated from major population centers, interests must employ a full-time spokesman who can live in the capital and have the opportunity to interact with legislators.

After committee deliberation and recommendation, debate, amendment, and approval by the full legislative body—as well as agreement with the second legislative body in bicameral state legislatures—the legislative action step ends with a decision and a document. The document is the text of a law, resolution, statute, or directive; it is an order or authorization for certain action to be taken by the officers of the government. The text also specifies the effective date of the legislation. The communication of the official legislation document to the chief executive ends the legislative action step.

SUPPLEMENTARY DECISION

THE LEGISLATIVE action step produces a formal document, which is an order from the legislature, council, or school board to other governmental officials. Only a small proportion of these orders are meant to be implemented immediately. Typically, there is a lag time between legislative action and implementation. For example, changes in statutory law made by state legislatures and city councils are normally made effective sixty or ninety days following enactment, or sometimes on the following January 1. In states where the legislative session ends in June, or earlier, a six-month interval between enactment and enforcement is not uncommon.

The rationale for this delay between legislative action and implementation is threefold. First, it gives time for the development of enforcement procedures by government officials; second, it provides for a transition period between the old and new program during which time affected parties can be informed of the change; and third, it provides a final opportunity for minor adjustment, major change, or even revocation of legislation *prior to its implementation* based on later developments. The supplementary decision step involves changes in policy which are made after legislative action and before implementation.

Updating

Supplementary decisions often reflect a need to update legislation because of minor developments after the passage of the original legislation. For example, a legislative body may amend an agency or department's appropriation to take advantage of a minor unexpected revenue increase or to compensate for a revenue shortfall. Legislation involving estimates of residents, clients, or students may be updated before enforcement by a more recent survey or census. State and local governments initiating programs to qualify for state aid or federal matching funds may make amendments that reflect last-minute changes by the funding agency. Supplementary change legislation to correct a clerical error in a previously passed bill is another example. Updating involves simple, marginal, noncontroversial changes in original legislation made in reaction to minor developments after enactment.

Plebiscites

Some policy decisions require a popular vote of approval following legislative action and prior to implementation. Referenda, bond issues, and constitutional amendments are examples of plebiscites as supplementary decisions. In a sense, plebiscites allow for maximum responsiveness: constituents can participate directly in the decision-making process. Unfortunately, as was discussed in chapter 2, these plebiscite elections are the object of lowest voter turnout. Thus, while plebiscite supplementary decisions have great potential for responsiveness, that potential is rarely attained.

Executive Veto

A supplementary decision step can be initiated in state and municipal government by an executive veto. All governors (except North Carolina's) çan veto acts of their state legislatures; forty-three enjoy some form of

Table 4.3.   Introductions, Enactments, Vetoes, and Overrides in 1973 and 1974 State Legislatures

State	Introductions	Enactments	Vetoes	Overrides
Alabama	3669	1308	6	
Alaska	1928	250	7	
Arizona	1567	400	3	
Arkansas	2058	1055	72	
California	8139	3327	371	1
Colorado	1598	630	1	1
Connecticut	8469	1476	32	

State	Introductions	Enactments	Vetoes	Overrides
Delaware	1931	631	9	
Florida	6941	1367	30	
Georgia	3136	1556	97	
Hawaii	7357	1424	25	
Idaho	1464	795	11	
Illinois	4756	1344	224	14
Indiana	3219	497	15	
Iowa	2387	598	3	
Kansas	2102	861	32	7
Kentucky[a]	1425	406	18	
Louisiana[a]	6266	2430	26	
Maine	2312	1128	3	
Maryland	6212	1939	91	
Massachusetts	18498	2193	125	24
Michigan	3900	595	9	
Minnesota	7617	1376	3	
Mississippi[a]	5938	1772	42	9
Missouri	2630	372	32	
Montana	3947	463	13	1
Nebraska	1059	633	33	13
Nevada	1842	938	1	
New Hampshire	1504	649	29	1
New Jersey[a]	7082	1007	67	28
New Mexico	1542	516	36	
New York	23413	2303	548	
North Carolina	3701	1658	b	b
North Dakota	1131	602	10	3
Ohio	2186	419	1	
Oklahoma	2283	1206	10	
Oregon	2631	979	18	1
Pennsylvania	5091	725	58	2
Rhode Island	4207	785	57	
South Carolina	2707	1539	6	
South Dakota	1316	733	6	
Tennessee	4972	1196	53	13
Texas	3222	913	29	
Utah	854	325	3	
Vermont	881	357	0	
Virginia[a]	3324	1504	49	
Washington	3157	633	100	7
West Virginia	3573	446	55	3
Wisconsin	2503	342	13	
Wyoming	737	276	0	

Source: *The Book of the States 1976–77,* Vol. **XXI** (Lexington, Ky.: The Council of State Governments, 1976).

[a] 1974–75 state legislatures

[b] No executive veto

Table 4.4. Enactment, Veto, and Veto Override in 1973 and 1974 (in percentages)

State	Enactment	Veto	Override
Alabama	36	*	—
Alaska	13	3	—
Arizona	26	1	—
Arkansas	51	7	—
California	41	11	*
Colorado	39	*	100
Connecticut	17	2	—
Delaware	33	1	—
Florida	20	2	—
Georgia	50	6	—
Hawaii	19	2	—
Idaho	54	1	—
Illinois	28	17	6
Indiana	15	3	—
Iowa	25	1	—
Kansas	41	4	22
Kentucky[a]	28	4	—
Louisiana[a]	39	1	—
Maine	49	*	—
Maryland	31	5	—
Massachusetts	12	6	19
Michigan	16	2	—
Minnesota	18	*	—
Mississippi[a]	30	2	21
Missouri	14	9	—
Montana	12	3	8
Nebraska	60	5	39
Nevada	51	*	—
New Hampshire	43	4	3
New Jersey[a]	14	7	42
New Mexico	33	7	—
New York	10	24	—
North Carolina	45	[b]	[b]
North Dakota	53	2	30
Ohio	19	*	—
Oklahoma	53	1	—
Oregon	37	2	6
Pennsylvania	14	8	3
Rhode Island	19	7	—
South Carolina	57	*	—
South Dakota	56	1	—
Tennessee	24	4	25
Texas	28	3	—
Utah	38	1	—

State	Enactment	Veto	Override
Vermont	41	—	—
Virginia[a]	45	3	—
Washington	20	16	7
West Virginia	12	12	5
Wisconsin	14	4	—
Wyoming	37	—	—

Source: *The Book of the States 1976–77,* Vol. **XXI** (Lexington, Ky.: The Council of State Governments, 1976).

[a] 1974–75 state legislatures

[b] No executive veto

* Less than 1 percent

item veto. Approximately 38 percent of mayors have some form of veto power. State and local executive veto resembles that of the presidential veto. The signature of the chief executive is the final step in the legislative process. By refusing to approve legislation the governor or mayor prevents the passage of a bill or resolution into law. Override of an executive veto is possible, but it requires reapproval of the entire legislature and usually requires a legislative majority of two-thirds or more.

As tables 4.3 and 4.4 show, use of the veto varies greatly from state to state. The uniformly low rate of override of gubernatorial vetoes by legislatures across states suggests that all governors make effective use of the veto to cancel some legislative policy decisions. However, these statistics do not reveal the full impact of the veto in the policy-making process. The mere threat of veto is often sufficient to achieve a modification in the original legislative proposal that is satisfactory to the chief executive.

The institution of the executive veto gives constituents one last chance to appeal and modify or cancel a legislative decision before its implementation. Governors and mayors can be influenced to overturn a legislative decision by a mass of communications from the general public. Thus, legislatures will tend to be more responsive to organized interests—regardless of size—that have the resources to support lobbyists who provide expert information. Chief executives—who have their own sources of expert information—will be more responsive to the desires of large numbers of average citizens at the supplementary decision step.

Two factors make it easier to generate mass interest and communication at the supplementary decision step than at the legislative action step. First, the short time period when executive veto is possible after legislative action creates a sense of urgency that helps stimulate mass constituent action. Second, all communications are channeled to the chief executive's office, which amplifies the impact of mass communication; the same number of letters, telegrams, and telephone calls distributed among hundreds of legislators would cause much less impact. Executive veto as a supplementary decision mechanism is more responsive to the preferences of the mass public than of isolated special interests.

In 1971 the Indiana legislature passed a series of laws to change the age of majority from 21 to 18. The U.S. Supreme Court had decided on December 21, 1970 that 18-year-olds should be eligible to vote in federal elections. Indiana was one of a number of states that decided to give full adult status to 18-year-olds and made changes in laws governing such areas as minimum age for property ownership, responsibility for personal debt, and marriage without parental consent. One item in the legislative package lowered the legal age for purchase and consumption of alcoholic beverages to age 18. After legislative approval of the measure to lower the drinking age, a mass communications campaign was quickly initiated by the religious community. Local newspapers were filled with letters opposing lowering the drinking age and, more importantly, the governor's office reported receiving thousands of letters, telegrams, and telephone calls urging veto of the bill. Governor Whitcomb, who had not indicated any strong opposition to the new drinking law before the public outcry, vetoed the law in accordance with the timely popular mandate.

Advisory Opinion

Legislative bodies may be persuaded to modify or rescind an action by an expert advisory opinion rendered after a bill has been enacted. Governors, mayors, city managers, and superintendents suggest changes in their roles as chief administrators, most frequently when their executive recommendations are not accepted.

A more important stimulus of supplementary decision is legal opinion. State legislatures, city councils, and school boards often invite their legal counsel to review and evaluate their legislative acts. State legislatures are mainly concerned with the constitutionality of their acts and often ask the state attorney general to evaluate any possible inconsistencies between new legislation and state and federal constitutions.

City councils and school districts are concerned both with the constitutional legality of their decisions and the legal status of their decision-making procedures. Legal counsel comment on both the legal content and the process of decisions. An adverse advisory opinion is sufficient to cause the legislative body to revoke its decision and reinstitute the deliberative process.

Judicial Intervention

When courts are the source of proposal development, they often review legislative action and sometimes require supplementary decisions. When the U.S. Supreme Court required several state legislatures to reapportion voting districts in the 1960s, the court reviewed and, in some cases, rejected reapportionment schemes. State courts that have ordered school districts to redistribute students among schools to achieve greater racial balance have reviewed school board plans and indicated necessary changes. Supplementary action based on advisory opinion is optional; supplementary action is mandatory when initiated by executive veto or court order.

Strong Reaction

A strong negative reaction to legislative action directed at the legislative body itself can stimulate a supplementary decision prior to program implementation. In most municipal governments and all school districts opponents of legislation have no opportunity to appeal for an executive veto; thus, dissidents must ask the council or school board directly to reconsider its decision. The problem of declining student enrollments mentioned earlier in the chapter has prompted many school boards to resolve to close some neighborhood schools and transfer students. This action is universally met with loud and persistent protest from the parents of children attending affected schools. Many school boards have been convinced by such demonstrations of constituent preference to cancel the school closings and to seek economies elsewhere.

Strong protest that stimulates supplementary change in legislative action may originate within government. Line employees who will ultimately be responsible for enforcing legislative decisions may raise objections that lead school boards, councils, and legislatures to amend original decisions. The growing importance of unions composed of

teachers, municipal employees, and state employees has given government workers a stronger voice to make their opinions known. The threat
or implementation of union protest activities such as work slowdowns
and strikes is often sufficient to make a legislative body react favorably
to a grievance.

Secular Change

When a lag period of several years is specified between legislative enactment and administrative enforcement of a program, a supplementary
decision may be desirable or necessary because of changes after the
original enactment. One change that is virtually assured by such a long
lag period is turnover in legislative personnel; turnover of top administrators is also a strong possibility. The new officials may hesitate
to follow through on legislation passed before their tenure, or they may
reinitiate the legislative process to amend the as yet unenforced statute.
Generally speaking, the greater the change in policy, the longer the lag
period between legislation and enforcement. And the greater the lag
period, the greater the probability that the policy will be changed before
its implementation.

   In 1971 the Oregon legislature, responding to the proposal of then
Governor McCall, passed environmental quality legislation aimed at
eliminating air pollution caused by field burning. The major crop in the
Willamette Valley is commercial grass grown for seed. For years seed
growers burned their fields after harvesting to clear the waste and
sterilize the land. Although burning was a convenient and inexpensive
solution to the problems of the growers, the smoke that resulted from the
burning of thousands of acres of grass caused problems for other valley
residents. Thus, the McCall proposal called for yearly reductions in
acres to be burned, with burning to be completely eliminated by 1975.
The long lag period between the legislation and the elimination of burning was intended to allow growers to develop alternative ways of
eliminating waste.

   In early 1975 seed growers requested that the burning ban policy be
reconsidered. A new governor and a new legislature were receptive to
their arguments that the hardships the ban would impose on them
should be balanced against the "temporary inconvenience" of six weeks
of burning. The pollution control act was modified to eliminate the ban
and continue a flexible program to reduce the number of acres burned.
Seed growers took advantage of the lag period to mobilize their resources

and to deal with state officials in 1975 who were more receptive than their 1971 counterparts. The decline in public interest in and attention to this environmental quality issue between 1971 and 1975 also made the achievement of the supplementary decision possible.

IMPLEMENTATION

THE IMPLEMENTATION step is the actual execution of policy directives of the legislature as amended by supplementary decisions. Implementation is the carrying out of decisions made during the earlier steps—the business of hiring personnel, purchasing raw materials and services, administering regulations, enforcing laws, and delivering goods and services as prescribed by law and administrative regulation. At the implementation step government takes action which may be responsive or unresponsive to the demands of its citizens.

The agents of policy implementation are the millions of employees of state and local government. Most are making a career of government service; most are civil servants who gain their jobs and promotion by open competitive examination; most are called bureaucrats by their fellow citizens. Policy implementors in school districts include school bus drivers, cooks and cafeteria workers, custodians and grounds crews, office personnel, and, of course, teachers and administrators at local schools, and the superintendent and his central office and administrative staff.

Policy in municipal government is carried out not only by the mayor or city manager, but also by police officers, firemen, public transportation workers, city librarians, clerks in zoning and building departments, and recreation leaders at city parks and greenskeepers at municipal golf courses. State policy is carried out by the governor, secretary of state, treasurer, and auditor, and thousands of state employees in the capital, as well as by highway patrolmen, social service employees, employment opportunity and unemployment compensation officers, and administrators, faculty, and support staff at state universities, colleges, and junior colleges located throughout the state.

The listings in your local telephone directory under city, county, and state government and public schools underline both the wide range of services provided by state and local governments and the variety of government employees who are responsible for policy implementation.

The overseer of policy implementation is the chief executive whose major task is to see that the decisions of the legislative body are faithfully executed. Early students of public administration were committed to the idea that "politics" ended with the passage of legislation and that the administrative process consisted of the automatic enforcement of the legislative mandate.[36] However, legislation is rarely so comprehensive and clearly written that implementation is merely following the letter of the law. The upshot is that administrators of government policy enjoy wide latitude in deciding how legislative programs will be carried out. Thus, a school board may approve a sex education curriculum, but instructional staff and textbooks are selected by principals, central administrators, and the superintendent of schools. Likewise, a city council may approve a campaign against robbery, but patrol routes are chosen by police administrators. The implementation step is influenced and constrained by earlier steps in the decision-making process, but by no means is it entirely determined by executive, legislative, and supplementary decisions. The questions of expertise, interest-group activity, and responsiveness to community desires are extremely important for policy implementation.

Ira Sharkansky speaks of four intellectual roots that are prominent in the structures of government administrative organizations in the United States: (1) the desire to maintain political accountability in public administration; (2) the desire to maintain the traditional equilibrium among the three constitutional branches of government by preserving the system of separation of powers and of checks and balances; (3) the desire to ensure that professional and technical skills are brought to bear on relevant matters of policy formation and implementation; and (4) the desire to maximize the efficient use of resources by means of a hierarchical form of organization.[37] Professor Sharkansky notes that each principle promotes an important goal, yet in practice the principles are not always mutually compatible. Our discussion of policy implementation will follow Sharkansky's four principles to point out some of the inconsistencies of policy administration in state and local government and to underline that the struggle present in the earlier steps in the policy-making process continues during implementation.

Political Accountability

The most basic idea of political accountability in policy implementation is that elected officials should have the final control over the activities of administrative agencies. Appointing top administrative personnel and overseeing administrative activities by elected officials are the most important factors that promote political accountability.

The procedures for selecting and removing senior administrative decision-makers—including chief executives—in most state and local governments provide for regular review of administrators either by elected officials or by the voters themselves. In state governments and mayor-council forms of municipal government, a wide variety of administrative officials are popularly elected. It is not unusual for state and local attorneys, treasurers, and auditors, and state superintendents of education and secretaries of state to be chosen by election. Thirty-nine states select judges by elections. Their terms are limited, and their regular participation in electoral politics presumably increases their political accountability. Furthermore, most elected officials are subject to removal from office by either legislative action (impeachment and trial) or direct popular action (recall) at any time.

Most top administrative officers who are not subject to appointment and removal by popular vote are only once removed from the political process. They are subject to appointment and removal by those who are popularly elected—for example, school district superintendents and city managers are appointed by school boards and city councils. They are typically given one- or two-year contracts, so they must win a regular vote of confidence from elected officials. Legislative bodies have the power to remove an appointed chief executive before the end of the contract period, so appointed officials are also subject to immediate dismissal via the political process.

Political accountability is also promoted by the power to review personnel actions granted to legislative bodies. The range of this power varies considerably but is generally stronger in local than in state governments. Important appointments by the governor are usually subject to confirmation by the senate, but the typical city council or school board must consent to such routine personnel matters as hiring, firing, and assignment of individual policemen and teachers. School boards and city councils normally consider the agenda of personnel matters in executive session. However, once a decision has been made, it is subject to consideration and reversal at a subsequent public meeting.

The most dramatic examples of the role of political accountability of administrators to elected officials occur when school boards must decide in public hearings whether or not to dismiss an individual teacher or principal on the grounds of "unethical or immoral conduct." Whatever the particulars of the case, there are always a number of interested parties, including students, parents, colleagues, and such interest groups as teachers' unions or administrators' organizations, PTAs, and religious and civil rights organizations, who want their preferences to be known and acted on by school board members. Political accountability comes full circle when school board members themselves are subject to a recall election because of their decisions to dismiss or retain controversial employees.

In addition to influence over individual administrators, elected officials maintain influence over individual policy decisions by participating in the various steps in the policy-making process, most notably executive recommendation, legislative action, and review. Political accountability is promoted by the requirement that nonelected administrators must regularly report to, interact with, and obtain the approval of elected officials.

Equilibrium

By and large, state and local governments have followed the federal model of division of powers and checks and balances among the executive, legislative, and judicial branches. Most state and local officials are granted powers held by their federal counterparts to protect themselves from the other branches. For example, chief executives can veto or otherwise prevent the implementation of legislative acts and can appoint some executive and judicial officials; legislative bodies can override executive vetoes and review executive appointments and personnel action; and the judiciary maintains a right to review the actions of the other branches for their constitutionality.

"Overlap of powers" is probably a more accurate description than "separation of powers." This overlap has important implications for policy implementation. The control of administrative units is not entirely given to any one branch. Although the executive branch maintains primary responsibility for policy execution and administration, the judicial and legislative branches retain important powers. The judicial branch shares the responsibility with the executive branch in state and municipal governments of enforcing criminal and civil law and, through its power to evaluate the constitutionality of administrative procedures, may void or restrict power that an administrator had exercised. The legislative branch can also affect the execution of policy through its powers to approve personnel, appropriate monies, investigate current programs, and initiate new ones.

A positive aspect of the overlap is that multiple channels allow constituent input and influence on policy administration. This, however, is overshadowed by a negative aspect: administrative units are frequently subject to the demands of competing superiors. This situation not only presents problems for administrators—To whom should they be responsive?—but it presents a problem for citizens—Whom should they hold accountable for policy execution? As a result, the principle of equilibrium is somewhat inconsistent with the principle of accountability.

Professional Expertise

The movement to replace the "spoils system" of personnel management was part of the larger reform movement of state and municipal governments that gained momentum in the late nineteenth and early twentieth centuries. Under the spoils system, party membership, loyalty, and activity were the chief qualifications for obtaining employment in state and local government. Wholesale changes in government personnel were likely to occur after each election. According to reformers, this uncertainty of employment both deterred the most capable individuals from entering government service and inhibited current employees from developing professional expertise.

The original emphasis of the civil service movement was merely to prevent personnel decisions from being made solely on a partisan basis. As the tasks of public administration have become increasingly technical and complex, and as university programs of public and educational administration have grown and the ranks of administrative professionals have increased, the civil service network has become much broader in scope. The task has grown from the essentially negative service of screening out grossly unqualified candidates to include recruitment of candidates, testing and certification of competencies, ranking of candidates, training, education, and periodic evaluation of employees. State and local civil service systems also maintain position classification schemes, which group jobs according to duties and necessary qualifications. A position qualification plan allows equal pay for equal work and also provides the basis for rational recruitment, examinations, and placement.

As the tasks of state and local government have become more complex, the requisite expertise for state and local government employees has increased. In larger units of government, professional degrees and prior experience are required for employment in management positions.

As a result, civil servants charged with the daily implementation of policy are experts by training and experience.

Elected officials who oversee these staff and line implementors cannot match their expertise. Furthermore, the authority of elected officials is limited by their terms of office. In comparison, civil servants enjoy un- limited tenure. As a result, bureaucrats can often circumvent the at- tempts of elected officials to oversee policy implementation. Thus, the principle of professional expertise is sometimes inconsistent with the principles of equilibrium and accountability.

Hierarchical Management

Sharkansky's fourth intellectual root of administrative organization is hierarchical management. The benefits of hierarchical organization are twofold. First, accountability is promoted by grouping personnel under the control of clearly defined supervising units. There should be a clear chain of command so that superiors will have full information about the activities of subordinates and be assured that subordinates will be responsive to their directives. Second, efficiency is promoted by organiz- ing work units hierarchically according to activity. By limiting the span of control of each supervisor, executives can acquire the information necessary to understand and control the activities of subordinates and can give sufficient attention to maintain efficient performances.

State and local governments have generally organized their bureaucracies along hierarchical lines. Unfortunately, as governments increase in size and complexity, the principle of hierarchical manage- ment becomes inconsistent with the principles of accountability, equilibrium, and expertise. Expertise and hierarchy are incompatible in the growing number of cases in which executives at the top of organiza- tions are unable to master all the information necessary to control subor- dinates, because of either its technical nature or its sheer volume. It is unrealistic to expect that governors, for example, will be experts in all phases of environmental protection; public finance and budgeting; law enforcement; primary, secondary and higher education; and the myriad of other activities they are expected to supervise. This also frustrates the contribution of hierarchy to the accountability of employees to elected officials. Rather than promote accountability, hierarchy can insulate employees charged with policy implementation from elected officials with layers of bureaucratic managers who cannot control their subor- dinates. Even when authority and control does exist, hierarchical management cannot completely overcome the inertia of large, complex organizations.

As we have seen, hierarchy and equilibrium are incompatible when administrators are subject to the intrusion of executive, legislative, and judicial authorities. The three branches are independent. Thus, allowing all three to exercise oversight authority violates the principle of hierarchical management.

The Paradox of Mobility

An important element of the civil service system is mobility for career bureaucrats. There are several kinds of mobility.[38] One can speak of *organizational mobility* (for example, movement from one department, bureau, division or branch to another), *occupational mobility* (movement from one job to another, such as a move from budget analyst to personnel specialist), *vertical mobility* (movement from one rank to another), and *geographical mobility* (movement from headquarters to field offices or from one region to another).

Students of public administration generally agree that the public's business is best managed by a mobile civil service, and that civil service reform ought to enhance that mobility rather than hinder it. The view is that mobility increases the control that chief executives and members of their administration have over civil servants. Organizational, occupational, and vertical mobility provide incentive for efficiency and organizational loyalty by rewarding employees for superior performance of duties (that is, their expertise). Geographical mobility reinforces hierarchical management and accountability to elected officials by preventing the long-term capture of bureaucrats by local interests. Mobility is therefore consistent with the principles of accountability, expertise, and hierarchical management.

However, another line of reasoning argues that mobility is inconsistent with the principles of expertise and accountability. Whenever any employee changes duties, location, or rank, a period of adjustment and learning occurs. To the extent that tasks, surroundings, standard operating procedures, clients, and colleagues are unfamiliar, the civil servant's efficiency is reduced. Though professional expertise is, to a degree, transferable, what might be called localized expertise must be freshly acquired. Thus, mobility can serve as an impediment to expertise.

Mobility can also impede accountability. The problem is essentially the same as when there is frequent turnover of elected officials. Most governmental programs have a considerable time lag between proposal development and implementation of policy and when the effects of the policy are known. When turnover of those involved in developing and implementing policy occurs, it is very difficult for elected officials to locate and hold accountable (that is, reward or punish) responsible civil servants. Furthermore, the knowledge that some sort of transfer is probable that will prevent an individual from receiving credit or blame for his current service may well reduce his incentive to do the best job possible.

The role of most elected officials in the daily implementation of policy decisions is limited to overseeing civil servants. Accountability, equilibrium, expertise, and hierarchy are principles of public administration that are supposed to promote bureaucratic efficiency and responsiveness to elected officials and government clientele. Unfortunately, these principles are sometimes incompatible. There is no universal theory of public administration in the United States which successfully integrates these four principles. The evolution of administrative organizations in state and local governments is a continuing process. Like other steps in the decision-making process, implementation involves many different kinds of actors whose preferences are often in conflict.

POLICY REVIEW

THE FINAL step in the policy-making process is review and evaluation of past decisions and programs. Of necessity, review must follow implementation. But, as we shall see, the review process is continuous and for some actors is concurrent with other steps in the policy-making process.

Internal Review

Internal review is undertaken by those who were involved in the development and implementation of the policy under review. External review involves participation by those outside the governmental unit. There are two major types of internal review: executive review and legislative review.

EXECUTIVE REVIEW   Most executive review occurs within the context of the executive recommendation step. Evaluation of current programs and procedures is a prerequisite to a governor's, mayor's, or superintendent's recommendation to continue or replace those programs. There is also an ongoing process of executive review in the context of policy implementation management. On the lower levels of management, principals, office managers, or section heads periodically review the performances of the line employees directly under them. On the higher levels, superintendents, city managers, or governors meet with their cabinets to assess current government-wide programs.

Unfortunately, several factors make review and evaluation extremely difficult. Evaluation involves comparing actual performance with an expected performance or goal. For a great number of state and local government activities, goals are either vague or subject to debate. Some programs have multiple goals that may not always be consistent. As a result, there are no accepted indicators that can be used for evaluating the overwhelming majority of government programs.

The nominal purpose of unemployment insurance programs is to provide individuals assistance while they are between jobs. Not all unemployed persons are entitled to this compensation. Eligibility is commonly limited to those whose separation from employment was justified and who are actively seeking reemployment. The task of establishing and limiting eligibility is assigned to state agencies. Performance indicators include statistics on claims taken, claims accepted, claims rejected, benefit periods, benefit payments, reemployment rates, fraud investigations, fraud convictions, and so forth. Obviously, no one indicator or single composite index can be used to assess a state's unemployment compensation program.

The goal of public elementary and secondary schools is to educate children. There are, however, a number of indicators of success, such as enrollments, promotions, test scores, student-teacher ratios. A duplicate set of indicators relates benefits to costs. Again, there is no technique which measures the performance of local schools to the satisfaction of educational professionals, students, parents, and taxpayers.

The problems of review and evaluation are even more complicated in policy areas that are so technical that the average person cannot assess relative success or failure. Environmental protection and public health programs must be evaluated in such technical terms as toxins per million particles, disease occurrence per thousand inoculations, or

deaths per ten thousand. The increasing professionalization of government service has increased reliance on performance indicators that are
extremely difficult for the untrained and uninitiated to interpret.

Yet another difficulty for program evaluation occurs when the effects
of an ongoing program are cumulative or when program efforts are not
easily separable from other factors affecting outcomes. Cumulative effects, for example, occur in vaccination programs against communicable
diseases. This year's incidence of tuberculosis and polio are partially
caused by the fact that a given number of people received inoculation
during the preceding twelve months. However, the low rates of these
communicable diseases is more a result of nearly universal immuniza-
tions in the past and the resulting small populations susceptible to the
infection.

The Connecticut crackdown on speeding which was initiated in
December 1955 is an example of uncertain policy impact. Distressed at
the number of deaths on state highways, the governor of Connecticut ordered that speed limits be strictly enforced and encouraged judges to
suspend driver's licenses of convicted speeders. The highway death rate
soon declined and the crackdown was declared successful. Years later,
researchers compared Connecticut's accident statistics with those of
neighboring states and found similar declines in death rates—even in
states without similar crackdown programs. They concluded that the
decline in the Connecticut traffic death rate probably resulted from
weather, auto safety improvements, changing driving habits, and other
factors unrelated to the state policy.[39]

We have argued that state and local government executive officials
command the greatest resources of information and expertise. Nevertheless, executive review of existing policies is still difficult when
performance indicators are complex, extremely technical, or not easily
separable from nonpolicy effects. Public participation in executive
review in state and local governments is almost nonexistent. Inquiries
are carried out by executive staff, sometimes assisted by professional
consultants. The major role nongovernmental actors can play is to encourage review of certain programs and policies to be placed on the executive agenda.

LEGISLATIVE REVIEW   Legislative review is another form of internal review and occurs within the context of the legislative action step.
The tenet of the principle of separation of powers among the three
branches of government is legislative oversight of the executive branch.
The common vehicle of legislative review in the U.S. Congress—in-

vestigations and reports by committees—is also used by state and local legislative bodies.

The problems of evaluation are even more serious for state and local legislative bodies than for executive officials because most legislative positions are part-time jobs held by amateurs. State legislators, city councilmen, and school board members have neither the time nor the expertise to carry on an effective review and evaluation of public policy. The fact that the time lag between legislative authorization, implementation, and assessment often spans several years—and several legislatures—further impedes the effectiveness of the legislative review process.

It should come as no surprise that state and local legislators are increasingly turning to nonlegislative experts to aid them in reviewing and evaluating current programs. Karl T. Kurtz has noted that state legislatures are making greater use of postauditors to fulfill their oversight responsibilities.[40] There are three important trends:

1. There has been a long term trend toward placing state postauditors under the legislative branch rather than under the executive or as an independently elected official. Postauditors are chosen by the legislatures of twenty-eight states; in another five the auditor is at least partially responsible to the legislature.

2. Postauditors are developing more interest in carrying out evaluations of agency performance and program effectiveness.

3. Several legislatures have established separate committees whose major function is program review and performance evaluation.

Legislative reference service personnel are another source of experts for state legislators attempting review and evaluation. In the context of special reviews, state legislative committees may also hire outside consultants and take testimony from the public.

"Sunset laws" are an increasingly popular innovation in the legislative review process. Sunset laws provide a formal mechanism for periodic legislative review of state agency functions and make necessary a decision that continued existence is justified. The common practice in most governments is to continue the status quo unless review indicates a change is necessary. However, review is often sporadic and agencies, once created, are seldom terminated. The important provision of sunset laws is that certain laws, regulations, programs, and agencies will be *automatically abolished* unless review and renewal take place.

Sunset laws are probably not the panacea they seem. Legislative bodies can easily circumvent the requirements for periodic review by passing continuing resolutions, which they currently do to avoid deadlines for establishing state budgets. More important, because agencies know that periodic performance reviews will have life-and-death consequences, it is likely that they will take steps to ensure survival. One tactic might be to divert resources from providing mandated goods and services to building a strong case in support of agency renewal. The *appearance* of performance may become more important than the *substance* of performance. Alternately, agencies may seek to circumvent legislative review by employing increasingly technical and sophisticated indicators of performance to prevent legislators from conducting their own evaluations.

Possibilities for agencies to defeat the purpose of sunset laws are legion. Suffice it to say that state legislatures with part-time, amateur members cannot match the resources or incentive of full-time professionals in state agencies. It seems likely that the main benefit of sunset laws will be to formalize and regularize the process of state legislative review.

There do not seem to be parallel trends in city and school district legislative bodies. City councils and school boards lack staff research support and typically do not secure outside experts to aid them in the review process. These local legislative bodies must draw upon the expertise of their members and the public who may attend public hearings to interpret and evaluate information provided by the executive branch. The result is that legislative review is relatively weak in local units of government.

External Review

Internal review is conducted by actors who participated in one or more of the earlier steps of the policy-making process. External review is conducted by actors who have not participated at earlier steps. Proponents of internal review stress that having program evaluation under the auspices of those responsible for development and implementation is desirable because it makes use of the expertise of those most familiar with policy. Proponents of external review stress the desirability of having outsiders evaluate ongoing programs because people tend to be less critical of their own efforts than the efforts of others. In short, the expertise advantage of internal review may be balanced by the problems of self-evaluation. External review is a useful complement to internal review.

AUDITING   The original purpose of auditing was to review government expenditures to guarantee executive compliance with legislative appropriations. State and local auditors have retained this financial review function. All government activities involving the expenditure of money are subject to review by auditors. A major issue has brewed for decades; it centers on fixing responsibility for auditing.[41] Some states and cities elect auditors on the assumption that objective audit can be achieved only by an official who is independent of both the executive and legislative branches. The opposing argument is that, because the electorate cannot suitably judge the qualities of candidates for auditor, auditors should be selected by legislatures or executives. Because most state and local auditors maintain autonomy from the executive and legislative branches by mandate or selection process, we will consider auditing as an external source of review.

The auditing function has evolved from its origins of enforcing uniform accounting procedures and reviewing agency accounts. Contemporary auditors see their mandate as promoting the accountability of nonelected government employees to elected officials. Elmer B. Staats, former comptroller general of the United States, has argued that the demand by public officials and the general public for information on the efficiency, effectiveness, and economy of governmental programs has necessitated broadening the scope of auditing.[42] The auditor must be concerned with three types of accountability:

1. Fiscal accountability, which includes financial integrity, disclosure, and compliance with applicable laws and regulations. This is the traditional role of postaudit review.

2. Managerial accountability, which is concerned with efficient and economical use of resources. This is a more difficult task which has become a common component of postauditing. The goal is to identify and eliminate wasteful procedures. This kind of assessment is difficult because there are no generally accepted criteria of efficiency.

3. Program accountability, which is concerned with objectives and accomplishments. A number of state and local governments have tried to link expenditures and objective indicators of program success to expand the scope of auditing to include review of program substance as well as procedure.

The third type of accountability is the most ambitious and important. As noted earlier, most legislators and members of the public lack the necessary expertise to evaluate government programs. An independent assessment of continuing programs and policies is desirable but, at present, the traditional auditor lacks the skills necessary to provide substantive as well as financial review.

In a larger sense, program accountability cannot be achieved satisfactorily by a government auditor alone—no matter how independent of executive branch officials. A crucial element of program evaluation must be clientele and constituent satisfaction. The auditor's quest for objective indicators of performance often overlooks this important subjective dimension of evaluation. At present, opportunities for public participation in auditing review are virtually nonexistent. If auditing is to include responsiveness in its concept of program accountability, then performance indicators must include measurement of constituent satisfaction and preferences.

Judicial Review

There is widespread agreement among scholars that state and federal courts are important actors in the state and local policy-making processes. Although state courts play a policy role in the implementation step, as discussed earlier, the most important policy role for state and federal courts comes at the review step.

The role of state courts as policy-making institutions is often neglected. This neglect is unfortunate because practices vary among states and because state courts can and do make important decisions that affect political, social, and economic life.

> For example, a series of decisions reviewing local zoning practices may have important effects on local commerce, the development of the economy, and the benefits obtained or lost by various economic interests in the community. Decisions in labor-management disputes, workmen's compensation claims, criminal cases (especially those involving constitutional questions), creditor-debtor conflicts, regulation of business practices, and other cases establish state courts as important policy-making institutions affecting numerous aspects of our daily lives. Moreover, many of these kinds of cases are rarely heard by federal courts, which gives state courts an added importance in the policy-making process.[43]

Even though most Americans do not usually think of courts as policy-makers, important controversies are often brought to them for resolution. The power of courts to review the constitutionality of legislative and executive action, commonly called the power of "judicial review," constantly involves American courts in conscious policy-making.[44] State and federal courts have the power to review and evaluate state and local governments' policies and programs. Courts can find practices contrary to statutory or constitutional law and order them modified or discontinued.

Judicial policy-making is much narrower in scope than other governmental policy-making. Jacob notes that appropriating funds and taxation are still the "almost exclusive domain" of the executive and legislative branches.

> Most judicial policies are concerned with the regulatory activities of government. Judicial concern with government regulation arises from the constitutional guarantees of individual freedom and the right to hold property subject only to government action through the due process of law. All regulatory policies restrict freedom and property. Therefore, courts have often been asked to determine whether such regulations were imposed through due process or not. Such conflicts have required the courts to develop judicial policies restricting government regulation to reasonable acts adopted through lawful procedures.[45]

Another most salient aspect of judicial policy for the present discussion is that courts are entirely passive in the initiation of judicial proceedings. They must wait until a case that raises a question which they can settle is brought before them. State and local executives do not suffer such limitations; legislators are restricted only by limitations on length of sessions. The passive nature of the judicial process creates extraordinary opportunities for public participation and responsiveness.

Access to the courts is governed by a special set of requirements:

1. A potential plaintiff must have sufficient resources to engage a lawyer and to bear the expense of a court suit.

2. The courts must recognize their jurisdiction over the conflict; if they do not, they cannot settle it.

3. The courts must offer appropriate remedies if they are to be used.

4. Those involved in disputes must perceive the courts as forums they can use.

5. The rules of the court must give the potential plaintiff (the one who will initiate judicial action) a chance to win. When each of these five conditions is met, a case may be brought to court.[46]

Individuals can and do seek review of policy by initiating lawsuits against state and local governments. The courts are always responsive to the extent that suits are either accepted for consideration or rejected, and those accepted are subject to decision. As in executive and legislative decision-making, gaining a place on the policy agenda may be difficult. Unlike other forms of decision-making, the judicial process takes explicit action on all agenda items. The courts cannot table, bury in committees, ignore, or otherwise avoid the matters they accept for consideration. Those who do gain entry to the judicial agenda are assured that some timely action will be taken.

Though individuals are able to seek policy review and change through the courts, judicial review is pursued more often by organized interest groups who can afford the time and money necessary to see the case through. According to Jacob, individuals must be "personally involved" to sue—that is, their personal property or rights must be threatened in some way. Therefore, groups sometimes deliberately break laws to force the courts to examine the constitutionality of a contested law or to change its usual interpretation.

> Interest groups sometimes search for persons who are willing to serve as the formal plaintiff or defendant in a test case. They must find someone who can maintain standing as a litigant and who can be counted on to stick with the court fight over the several years that are required to bring a case to an appellate court. If the litigant is fighting segregation in schools, for instance, he must have a child so young that it is still in school when the case reaches the high court; otherwise, his case will be declared moot, for he no longer has a personal interest in the matter. Such a litigant must also be firmly settled in his locale, for moving to another city or state might moot his case.
>
> A test case not only requires careful selection of the individual litigant whose name is lent to the suit but also necessitates careful planning of courtroom strategy. The action protested against must be challengeable only on constitutional grounds. If

a judge rules that is wrong because some procedure has not been
followed or because the law does not apply to the particular case
in question, the group will have won its case without gaining its
broader policy objective. Such a victory is a Pyrrhic one, for
other officials may still proceed against the group as before. The
group's lawyers, therefore, must plan its case so that a decision
can only be reached on constitutional grounds. All other avenues
of deciding the case must be foreclosed; no gaps may remain
open that might allow a court to avoid the issue the group wishes
to press on it.[47]

Groups can also participate in the policy-making activities of the
court other than by bringing suit. They can provide financial support to
individuals or other groups involved in litigation. They can also participate by providing testimony or other evidence or by submitting an
amicus curiae ("friend of the court") brief to the court, which places the
group's opinions and attitudes on record, gives additional information,
and sometimes more substantial legal arguments.[48]

Judicial review is classified as an external form of review because of its
great opportunity for nongovernmental individuals and groups within a
polity to initiate the process. Judicial review is also an external form
because other governments can also bring court action. Courts with
power of review are within state and federal governments. Thus, any
proceedings involving municipalities, school districts, or other local
units of governments involve intergovernmental relations. Likewise,
federally initiated suits against state and local governments are also intergovernmental. This situation is potentially detrimental to the responsiveness of state and local governments.

State and local governments may be prevented from pursuing policies
or employing procedures that are favored by a majority—or even all—of
their constituents, but are found unacceptable by the courts of more
central levels of government. Ironically, some state judges must be
responsive not only to the legal structure of their own state, but also to
federal laws. As a result, state and federal governments can intervene in
the affairs of other levels of government through judicial processes and
frustrate state and local responsiveness to constituent preferences.

The role played by courts at the review step of the policy-making
process is as important as the role they play at the implementation step.
The openness of the judicial agenda to individuals and groups promotes
responsiveness in the sense of widespread participation in decision-
making. This openness is balanced by the fact that the decision-making
process itself is restricted to members of the legal profession. All com-

munications from the public must be made through the medium of lawyers. Furthermore, judicial proceedings make the actions of state and local governments subject to review by other levels of government. As a result, courts must serve many clients, who often make conflicting demands. These demands are supposed to be resolved by application of legal principles, established in part by state and local governments. The division of labor and legal authority of local, state, and federal law is unclear. Judicial review can prevent the responsiveness of state and local governments to constituent preferences by making them subject to the laws of more central levels of government.

Finally, we should clarify an implicit argument throughout this discussion of the review step of the policy-making process—review of the past is never undertaken solely for its own sake. Review is always part of the process by which current practices are improved and future proposals are developed. The review step not only completes the cycle of decision-making, it feeds into future cycles.

CONCLUSION

THE DIFFERENT stages of the policy-making process are dominated by different government actors and allow varying opportunities for public participation and government responsiveness. The greatest opportunities for responsiveness are at the proposal development and legislative action steps. Moderate opportunities exist at the executive recommendation, supplementing change, and review steps; virtually no public role occurs during policy implementation. Executive officials are clearly the most influential actors. They control proposal development, executive action, supplementary change, and implementation. They dominate legislators, who defer to them at the legislative action step. And, though they share review authority with legislative and judicial officials, they control the flow of information and the content of policy.

Ironically for the representational model of responsiveness, those state and local officials presumed to be most attentive to citizen preferences—legislators—have the least power in the policy-making process. Furthermore, the executive officials with greatest power are the career civil servants, not the few who are elected. Government decision-makers are most consistently responsive to other government decision-makers. The content of their decisions might, of course, be congruent with public opinion. However, since opinion normally follows policy rather than influencing it, such congruence (if it exists) is likely to be a congruence of public opinion being responsive to policy.

As the content of decisions and the criteria of choice become more complex and technical, executives, in turn, will increasingly tend to rely on bureaucratic experts. The growing authority of experts at the expense of laymen is well illustrated by the example of educational policy, toward which we now direct our attention.

NOTES

1.
For an application of a similar model in an international organization, see Francis W. Hodle, *Politics and Budgeting in the World Health Organization* (Bloomington, In.: Indiana University Press, 1976).

2.
Stuart H. Rakoff and Guenther F. Schaefer, "Politics, Policy and Political Science: Theoretical Alternatives," *Politics and Society* 1 (November 1970): 56.

3.
Joseph P. Chamberlain, *Legislative Processes: National and State* (New York: Appleton-Century, 1936), p. 3.

4.
Ibid., p. 64.

5.
Ibid., pp. 189–90.

6.
See, for example, Harmon Zeigler and Michael Baer, *Lobbying: Interaction and Influence in American State Legislatures* (Belmont, Calif.: Wadsworth, 1969).

7.
Morris J. Levitt and Eleanor G. Feldbaum, "Council Members, Lobbyists, and Interest Groups: Communication and Mutual Perceptions in Local Politics," *Journal of Voluntary Action Research* 4 (January–April 1975): 100–101.

8.
Daniel Katz, Barbara A. Butek, Robert Lokahn, and Eugenia Barton, *Bureaucratic Encounters: A Pilot Study in the Evaluation of Government Services* (Ann Arbor, Michigan: Survey Research Center–Institute for Social Research, 1975), p. 23.

9.
Ibid., pp. 34–37.

10.
S. M. Meyers and J. McIntyre, *Welfare Policy and Its Consequences for the Recipient Population: A Study of the AFDC Program* (Washington, D.C.: Government Printing Office, 1969).

11.
Jack L. Walker, "Innovation in State Politics," in Herbert Jacob and Kenneth N. Vines (eds.), *Politics in the American States,* 2nd ed. (Boston: Little, Brown, 1971), pp. 365–68.

12.

Ibid., p. 365.

13.

Ibid., p. 375.

14.

Ibid., p. 376.

15.

Reynolds v. *Sims,* 377 U.S. 533, 845.Ct.1362, 12 L.Ed.2d506 (1964).

16.

For a discussion of Dillon's Rule see John G. Grumm and Russell D. Murphy, "Dillon's Rule Reconsidered," *The Annals of the American Academy of Political and Social Science* 416 (November 1974): 120–32.

17.

Ibid., p. 127.

18.

Chamberlain, *Legislative Processes,* p. 6.

19.

The Municipal Yearbook, 1972 (Washington, D.C.: International City Management Association, 1972), pp. 20–21.

20.

L. Harmon Zeigler, M. Kent Jennings, with G. Wayne Peak, *Governing American Schools: Political Interaction in Local School Districts* (North Scituate, Mass.: Duxbury Press, 1974).

21.

Malcolm E. Jewell and Samuel C. Patterson, *The Legislative Process in the United States* (New York: Random House, 1966), p. 5.

22.

The discussion in the next few paragraphs is adapted from Jewell and Patterson, ibid., pp. 8–15.

23.

Alan Rosenthal, "Turnover in State Legislatures," *American Journal of Political Science* 18 (August 1974): 611; *Book of the States 1974–1975* XX (Lexington, Ky.: The Council of State Governments, 1974), p. 59.

24.

The Municipal Yearbook, 1972, p. 17.

25.

Zeigler, Jennings, with Peak, *Governing American Schools,* p. 56.

26.

Chamberlain, *Legislative Processes,* p. 63.

27.
Ibid., pp. 92–93.

28.
National School Boards Association, *Survey of Public Education in the Nation's Big City School Districts* (Evanston, Ill.: National School Boards Association, 1975), pp. 48–50.

29.
Robert L. Morlan and Leroy C. Hardy, *Politics in California* (Belmont, Calif.: Dickenson, 1968), pp. 103–104.

30.
Sidney Verba and Norman H. Nie, *Participation in American Political Democracy and Social Equality* (New York: Harper & Row, 1972), p. 31.

31.
See, for example, Zeigler and Baer, *Lobbying,* and Levitt and Feldbaum, "Council Members, Lobbyists, and Interest Groups," pp. 98–103.

32.
Zeigler and Baer, *Lobbying,* p. 102.

33.
Ibid., p. 61.

34.
Ibid., p. 62.

35.
Levitt and Feldbaum, "Council Members, Lobbyists, and Interest Groups," p. 98.

36.
L. Harmon Zeigler and G. Wayne Peak, *Interest Groups in American Society,* 2nd ed. (Englewood Cliffs, N.J.: Prentice-Hall, 1972), p. 160.

37.
Ira Sharkansky, *Public Administration: Policy-Making in Government Agencies* (Chicago: Markham, 1970), pp. 74–82.

38.
For a discussion of the several kinds of mobility that exist for career bureaucrats, see Eugene B. McGregor, Jr., "Politics and the Career Mobility of Bureaucrats," *The American Political Science Association* 68 (March 1974): 18–26.

39.
Donald T. Campbell and H. Laurence Ross, "The Connecticut Crackdown on Speeding: Time Series Data in Quasi-Experimental Analysis," in Edward R. Tufte (ed.), *The Quantitative Analysis of Social Problems* (Reading, Mass.: Addison-Wesley, 1970).

40.
Karl T. Kurtz, "The State Legislatures," *Book of the States 1974–1975* (Lexington, Ky.: The Council of State Governments, 1974), pp. 53–65.

41.
See, for example, Robert D. Lee, Jr., and Ronald W. Johnson, *Public Budgeting Systems* (Baltimore: University Park Press, 1973), p. 94.

42.
Elmer B. Staats, "Intergovernmental Relations: A Fiscal Perspective," *The Annals of the American Academy of Political and Social Science* 416 (November 1974): 36.

43.
Henry Robert Glick, *Supreme Courts in State Politics* (New York: Basic Books, 1971), p. 5.

44.
Ibid., p. 27.

45.
Herbert Jacob, *Justice in America* (Boston: Little, Brown, 1965), p. 31.

46.
The requirements governing access to the courts are taken from Jacob, ibid., pp. 6–8.

47.
Ibid., pp. 27–28.

48.
Ibid., p. 30.

5

THE POLITICS
OF EDUCATIONAL
GOVERNANCE

THE MAJOR point of the last chapter—the responsiveness of government elites to each other rather than to segments of the public—is well illustrated by the case of educational governance. Only within the past decade has educational policy-making come to be widely recognized as a political process. If systematic studies of educational decision-making are still rare, it is because students of politics have traditionally directed their attention toward the more obviously political institutions of society such as political parties, interest groups, the courts, and legislatures. There is certainly no reason to argue that schools are not political. Even when nobody noticed them, they were performing distinctly political functions, for school districts have always been involved in decisions concerning taxation and distribution of public resources.[1] The past decade of student protests, teacher strikes, and taxpayers' revolts has thrown the schools into a sharper political focus.

The source of turmoil has, in most cases, been the inability of schools to respond to the changing needs of students and the larger community.

Indeed, the National Institute of Education (NIE) has recently described American primary and secondary education as a system "unable to renew itself by responding rapidly, confidently, and openly to diverse client needs and expectations."[2] This chapter is an inquiry into the failure of public education to be responsive. Education policy has been selected for intensive consideration here because it is the largest and most expensive policy enterprise shared by state and local governments.

SETTING EDUCATIONAL POLICY

Policy Levels and Participants

School policy is made by a variety of participants at all levels of government. The federal government—though it does not usually provide direct financial support—affects lower education through such activities as subsidizing teacher training, giving aid to federally impacted areas, supporting demonstration and innovative projects, providing the "hot lunch" program, sponsoring research, and overseeing such controversial national policies as desegregation. State legislatures finance education to the tune of between 20 and 50 percent of the educational expenditure of local school districts. State boards of education establish—to a greater or lesser degree depending on the state—curriculum and text requirements and certification procedures. Local boards of education and superintendents are legally in charge of the basic educational program of a district. School principals must interpret district-wide policy, and the classroom teacher (in most cases effectively shielded by the classroom door) must instruct within the guidelines established by this multi-layered decisional apparatus.

Despite evidence of growing nationalization, most important routine and episodic decisions still seem to be made at the local level. Although demands for decentralization and community control are increasing, American schools, compared with those of other Western nations, are decentralized. Out of a variety of diffuse historical trends (including the Pilgrims' deep commitment to localism), the "traditional" American pattern of school governance emerged: a weak state education department providing limited leadership to a very large number of local units.[3] Despite the decline in the number of districts, this pattern remains intact. Our discussion of educational decision-making will therefore concentrate on local school districts.

The differentiation of hierarchical levels is a helpful initial step in the process of narrowing down our examination. We also need to know who is usually most active in local decision-making. Obviously the school board and superintendent are consistently involved. Additionally, however (again, in various degrees), so are organized interest groups, teachers, students, and informal community power elites. Though this list is not exhaustive, it does include the most visible participants. A major task of this chapter will be to indicate the way in which these participants influence local education policies.

WHO MAKES THE DECISIONS?   Common sense and empirical evidence indicate that the influence of specific participants in a decision varies with, among other things, the nature of the decision. School systems, like all organizations, must make decisions of diverse magnitudes and impacts. School district authority is invoked to decide educational programs, salary levels of custodial employees, and the purchase of office supplies. Organizational theorists have attuned themselves to the problem of types of decisions with varying degrees of clarity. In all cases, the goal is to classify decisions along a continuum ranging from almost purely routine to those which fundamentally alter goals. Downs, for example, uses the notion of "depth of change." Minor changes in everyday behavior that can be made without changing organizational goals. However, new organizational purposes require (theoretically) changes in day-to-day behavior.[4] A similar, if dichotomous, distinction is offered by Agger, Goldrich, and Swanson:

> An *administrative* demand or decision-making process is regarded by its maker or participants as involving relatively routine implementation of a prior, more generally applicable decision; it implicates relatively minor values of a relatively few people at any one time and has "technical" criteria available to guide the technically trained expert in selecting one or another outcome as *the* decision. A *political* demand or decision-making process is thought to involve either an unusual review of an existing decision or an entirely new decision, it implicates

relatively major values of a relatively large number of people and has value judgments or preferences as the major factors in determining selection by "policy-makers" of one or another outcomes as *the* decision.[5]

As applied specifically to schools, Martin has distinguished between "internal" (administrative) and "public" (political) decisions.[6]

Most decisions made in school districts are administrative, routine, or internal. As we shall see, the routinization of decision has considerable impact on the influence of various participants.

Distribution of Resources

When two or more participants are vying for decisive influence over the same outcome, the exchange of resources is similar to primitive economic bargaining. In the situation under consideration here, for instance, formal control of educational policy rests with the school board. The board appoints the superintendent and may remove him at any time. The superintendent is an administrative officer similar to a city manager.[7] In most instances, the school board is the elected representative body speaking for the public. Even when the board is appointed, its function is still representative.

However, as is too easily the case when elected officials confront their administrative employees, the legal and the actual distribution of influence varies considerably. Frequently, the resources of the superintendent are of sufficient value to cause the board to defer to him in the actual establishment of authority. The "rank" authority of the board loses out to the "technical" authority of the superintendent.[8] Clearly, if school boards were to maximize their fundamental resources—formal authority—there would be no question of their supremacy. Obviously, as will become clear, this resource is underutilized.

Another potential school board resource is representative responsibility. From the normative view of lay control of education, school boards speak for the people. In a society in which symbols associated with popular sovereignty have such high salience, the mere *act* of representation is a potential resource. If the school board is perceived—at least by the superintendent—as being a potential mobilizer of various publics, its power is enhanced. The amount of public, or external, support available to a board varies with several factors, including the recruitment pattern of a particular board, the visibility of the board to its publics, and the salience of, and satisfaction with, educational policy.

Although legal authority and representative function are the most universal of the potential resources available to school boards, others may exist in specific districts. In their study of a rural community in up-state New York, for instance, Vidich and Bensman discovered that the school board was closely allied with prevailing community elites.[9] Others have found this to be the case in communities characterized by homogeneous elite desires and preferences.[10] The whole question of utilization of political elites by school boards is complex, and needs further explanation than is possible here. Early studies suggested that major educational decisions were shaped directly by "prime movers" in the community. Hence, school boards could mobilize key members of the power system to do battle (if need be) with the superintendent. By the same token, small groups of lay people influential in local politics were said to set the major policies of the educational system. We suggest that the political elites of a community may—depending on the issue, the community, the style of the board—be unavailable as a board resource.

The superintendent's potential resources are more limited but potentially more effective in an exchange. His primary resource is his professional reputation for expertise in education. The exchange between bureaucratic experts and elected laymen is hardly unique to school boards. The most obvious analogies are the exchanges between city council and city manager and between legislative committees and executive departments. The medium of bargaining is similar in all these situations, yet the resources of the superintendent of schools are both unique and puzzling. We have a tradition of "lay control." The existence of local school boards—almost uniquely American—attests to this tradition. In contrast with, say, the British, Americans believe that laymen should influence educational policy-making. Simultaneously, however, we accord greater deference to superintendents than is accorded most other public professionals.[11] This curious ambivalence actually strengthens the value of expertise, because there are virtually no institutional controls on superintendents other than accountability to the board. Superintendents, then, use their expertise in a disguised fashion, insisting that they are held in check by an alert board while attempting to establish a monopoly on technical skills and information. As Minar notes:

> The technical expert, the district superintendent, is likely to flourish in those community settings where expertise and divi-

> sion of labor are assigned intrinsic value. . . . Where his "em-
> ployers" on the board and in the community trust and value
> *expertise* [the superintendent] is likely to have much more dis-
> cretion and initiative, right up to the highest policy level.[12]

The claim for expert status by the superintendent is buttressed by
another belief that can be used as a resource to evade lay control: the
separation of education and politics and the consequent insulation of
educational decision-making from broader based political conflict. The
reforms of 1890–1910—initiated in response to the growing influence of
urban political machines—produced a convention that is still intact
among administrators: the separation of policy-making from administration and the concentration of authority in the office of the superintendents.

Keeping schools out of politics also meant minimizing the legitimacy
of political conflict, and hence the legitimacy of outside influence as
represented by pressure groups.[13] In contrast to such overtly political
bodies as state legislatures or city councils, school boards and administrators define pressure groups as outside the proper influence
system.[14] The normal resource of an interest group is the perception of
its legitimacy by a decision-maker.[15] Admittedly, perceptions of
legitimacy vary from group to group and issue to issue, but most politicians generally assume that groups have a right to be heard. Superintendents do not share in this assumption.[16] Further, it has been found that
only about half the school board members accept the legitimacy of
group-originated demands.[17] When the claim for expertise is successful,
interest-group influence will be minimal, as in New York:

> In the last two decades, education in New York City has become
> amazingly insulated from political and public controls. One
> could accurately describe the situation as an abandonment of
> public education by key forces of political power within the
> City. . . . Weber's theory of the emergence of a specialized
> bureaucracy monopolizing power through its control of expertise
> characterizes the role of the education bureaucracy in New York
> City. The claim that only professionals can make competent
> judgments has been accepted. Civic and interest groups have
> responded ambivalently. On the one hand they accept the no-
> tion of the professional competence of the bureaucracy, but at
> the same time express a hopelessness regarding their ability to
> change the system.[18]

To a lesser degree, teachers suffer from a comparable denial of
legitimacy. They are *employees* of the school district. Employees, in the

official argument, have a right to be heard but not to participate. If teachers accept the employee role, their organizational influence will be minimal. Similarly, students and parents have not yet been accorded a legitimate voice as the consumers of the educational product. They are accorded considerably less voice than consumers normally exercise. They are not free to "vote with their feet." Schooling is compulsory, and it is monopolized by a single public agency. Hence, consumers can exercise few options, unlike consumers in a free market. Because their choices are limited, their resources are largely confined to protest. Protest normally isolates the protesters from sources of power, thus proving to be an inefficient mechanism.[19]

Strategies of Influence

We have described the most persistent actors and their resources. We now turn to another key concept: strategies of influence. The point here is that the new existence of a potential resource is insufficient to warrant the conclusion that it will necessarily be used in political exchange. Power requires, in addition to resources, the ability of the resource holder to convert the resources and their relevance to the stakes of the political exchange. One norm, for example, provides criteria by which resources are evaluated. The goal of the participants is to arrange for issues to be defined in such a way that their particular resource will be highly valued. Therefore, for example, superintendents seek to achieve a definition of all issues as "technical." They attempt to routinize decision-making by constructing the agenda for board meetings and establishing themselves and their staff as the most reliable sources of information. Because boards typically do not have staffs, they have no alternative source of information. The superintendent's expertise will dominate if the decision to purchase science textbooks is made in terms of reading levels, correlations with national achievement test scores, or other technical criteria. If the main criterion becomes the presentation of the evolution-creation controversy in the textbooks, public opinion and representation will come into play.

The board, to counter the superintendent's monopoly on information and expertise, must perceive the issues as nonroutine or external. The most obvious way to accomplish this goal is to keep the agenda loaded with problems of resource allocation rather than resource utilization, thus engaging the interest of organized groups. Thus, while the superintendent's best strategy is to constrict the range of debate, the board's best strategy is to expand the range of debate, thus arousing the public passions and embedding the decision-making process within the general framework of the representational process or, if necessary, community conflict. The board can stimulate public input on a proposed program of art education, for example, by making it clear that resources allocated to such a program will be subtracted from the pool available for, say, high school athletics. Rephrasing the policy question from—Do we want new program X?—to—Do we want new program X at a cost to existing program Y?—will increase the number of school patrons who see their interests affected by the decision.

A key component in this description of exchange is that of *perception*. For a resource to be applied, the potential user must view it as appropriate. Perceptions are not easily explained, but we do have some clues—particularly recruitment and environment. We shall direct our attention to patterns of recruitment, images of representative obligations, and response to outside influences. We shall then turn our attention to general patterns of interaction between school boards and superintendents. Finally, we shall address the policy outcomes of such interactions.

Recruitment

SCHOOL BOARD MEMBERS   When compared to the general public, board members have the qualities that—right or wrong—are more valued and esteemed in American society. Specifically, they are more male, white, middle-aged; longer residents of their communities; much better educated and have more prestigious occupations; more Protestant, more devout, and more Republican.[20] Although the fallacy of inferring attitudes and behaviors from the social origins and positions of public officials is by now well established, social characteristics are important in that certain perspectives or *Weltanschauung* are inevitably underrepresented on governing bodies by virtue of their status bias. Thus, though specific decisions or policies might not be attributable to a middle- and upper-class ethos, it does seem likely that the agenda of problems and possible solutions as well as the style of decision-making are affected by composition factors.[21]

The upper-class bias of school boards is hardly unique; indeed all governmental bodies exhibit such a bias. Nor is it surprising that school boards attract a disproportionate share of people who, along with their families, have been associated with education. What is unique is the isolation of board members from political involvement. Because governing schools is part of the political process, we might expect board members to spring disproportionately from politicized homes. Such is not the case.[22] Board members are no more likely than the general public to come from homes more involved in public affairs. For all the usual findings about the political backgrounds of political elites, the pattern obviously does not apply to local elites in education. Thus, the recruitment process provides more evidence of a recurrent theme of this discourse: the apolitical character of school politics.

Another way we can discern the insulation of school board members is by looking at the positions held by board members before their elections. Most members serve an apprenticeship in public affairs, either in civic-business, political-governmental, or educational spheres.[23] Though all three avenues to the school board are used, the civic-business path is the most prominent. The senior position of civic-business apprenticeship again is not unique, as a variety of community studies has shown. Such organizations as the Chamber of Commerce are prominent actors in the drama of local politics. Yet boards of education provide an even more congenial destination than, say, city councils or state legislatures. What could be better preparation for service in a nonpolitical agency than proven ability in the civic-business world?

Obviously there are other paths to the school board. One alternative path of considerable theoretical interest is the political. Those board members whose careers interface with the community's manifest political process are likely to approach their jobs with markedly different attitudes than those whose careers are in civic and business organizations. Boards with strong political orientations (when they can be found) stand in stark contrast to the normal board. Crain notes that:

> the appropriate model for studying school board recruitment is one of conflict between the two most powerful groups in the city—the political party and the civic leadership . . . this is simply a continuation of the pressures which divided those two groups over fifty years ago, when the industrial cities of the North developed professional politicians who could use ethnic and class conflict as a resource to compete with Yankee money.[24]

Crain went on to assert that because boards recruited from the civic-business sector were more sympathetic to desegregation demands, they were high on "reform orientation." This conclusion fits well with what we know of upper-class attitudes, but hides some other consequences of recruitment patterns. Jennings and Zeigler found that board members with strong links to the political process (20 percent) are more likely to

(1) have been originally elected to a board; (2) have attracted the support of various publics during the campaign; (3) want to institute changes in the educational program; (4) have differed seriously with their opponents; and (5) be more unhappy with the role of the board in making decisions.[25]

On every one of these dimensions, the civic-business–oriented board members (32 percent) ranked considerably lower. Such persons, though perhaps satisfying the reform values of being "above politics," hardly satisfy requirements for meaningful lay control: contested elections, issue differences, challenging the status quo, and looking back over one's shoulder at the mood of the constituency:

> of all those board members with prior public affairs experience the civic notables are the blandest and gained office in the least competitive fashion.[26]

It hardly need be added that political paths and civic-business paths occur in reasonable correlation with the institutional relationship between the school and the political community. Political careers occur more often in partisan districts with ward elections; civic-business careers abound in nonpartisan, at-large districts.

Adding to the noncompetitive nature of the recruitment process is the strong tendency of boards to perpetuate themselves. Elections to school boards are only moderately competitive. Only about half of the board members are elected in a contest with an incumbent.[27] Those who challenge incumbents are likely to stress ideological concerns and specific issues as opposed to such symbolical euphemisms as "better schools." Still, most board members can cite only one difference with their electoral opponents, and such differences are not likely to relate directly to the educational program.

In addition to self-perpetuation by default, there is deliberate self-perpetuation.[28] The best way for any elected body to perpetuate its style and policies is to handpick its successors. True, such designees do not always fulfill the promise of their supporters. Moreover, the lone dissident or two might be most active in encouraging others to run. Over the long pull, however, it seems probable that board members encourage like-minded individuals to join them and that those who are successful prove compatible with existing board members. Adding to this probability is the socialization of new members into the norms and folkways of the board. If the new entrant initially considers diverging from his fellow members, such deviance is quickly attenuated by the socialization process, especially because the new member owes his position on the board to the instigation of board personnel. If one adds the activity of the PTA (closely identified with the "establishment"), superintendents, and teachers to the recruitment by the board, about one-half of the members of school boards are the products of self-perpetuation. To a substantial degree the pool of eligibles comes to be those people recognized by local educational elites as potential board members.

To return to the notions of resources of boards, representative capacity and legal authority are underutilized. It is not surprising that school boards are Waspish; what does bear directly upon resource utilization is the low-keyed, self-perpetuating selection process that minimizes conflict. Such a selection process subverts the notions of lay control and hence the public orientation of board members. Orthodoxy and tradition are cherished; controversy is not. There is little intensive lay, or group, involvement in elections. Thus, boards emerge as relatively impermeable. The early educational reformers have succeeded too well: politics (that is, partisanship) and education are normally separate. Thus, the superintendent's basic resources—technical skills, information monopoly, expertise—are not matched by an equally resourceful board. As we continue to describe the decisional culture of school systems, the lack of a balance of power between board and superintendent will become apparent.

ADMINISTRATORS   Superintendents, too, have a clear, even more homogeneous, recruitment pattern. Like school board members, they are Waspish, Republican, and devout. Here, however, the similarity ends. Superintendents are far more likely to have been reared in a small town, and to have a lower middle-class background. Very few have urban and professional origins.[29] For most school board members, board service is neither a route nor end goal of upward mobility. Very few seek to better themselves politically. For superintendents, the job represents the culmination of a struggle out of the lower middle class.

To be a superintendent, one must first be a teacher. To survive as a teacher—or to become an administrator—one must learn to understand and accept occupational norms. The norm for teachers—less so now, but certainly so when today's administrators were teachers—is quiescence, acceptance of authority, and conservatism.[30] Those who cannot accept the norms drop out.[31] Surviving long enough to become an administrator requires more than an employee orientation. In addition to "knowing one's place," male teachers (superintendents are universally male) have to face the financial and psychological deprivations of existing in a highly feminized occupation. Ninety percent of all elementary teachers and about half of high school teachers are female. It is not surprising that only about 10 percent of the male teachers last longer than five years.[32] The pool of eligibles is thus reduced considerably to those male teachers who, through keeping free of controversy, are able to survive. As Carlson notes, sheer *perseverance* seems to be a contingency of the career path of the superintendent.[33]

It is perhaps here as a teacher, or more specifically, as a fraction of those males that survive, that future superintendents first develop their suspicion of lay control. In competition with parents for the obedience of the child, teachers develop defensive reactions: opposition to para-professionals, resentment of parental interference, belief in certification, and using methods courses. Surviving male teachers, buffeted by the tensions of their jobs, tend to become more politically conservative and develop an unusually high need for respect, an exaggerated concern for authority, and a personal rigidity and a fear of risk-taking behavior.[34]

The occupational recruitment of superintendents—coupled with their unusually high small-town representation and working-class origins—helps considerably in understanding their view of school boards—which are usually upper middle-class laymen (even though they reflect the values of the local educational establishment). Given their humble origins and the development of a defensive response to criticism, overcompensation is virtually guaranteed. Thus, the development of expertise as a resource comes naturally. Curiously, the militant defense of expertise comes from an occupational group quite un-distinguished academically. Among graduate students in seventeen fields attending universities that grant doctoral degrees, those in educational administration have the lowest mean score on the Miller Analogies test.[35]

Taken together, these various strands of the recruitment process add up to the superintendents perceiving their roles as "narrow and defensive."[36] They are often intolerant of lay criticism and frequently unwilling to engage in dialogue with outsiders. Criticisms may be answered with either complete disagreement or with irrelevant replies loaded with trivial detail.[37] For superintendents expertise is not only a resource, it is a way of life learned early and necessary for psychic and occupational survival. Small wonder that superintendents use their resources more relentlessly than school boards.

LINKAGE: THE COMMUNITY AND THE SCHOOLS

VARIOUS ARTICULATE publics have found this relatively closed educational system remarkably impermeable. At the risk of redundancy, American education is *symbolically* democratic. As we have seen, however, a few insiders pay more than lip service to the concept of lay control and many actively oppose it. Roscoe Martin, perhaps most severe among those who expose this conflict between symbols and reality, laments:

> Thus is the circle closed the paradox completed. Thus does the public school, heralded by its champions as the cornerstone of democracy, reject the political world in which democratic institutions operate.[38]

Isolation from the Community

Legitimacy—the key to successful negotiation between elected officials and various publics—is difficult to establish. Information—a basic resource in the arsenal of the lobbyist—is hard to pry loose from the iron grip of the superintendent. Clearly, opening school districts to environmental demands hinges on the extent to which educational decision-makers conceive their role as legitimately entailing acknowledgment of and response to such demands. On this score, we find that the mass public, in keeping with its attachment to the symbols of democracy, is disinclined to accept the notion that school board members should follow their own judgment; they want them to "do what the public wants." Though not denying that in most cases the public does not know what it wants, board members typically do not view their role as representing the public; two-thirds of them believe they should follow their own judgment. Even more adamant are superintendents. Three-fourths of them believe board members should be "delegates" rather than "representatives."[39] Needless to say, board members and superintendents misperceive the public's view and assume, wrongly, that it is congruent with their own.

Of course, such usages of various categories of role orientations are well known and well worn. They provide, at best, a clue about linkages between governing elites and public demands. Obviously, school boards and superintendents have some interaction with agents of the community. To get more precisely at the nature of this interaction, Jennings and Zeigler categorized school boards according to the legitimacy and responsiveness accorded to group demands and individual demands.[40] Though it is possible for boards to be equally responsive to both types of demands, in fact the two response styles are negatively correlated. Further, group-responsive boards and individual-responsive boards differ appreciably along a variety of dimensions. The conditions which lead boards to be responsive to group demands are those which *lessen* the responsiveness to individual sources of preferences and cues. Boards are considerably more group-oriented in the complex environments of metropolitan areas. Demands originating from individuals receive more sympathy in small towns. The ambience of small towns seems to be conducive to the sort of informal, almost casual inputs of information characteristic of our images of hinterland America.[41] Even if these constituents are formal group spokesmen, they are not recognized as such. They are seen as fellow merchants, farmers, luncheon club or church members, former high school classmates, relatives, friends, or perhaps just some residents with whom to pass the day. The exchange is nonthreatening, and the intensity is low.

INTEREST GROUP ACTIVITY   It is only when one moves into the complexities of urban life that there is any appreciable exchange between formal organizations and elected and appointed school officials.[42] Not only do such officials have a positive affect toward groups (for example, by according them legitimacy), but they see more of them. However, even in those urban, group-oriented districts, interest group activity is sporadic at best. Indeed, urban districts are "groupy" only in comparison to small towns and rural areas. A sizable portion of the districts are hardly boiling cauldrons of interest activity. To the contrary, they seem to be functioning with a minimum of formal group life.[43]

Whereas Jennings and Zeigler's conclusions about the paucity of group life are based on comparative surveys, Smoley's exhaustive case study of pressures on the Board of School Commissioners in Baltimore provides corroboration.[44] Using school board minutes and some additional published sources, he considered 2,389 issues during a seven-year period, Smoley revealed that interest groups are largely uninvolved even in a large city:

> Of the 2,389 issues considered by the Board of School Commissioners, only 207 included participation by outside groups—less than ten percent! Furthermore, much of the participation which did take place contained no hint of attempted influence, but was action in the performance of official functions to provide service to the Baltimore school system.[45]

Smoley's analysis also provides insight into how superintendents can use their resources to minimize external demands. Superintendents usually set agendas for board meetings and load them with trivia—nuts and bolts problems of administration that neither boards nor interest groups can understand. For example, school board members are inundated with lists of numbers: numbers of students, teachers, administrators, chairs, desks, books, test scores, and, of course, dollars. Since they lack the expertise necessary to form a picture of the state of the school district in personal terms from these detailed data, they must listen patiently to the interpretation of their administrators. School boards can thus be distracted from general discussions of curriculum goals by lengthy reports on isolated elements of the educational program. At first glance, including administrative tasks in the agenda may seem risky, but the strategy is successful. Immersed in trivial administrative matters rather than major issues of educational policy, boards do not provide a forum for interest arbitration. Over 2,000 of the 2,389 decisions concerned staff personnel and the school building program. Only a handful related to instructional affairs. Most issues were routine and quickly resolved. Trivia—skillfully used—is a powerful weapon.

Further evidence of isolation appears when we probe into the distribution of activity among types of groups. The results are unequivocal: the most active voice is that of the PTA, followed (distantly) by teachers.[46] Almost two-thirds of the board members in the Jennings and Zeigler study cited the PTA; about one-third recalled demands by teacher groups. After these two, the list declines through civil rights groups (29 percent); various business, professional, and service clubs, down through the much feared (but relatively quiescent) right-wing groups (13 percent) to the rarely active labor organizations (3 percent). PTAs and teachers are most active, and we will return to them for a more thorough analysis. At this point, let us point out that most of the interest-group action is controlled by "in-house" organizations whose major thrust is to create a climate in which the status quo goes unchallenged. There is an establishment tinge to the group spectrum.

TIMES OF CRISIS   If the usual decisional climate is ideologically cool, there is no gainsaying the fact that it does, on occasion, become quite heated. When issues lose their routine technical flavor and strike deep at emotions, the superintendent may find himself in the midst of group-dominated conflict. Such conflicts surrounding the resolution of episodic issues are rare but usually spectacular.

Granted that schools are now commonly described as the center of turmoil (teacher strikes, student revolts, taxpayer revolts, busing, community control, and the like), however, even in the 1960s relatively placid districts probably outnumbered the tempestuous ones. Some districts cope with their problems over a long period of time with a minimum of strife. Others, those which capture the imagination of the mass media, seem to be caught up in perpetual conflict. What may best characterize school district phenomena of this type is a model of episodic crisis—a situation that involves demands for a change in organizational goals.[47] Most districts experience crises and unrest at one time or another; the difference is that some few are marked by frequently recurring episodes whereas most enjoy rather long periods of calm between crises.

What happens when episodic crises erupt? When the district population becomes antagonized, support for school policy dwindles, group demands increase, and the interaction between educational decision-makers and unattached individuals decreases.[48] Imagine, for example, a school beset by scandal or fiscal chaos. As popular support dwindles, an increase in group demands sets in. As public confidence in the school continues its decline, the loss of confidence is articulated and given explicit focus by interest groups. They pinpoint, according to their own objectives and interests, the specific aspects of discontent to which they will address their efforts. The decline in popular support becomes less generalized as group activity increases. Groups clearly thrive in an atmosphere of conflict between the governed and the governors. Such a condition of stress is a precipitant condition for group activity, regardless of the social complexity of the community. The board and superintendent are in a state of siege.

The threatening environment of group activity surely sets educational governance apart from other public decision-making processes, where group activity is normal and considerably lower keyed. School boards, unlike most governmental bodies, are normally accustomed to individual exchanges, consisting of cues rather than demands.[49] Such cues may have affective content, but quite often simply consist of feedback to the board, signals about the reception of its actions. When individual cueing does consist of preferences on pending policies, such preferences are not seen as vigorously made demands. Because individual, unattached communications are typical of communities with a high level of satisfaction with educational policy, the content of the communications is usually supportive and not directed toward alterations in basic policy.

Group communications, more often reflecting the resentment of the masses, are addressed toward serious ideological conflict (except when coming from supportive organizations such as PTAs). Can organizations translate their anger into observable phenomena? If not, their activity would make little difference, because school boards and superintendents would have little evidence of the state of public opinion. The evidence is that group activity is strongly associated with financial defeats, teacher firings, and superintendent turnovers.[50] Small wonder that they are feared! Of particular interest is a strong association between the activities of political organizations and superintendent turnovers. When superintendents insist that education and politics do not mix, they are not just mouthing platitudes. Again, superintendents have strong incentives to use their resources as buffers against the assault of "outside" groups.

BARRIERS TO RESPONSIVENESS   In addition to their control of the agenda and their aggressive use of trivia, superintendents have the advantage of an institutional structure designed, as we have seen, to insulate schools from the erratic winds of community conflict. Such devices as at-large, nonpartisan elections minimize the link between public anger and group demands. Although it makes intuitive sense to argue that large electoral units increase social heterogeneity and hence increase group conflict, the opposite is true. Ward elections (a minority phenomenon in school district organizations) increase the likelihood that interest groups will provide a clearer focus for grievances that are likely to be neighborhood-based. Similarly, partisan elections place the educational decision-making process squarely within mainstream, conflictual politics, thus providing a visible target for interest groups.

Linkage opportunities are also reduced appreciably by the self-perpetuating recruitment pattern characteristic of school boards. When, as is frequently the case, incumbent board members are able to perpetuate their influence by bringing like-minded colleagues to the board, interest group activity (and individual communications as well) tapers off considerably. Boards in these circumstances appear almost akin to closed corporations, insulating themselves from the hue and cry of interest group politics. Popular uprisings or expressions of discontent come slowly to the attention of the board, because cues are internally generated. Boards and superintendents value a public display of unity, generally eschew identification with group-originated values, and avoid public conflicts. About 90 percent of the votes observed by Lipham and others in twelve Wisconsin districts were unanimous.[51]

The only groups welcomed into such dynasties are PTAs and, less often, teachers. Their comparative acceptance stems from their semi-official status. The PTA—with its membership strongly biased in favor of the social characteristics most comparable to those of school boards—functions not as a demand-generating group, but rather as a buffer or defense mechanism. It does not translate mass hostility into specific demands, but rather communicates the policy of the board and superintendent to its clientele. It coopts potentially disruptive parents, defusing conflicts before they begin.[52]

The Role of Teachers

Teachers' organizations (the local affiliates of the National Education Association and the American Federation of Teachers) occupy a curious place in the array of group activity. Of all the groups engaging—however sporadically—in efforts to influence the content of educational policy, teachers should have the highest legitimacy. They are not outsiders. Furthermore, they generally confine their activity to narrowly defined issues, such as teacher hirings, firings, conditions of work, and salaries. Yet teachers' organizations are a distant second to PTAs in group activity.[53] Despite some very visible political activities, such as lobbying at the state capital, public demonstrations, and strikes, teachers' organizations are apparently no more influential today than they were twenty years ago. In 1956, Griffiths concluded that "Teachers as a group have little or no say in the formulation of school policy."[54] In 1969 Rosenthal wrote that teachers' organizations "play a negligible part in determining school policies. . . ."[55]

A variety of explanations for the weak position of teachers has been advanced. Most relate, directly or indirectly, to the occupational norms of teaching and the authority structure of the school system. Most prominent among the explanations are (1) the employee status and orientation of teachers, (2) the nonpolitical tradition of education, as it translates into organizational acquiescence, and (3) the administrative domination of schools and teachers' organizations. Each will be examined briefly.

EMPLOYEE STATUS   Teachers—particularly teachers' organizations—use the word "profession" to the point of abuse, but it is difficult to agree with this self-concept. Among other attributes, professions are presumed to have some degree of autonomy in exercising their special competence. Yet teachers cannot exercise much independent authority even within the classrooms to which they are assigned. Nor do they control entry into teaching or assessment of colleagues' performance. Legally, they are employees, not professionals. More important, most teachers emotionally are employees. Traditionally, superintendents, principals, and other administrators have made decisions for teachers with the expectations that "teachers would be grateful for the generosity bestowed upon them."[56] The upsurge in militancy should not obscure the fact that most teachers accept their employee status, which requires a basic loyalty to the "boss." Some teachers—and the number appears to be growing slowly but inexorably—have adopted a genuinely professional orientation that impels them to seek to expand the power of teachers at the expense of administrators and lay authorities. However, Corwin's general conclusion is that teachers find the employee role more compatible. Two-thirds of the teachers he studied claim that they:

> Make it a practice of adjusting their teaching to the administration's views of good educational practice and are obedient, respectful and loyal to the principal: that they *do* look primarily to the judgment of the administration for guidance in cases of disputes in the community (over a textbook or speaker) . . . Approximately one half of the sample, too, agreed that their school's administration is better qualified to judge what is best for education . . . one half of the sample agreed that teachers who openly criticize the administration should go elsewhere . . . on the other hand, less than half of these believed that the ultimate authority over major educational decisions should be exercised by professional teachers.[57]

Corwin estimates that only about 10 percent of teachers have enough nonemployee characteristics to qualify them as militant. Zeigler found that going on strike was not considered professional by most teachers.[58] Even collective bargaining is viewed with suspicion.[59] The fact that most teachers are not militant should not be taken to minimize the teacher revolt. Obviously, some teachers are seeking more power and, equally obviously, administrators are resisting. Though the number of work stoppages (strikes) underwent an "irregular but gradual decline" from 1945 to 1966,[60] they began to surge upward around 1968.[61]

Nevertheless, predictions of increased militancy must be taken into account, particularly because school boards and superintendents regularly issue statements about dealing with teacher militancy (whether or not they have experienced it). Also, what we know about militancy may lead us to speculate about the future. Teachers are far more willing to challenge established authority in big cities, and in the North, East, and West than they are in small towns and in the Midwest and South.[62] Not surprisingly, large city school districts are more likely to experience teacher strikes. Further, popular support for strikes is also greatest in these areas. Indeed, segments of the public—particularly those with union affiliations—are more sympathetic to teachers than has popularly been assumed.[63] However, opportunities to form coalitions with various outside groups are constricted by the nonpolitical tradition of the teaching profession and the dominant position of administrators. In sum, one reason why teachers are not more active is that they do not wish to be. They are comfortable in their employee station. Even when strikes occur, the issues to be contested are usually salary and working conditions, not authority.

ORGANIZATIONAL ACQUIESCENCE   Closely related to the acquiescence that accompanies the employee image is the acquiescence of the nonpolitical organization. Of the two teacher organizations, the older, larger, still dominant National Education Association (NEA) sits clearly in the nonpolitical tradition in contrast with the smaller, urban-oriented American Federation of Teachers (AFT). NEA local affiliates have—until recently—opposed strikes and eschewed political activity of any kind. The NEA's official ideology was that the "professional" stature of teachers would suffer if the organization became involved in the rough-and-tumble world of politics. Hess and Kirst report, for example, that only tiny fractions of teachers even discuss school board elections, much less try to influence their outcomes.[64] Although leaders of NEA locals are more politically inclined than followers,[65] they are partially immobilized by a nonstable membership.[66]

ADMINISTRATIVE DOMINATION   Finally, there is administrator dominance of schools and associations. The National Education Association, in addition to stressing professionalism, emphasizes unity. Administrators and teachers, therefore, are in the same organization.

Until very recently administrators have controlled the NEA policy-making machinery, and they still dominate most locals. Pressure on teachers to join the NEA is fairly widespread, with administrators proudly announcing that their school is "100 percent."[67] The role of administrator in the NEA parallels their role in schools and even the influence of the administrative point of view in schools of education. Schools of education are typically more authoritarian, and products of such schools more acquiescent, than other portions of the university.[68] Further, there is a strong relationship between acquiescent behavior and administrative approval within the school.[69] The cry for unity, therefore, serves the administration well, and the NEA is the vehicle that enforces the ideology.

The AFT, which represents a minority of teachers, has a more militant, less acquiescent membership. It excludes administrative personnel from membership and has traditionally supported political action. Its success in winning representation elections in large cities—notably New York—has spurred the NEA to a substantially more militant position (so much so that administrators are considering pulling out). Still, the NEA is the major teachers' organization and it does speak more authoritatively for unity and administrative dominance than for teachers. Administrators are even more opposed to teacher militancy than school boards (especially when teachers' revolts have actually taken place) and are almost obsessed with authority. As the American Association of School Administrators (AASA) puts it: "We pledge to resist any effort to displace the superintendent and his authority in matters affecting the interest and welfare of school personnel."[70]

THE POLICY PROCESS IN EDUCATIONAL GOVERNANCE

WE TURN now to a consideration of the policy-making process in local school districts. The six-step model of chapter 4 will organize our inquiry. The focus will be on participation in the governing process. Broadly stated, the question is, How insulated is the decision-making process? This question has been the subject of intensive debate.[71]

The potential participants in school district decision-making are (1) the school board, (2) the superintendent, (3) the central administrative staff, that is, assistant superintendents, area supervisors, research directors, business managers, and other officials at the district level, (4) other professionals employed by the school district, including principals, assistant principals, curriculum specialists, and lawyers, (5) the public, and (6) other governments, including officials of other local, state, and federal governments. The range of participants may vary among the various steps of the policy-making process. By considering both the six potential participants and the six stages of the governmental process, we hope to reach some defensible answers to the question, Who governs?

Proposal Development

As we outlined in chapter 4, proposal development begins when the need for action is articulated and one or more policy alternatives are suggested. Proposal development can originate with either governmental or nongovernmental individuals or groups within the educational system or it can originate outside a specific decision-making unit. Indeed, many of the problems currently encountered by local school districts are the result of proposal development occurring at the federal level. Whatever the source, however, proposal development invariably requires that preferences be translated into *demands* that require a *response*. Hence, the question of responsiveness can be understood as an inquiry into which of the variety of demands placed on a school system are selected for a response.

AGENDA-SETTING   Proposal development is making a communication to school district officials that they can understand and take action on. Thus, proposal development includes preparation of a formal proposal for consideration by appropriate officials. The result of proposal development is setting the agenda (which demands shall be responded to), a formal commitment by the school district to consider particular policy alternatives.

Agenda-setting is the opening round in the struggle for influence, and by no means an inconsequential one. In Schattschneider's view, control of the agenda is analogous to, say, choice of a battleground in war. A group or individual will always select a battleground which provides the advantage.[72]

In education, participation in agenda-setting is largely in the control of a professional monopoly, with minimum involvement by the school board or the public. In about two-thirds of the districts surveyed in two national studies, the superintendent (and, in some cases, his or her staff) was solely responsible for setting the formal agenda for board meetings.[73] We define agenda-setting as the introduction of a topic for discussion at board meetings.

Though the parliamentary agenda document is controlled exclusively by school administrators and board members in most school districts, this less restrictive definition makes it possible for all actors to participate in setting the agenda. Indeed, district patrons and the general public are always invited to attend school board meetings and make their views known. The distribution of discussion initiation among our six potential participants in school district decision-making is presented in table 5.1.

Table 5.1.   Agenda-Setting at School Board Meetings (in percentages)

Agenda-setter	Mean	Low	High
Superintendent	47	18	73
Central administrative staff	19	1	43
School board	24	9	57
Other professionals	3	2	9
Public	7	1	33
Other governments	a	0	1

[a] Less than 1 percent.

Even by this most liberal definition of agenda-setting, educational professionals dominate all other actors. On the average, superintendents initiate nearly half of all discussions; educational professionals account for nearly 70 percent of the agenda. School board members control 24 percent of agendas, members of the public 7 percent, and representatives of other governments less than 1 percent.

The direct agenda-setting of school board policy-making is quite insulated from those outside the school establishment. Clearly, the administration occupies a powerful gatekeeping position. The administration is in a position to establish an agenda that will minimize controversy and maximize routine decision-making. That is, superintendents and other professionals can set an agenda that, because it emphasizes technical problems, requires administrative, rather than board, resolution. Thus, Boyd asserts that "many, perhaps even most, school administrators are inclined to be cautious in their policy initiations and reluctant to test the boundaries of their influence."[74] It is highly significant, from our perspective, that whether or not Boyd is empirically correct he concedes the control of the agenda to the administration.

PUBLIC PARTICIPATION   The matter merits further consideration. In addition to the problem of a public body, the school board, yielding its agenda-setting authority to its nominal employee, the superintendent, one wonders how much public participation can be initiated when the public enters the game after the issues have been defined.

The insulation of nonprofessionals from direct participation in the proposal development step should not be taken as evidence of a conspiracy. The public's knowledge of schools is substantially less than that of school authorities. When asked to do so, one-third of the public could not name any problems facing their school district. Among those who noted problems, most people could cite but one. Among this segment, the problem was generally vague and diffuse (for example, "bad teachers"). In contrast, school authorities cite problems with much greater certainty, specificity, and frequency.[75] Clearly, then, the mass public has little more than a rudimentary knowledge of the issues or, more important, the potential issues, within their schools.

The generally low level of public knowledge should not be equated with disinterest. Some evidence suggests that the public would like to know more about education provided it had access to information. Moreover, the high level of community involvement in isolated, episodic issues, such as sex education, the teaching of evolution or creation, school prayer, and busing to achieve racial equality, suggests a substantial reservoir of public interest, although it is only occasionally manifest. The key is the constraint placed upon the mass public in responding to selected, developed issues rather than participating in the generation of issues. To illustrate, of all the potential issues which might arise within the schools, perhaps the most important are those concerning the very substance of schools: the educational program, or curriculum. Indeed, all other issues are in some sense secondary to this fundamental issue. Yet, to the mass public, issues relating to the educational program have a very low salience. Fewer than one in thirty people cite problems directly or even generally concerning the educational program. In contrast, school board members and superintendents cite curriculum problems with up to fifteen times greater frequency.[76] The gap in saliency occurs because members of the mass public do not have the expertise to discuss or resolve most curriculum issues. They lack, for example, the vocabulary educational professionals and school board members employ in their consideration of curriculum. The problem is not one of disinterest, but of frozen access.

According to traditional democratic theory, political influence, in this case agenda-setting, follows lines of legal authority. The public elects a school board to make policy. The board appoints a superintendent to administer policy. Thus, administrators follow the mandates of legislators who follow the instructions of their constituents. The major source of power is electoral support, and the norm of policy-making is responsiveness to public demands and preferences. This model suggests frequent participation in agenda-setting by school board members and other laymen. Yet, at least in the formal meetings of school boards, this is not the case.

Another perhaps more apt model focuses on professional expertise as the essential element in decision-making. In this chain of influence the major source of power is information; the norm is deference to expertise. Problems are brought to the attention of the school board by the publicly proclaimed experts: superintendents and their staff.

This role of the public in proposal development under this latter model has been discussed in a variety of recent essays on "administrative representation."[77] Because the superintendent is the dominant policy actor, he or she can, through a variety of informal contacts, adequately represent the views of the public to the board.[78] Despite obvious problems with traditional democratic theory, such a notion is intriguing in its realism. After all, if the superintendent *is* in fact representing the diverse community needs, then the relative quiescence of the public and of school boards is of no concern. Perhaps superintendents receive sufficient communication from the public in forums other than public meetings to represent their desires and preferences for them. Our research casts doubt upon this sanguine view.

PRIVATE COMMUNICATIONS   Superintendents do receive a considerable number of private communications concerning school policy. The number of private communications made to superintendents is disproportionately greater than the sum of private communications received by any individual board member. The private communications to each board member in total normally exceed (54 to 46 percent) that of the superintendent. However, the superintendent receives far more private communications than any other single individual. Most significantly, nearly all privately articulated demands occur *after* the presentation of an agenda item. Superintendents tend to communicate with groups and individuals with a decidedly "establishment" tinge.[79]

Most communications support a position announced by the superintendent. Eighteen percent of the private communications received by the superintendents in our study were in disagreement, 34 percent were in agreement, and the remainder were either neutral or without issue content. This finding is consistent with numerous other examinations of the private communications of public decision-makers. On the basis of this evidence, it seems fair to conclude that, if superintendents hear largely from supportive constituents, their representative net is rather small. As a substitute for public dialogue, private communication is inadequate.

To sum up the proposal development phase of our model: (1) proposal development is clearly dominated by superintendents; (2) the active role of school boards and members of the public is substantially below that indicated by traditional democratic theory; (3) though superintendents receive sufficient volume of private communications to make a model of administrative representation plausible, the quality of those communications do not support a democratic model of administrative representation.

Executive Recommendation

The executive recommendation step consists of interaction between the source of a proposal and the office of the chief executive, deliberation and consideration of the proposal and alternatives, and recommendation of a policy to the legislative body. When proposal development originates within the executive branch—the norm in school districts—the interaction consists of negotiation between the executive office and the initiating department. When proposals originate within government but outside the executive branch, with other governments, or with nongovernmental individuals and groups, executive agency personnel are included in executive recommendation deliberations as expert consultants. Whatever the origin of a policy proposal, the goal of the executive recommendation step is to eliminate "bad" proposals and to modify "good" proposals to make them relevant, effective, and (perhaps most important) acceptable to all parties.

In educational governance, executive recommendations are expected and honored. Indeed, it appears only reasonable that those who set the agenda should also recommend appropriate policy actions. As studies of municipal, state, and federal government show, the dominance of executive recommendations hardly makes school district governance unique.

Superintendent preferences are explicit, on the average, for 66 percent of the votes taken by school boards. The frequency and importance of executive recommendation stem from a variety of sources.

The most important reason for executive recommendations by school district superintendents is to make use of their professional expertise. Although superintendents act as the chief executives of government units, their basic resource is expertise rather than more traditional political skills (such as bargaining). It is a curious anomaly in American popular attitudes that while the concept of local lay control of schools is so highly valued, the educational expert is accorded greater deference than perhaps any other professional in public life. As a recent survey concluded, "if the apparent weight of public opinion had its way, school boards would lose much of their present authority."[80] Schools of high quality are universally desired, and the quality of the educational program is thought to be best assured by placing it under the control of an expert.

Superintendents are called on to make policy recommendations because they will ultimately be charged with implementing decisions. Their opinions are sought, not only to tap expertise, but also to include consideration of policy execution. Policy execution is extremely important because school boards must, of necessity, grant wide latitude to chief executives in the actual implementation of the programs they pass. Even more than other legislative bodies, school board members are part-time, amateur, volunteer officials. They have neither the resources nor the time to pass legislation in such detail that administration is merely following instructions. Executive review gives superintendents an opportunity to explain how they intend to follow through after the school board acts.

Superintendents are also called on to make policy recommendations because they are the only actors who are presumed to be overseeing an integrated program. Other actors seek actions in limited spheres. While all assert that the interests of the children come first, administrators, teachers, parents, and other groups enter the policy-making process when their own interests are at stake. The superintendent is expected to weigh conflicting input from segments of the school district, and to present a balanced, comprehensive program. Because school boards are part-time, amateur, and volunteer bodies, they must rely on the superintendent to present a program that does not contain elements which are mutually exclusive or in conflict and which are appropriate to the district's financial and personnel resources.

Executive recommendations are also sought from superintendents because they enjoy significant political power in the traditional sense.

The superintendent is the single most visible representative of the school system. The average citizen can more readily name his superintendent of schools than his U.S. congressman, to say nothing of elected school board members. Unlike individual board members, administrators, principals, teachers, or parents, the superintendent's constituency is the entire school district. The mass popular identification of government with its chief executive makes the superintendent the "tribune of the people." Although they are not popularly elected, superintendents have a base of popular and elite support that they can use as a resource in the decision-making process.

Contrary to the professional maxim that superintendents should not engage in politics, superintendents are political actors with political powers. As in other units of government, school district governance involves conflict. For many superintendents, political conflict presents a crucial paradox: when conflict occurs, the technical skills so diligently developed not only are of no value, they are a liability. Trained in the tenets of an ideology that defines conflict as pathological and consensus as the most legitimate basis of a decision, superintendents may find conflict more painful than other executive officers. A defensive, hostile response to criticism may then generate more intense conflict. Thus, superintendents with doctorate degrees (the most ideologically committed) and little on-the-job experience, experienced substantially higher levels of decision-making conflict than other superintendents. Those with either less education, or more experience (which mediates the negative influence of education) were able to manage conflict with more skill.[81]

The basic resource of the superintendent, his expertise, is not accepted as negotiable. Because superintendents rely on expertise rather than more traditional political skills, the power base of the superintendent is destroyed when this resource is declared inapplicable. It is no surprise that issues such as busing and school closures made necessary by declining enrollments, which cannot be solved by technical skills, are troublesome to superintendents. As American schools move from an era of expanding resources to one of scarce resources, the essentially political issue of resource distribution will become dominant. School boards will continue to turn to superintendents for recommendations. Superintendents must use both their political and technical resources as the task of conflict management becomes more prominent in school district governance.

Legislative Action

Legislative action is the process of making authoritative decisions concerning the items of the policy agenda. Public school board meetings are the arena for formal decisions after superintendent and staff set the agenda and recommend a policy alternative.

The primary function of legislative sessions of school boards is decision-making. As table 5.2 summarizes, our study of school board meetings found that an average of nearly three-fourths of all discussions are intended to be concluded with some sort of formal decision. As the wide range of proportion of discussions intended for decision indicates, school boards differ in the character of their legislative sessions. Some boards combine decision-making and public hearing functions; others conduct separate meetings for public hearings.

Table 5.2.   Purpose and Resolution of Discussions at School Board Meetings (in percentages)

	Mean	Low	High
Decision intended	74	47	97
Decision reached when intended	90	58	99
Decision by vote	86	72	97

Table 5.2 also shows that school boards successfully reach decisions when they are intended, and that the vast majority of decisions are made by a formal vote. In other words, when boards begin discussion with the intention of reaching a decision (as opposed to a mere discussion), they do not become so bogged down in conflict that they cannot reach a decision.

We have already seen that superintendents and their staff members dominate agenda setting for school board meetings. However, school boards permit and encourage participation from all six of our potential participants during their legislative sessions. Tables 5.3 through 5.6 summarize participation at legislative sessions of school boards.

In table 5.3 the unit of analysis is the discussion, and the percentages given represent the proportion of discussions in which at least one member of a category of actors made at least one statement. As one would expect, school board participation is nearly universal. Superintendents participate, on the average, in less than half the discussions (the range is from 24 to 71 percent). Central administrative staff participate in 35 percent and other professionals in 17 percent. A member of the "school establishment" participates in virtually every discussion. The "outsiders" are the public and representatives of other governments. They participate, on the average, in one of five discussions.

Table 5.3. Participation in Discussions at School Board Meetings (in percentages)

	Mean	Low	High
School board	94	84	100
Superintendent	43	24	71
Central administrative staff	35	18	63
Other professionals	17	11	25
Public	20	6	42
Other governments	1	a	2

[a] Less than 1 percent.

Another definition of participation is shown in table 5.4, where the unit of analysis is the statement. For each group of actors the entry is the percentage of all statements made at school board meetings. Again, a picture of school officials talking among themselves emerges. Less than 10 percent of all statements are made by the public and government officials.

Table 5.4. Proportion of Statements Made at School Board Meetings (in percentages)

	Mean	Low	High
School board	60	47	74
Superintendent	12	7	18
Central administrative staff	14	7	28
Other professionals	6	4	9
Public	9	2	16
Other governments	a	a	1

[a] Less than 1 percent.

A low level of public participation is only partially demonstrated by these data. Equally important is *what* is said. If public participation, albeit infrequent, is visibly policy-laden, then the low aggregate participation may be misleading. Demand articulation from nonofficial sources is a key ingredient in democratic political theory. Political scientists typically assume a model of governance that begins with the articulation, usually through organizational activity, of preferences. Hence, the response to such requests is a key variable in evaluating the performance of public bodies.

However, such a model is inappropriate for school governance. Public participation is typically informational; few demands are made, as indicated by table 5.5. Clearly, public meetings do not promote an opportunity for demand articulation and response. Such demands do exist, as can be seen from other arenas of public discussion (such as letters to the editor and television coverage), and they rise and fall with the level of controversy. They do not, however, achieve visibility at public meetings. Indeed, as the level of controversy increased, the agenda and discussions of boards became even more heavily laden with routine matters. The norm of unity prevails.

Table 5.5. Types of Statements Made at School Board Meetings (in percentages)

	Demand favored	Demand opposed	Request information	Supply information
Superintendent	22	2	6	71
School board member	26	4	27	44
Staff official	11	1	3	85
Line official	11	2	2	85
Public	26	13	17	44
Government official	8	6	2	84

On the other hand, private communications are substantially more policy-laden. More than half of such communications are classified as demands. Yet, because such communications normally occur after agenda-setting and support the action intended by the administration, they are an inadequate substitution for a genuine public dialogue.

After the agenda has been set and discussion has been completed, some sort of decision is in order. Table 5.6 summarizes this important aspect of participation at school board meetings: who makes formal policy proposals that are considered by the school board. This is different from the question of agenda-setting because the person who initiates discussion may or may not make a policy proposal. A proposer is the first person who articulates a proposal that is decided on—favorably or negatively—by the school board. Although most boards require a formal motion be made by a school board member, this definition of proposal-making is less restrictive. All six categories of potential participants are potential policy proposers.

Table 5.6.   Policy Proposals Made at School Board Meetings (in percentages)

	Mean	Low	High
School board	65	25	97
Superintendents	26	1	69
Central administrative staff	6	a	23
Other professionals	1	a	6
Public	2	a	9
Other governments	a	a	1

[a]Less than 1 percent.

School board decision-making is even more insulated from the public by this measure of participation. Persons outside the school district establishment account for an average of less than 3 percent of policy proposals. In no district do outsiders make as many as 10 percent of proposals. Generally speaking, two-thirds of policy proposals are originally articulated by school board members, and the other one-third by the superintendent and his staff. Clearly, by design or chance, the public is insulated from direct participation in decision-making at the legislative action step. As table 5.7 shows, the superintendent was either asked for or he volunteered a policy recommendation, on the average, for two of every three voting decisions. Table 5.7 also shows that adoption of superintendent recommendations, usually unanimously, is also the norm.

Table 5.7.   Voting Decisions at School Board Meetings (in percentages)

	Mean	Low	High
Decisions made by voting	86	72	97
Unanimous votes	85	62	99
Superintendent position known	66	12	88
Superintendent position adopted	96	74	100

School boards react to their superintendents much in the way that Congress reacts to the initiative of the chief legislator, the president. The basic resource of the board is its representative capacity, yet few boards have been able to escape superintendent domination. The superintendent's professional expertise and control of information resources is a major factor, yet a more fundamental factor is the board's image of its role. As Dykes says, "What the school board does depends in large measure on the board's view of itself in relation to its responsibilities."[82]

Most American school board members perceive their roles as consistent with the values of professional educators. Lipham and his colleagues found that 90 percent of all school board members thought that they should not serve as spokesmen for segments of the community; yet slightly over one-fourth of the citizens thought this was a good idea.[83] Rather than serving as a conduit to channel popular views to administrators, boards define their job as "selling" the administration's program to segments of the community. School boards fail to assert their representative capacity partly because they find it difficult, and partly because they choose not to.

Supplementary Decision and Implementation

The next two stages in the governmental process are substantially less public than the preceding stages. The legislative action step produces a formal document, which is an order from the school board to school district employees. Only a small proportion of these orders are meant to be implemented immediately. There is typically a time lag between legislative action and implementation. For example, because of the academic calendar, curriculum decisions made in May will not take effect for months.

SUPPLEMENTARY DECISION   Supplementary decision in school districts is rare. A major reason why decisions are rarely returned to the school board agenda is the fact that superintendents, unlike governors or even mayors, do not have the right to veto legislative decisions. The legal position of the superintendent makes such authority impossible. Again, too, the reality of the distribution of influence between board and superintendent makes a veto power absurd, because nearly all board policies are proposed by the superintendent. What reason for a veto could exist? Consequently, supplementary change in school governance tends, more than in other governance situations, to be incremental and technical, involving at most a few central office staff and perhaps participation by affected teachers and principals.

In rare cases of a particularly conflictual decision—the decision to close a local school, for example—pressures from external sources may achieve reconsideration. However, such examples—although they create the illusion of widespread conflict—are not part of the normal routine of governance. More typically, supplementary change decisions enhance the domination of the superintendent over the school board. A recurring example is school boards acquiescing to administration proposals to transfer funds during a fiscal year. The entire budget, the district's "master plan," has been debated and resolved months before. The superintendent requests additional funds for favored programs late in the fiscal year when the alternative to increased funding is program cut-back or elimination. By changing routine decisions to crisis decisions, superintendents can use a supplementary decision step to reverse earlier adverse decisions or increase the probability of victory over the school board.

IMPLEMENTATION   Implementation, as an activity of low visibility that is limited to school district employees, is similarly dominated by professionals. Indeed, it is at the implementation phase of governance that linkages between policy intent and policy achievement can be most easily modified by professional hostility. The most apt example is the new militancy of teachers. Typically, teachers' organizations have virtually no influence upon educational policy. As compared to other professions, teachers have been less politically active and more reluctant to challenge the authority of superiors. However, even during their passive period, teachers shaped the educational process within the classroom, the level at which most constituent satisfaction or dissatisfaction could be expected.

As employees of the district, teachers were expected to implement district policy. In fact, they were free to implement or not, unless their non-compliance was so flagrant as to call it to the attention of administrative superiors. Organizationally impotent, teachers enjoyed substantial autonomy in delivering educational services to the client. This is not to say that they were not, if the occasion arose, subservient to administrators. Indeed, most teachers believed that the administration or central office was more capable of making pedagogical decisions than teachers and that teacher autonomy was no more than a consequence of the ever-increasing growth in size and complexity of the educational enterprise. As districts increased in size, both because of growth and consolidation, supervision became impossible.

However, this same increase in complexity also created an administrative bureaucracy, which in turn created a plethora of regulations that teachers were, at least nominally, expected to follow. As Guthrie puts it: "As school systems grew and came under the dominance of expert managers, teachers lost their ability to communicate freely with their employers, school trustees, or even with the superintendent and his staff."[84]

Alienation from work, as a consequence of bureaucratic expansion, contributed to the collectivization of teaching and the systematic redirection of individual classroom authority. At the same time that implementation became less individualized, it also began to feed more systematically into the policy proposal phase of governance.

TEACHERS BARGAINING COLLECTIVELY   It is true that money is the primary issue when teachers bargain collectively. Written agreements, which now govern more than half of the nation's public school teachers, also frequently specify working conditions.[85] Both these bread and butter items, which have quite properly been regarded as belonging to the implementation phase, have obvious policy implications. Money obviously affects policy formation, even if teachers are not (and they typically are not) involved in district-wide budget-making. Additionally, however, working conditions may be linked, at least indirectly, to policy implementation. Thus, for instance, some contracts include under working conditions the controversial topic of teacher evaluation. Finally, a growing number of contracts are overtly policy-oriented. For instance, contracts increasingly provide for teacher representation on groups that set curricular policy, select textbooks, and recommend educational programs.

It seems likely that overtly policy-linked items will increase in their negotiability. Corwin, for instance, has concluded that a desire for more influence over school policy and disagreement with central level decision-making seems to account for most of the dissatisfaction underlying increased teacher militancy.[86] The more such demands are granted, the greater will be the escalation of demands for more influence. Ultimately, the entire policy-proposal phase could be encompassed in the bargaining between teacher organization and professional bargainers representing the board and administration.

Such a development would not radically alter the distribution of influence between board and superintendent, but would substantially reduce the now dominant policy-proposal function of the administration. Pierce, for example, argues that, while the demand for lay participation did little to break administrators' control over schools, collective bargaining did quite a lot: "It was not until teachers began to organize and use collective bargaining to gain more control over educational policy that the monopoly of the school administration began to crumble."[87] An important point is that the challenge of collective bargaining not only threatens administrative dominance, it also reduces even further whatever policy initiation remains with school boards.

Although, as we have noted, collective bargaining agreements are laden with policy, they are normally regarded as personnel negotiations and then conducted privately. Public disclosure of bargaining positions or strategies is an unfair labor practice. Hence, not only is public scrutiny impossible, the board and superintendent find it necessary to hire a negotiator. Neither administration nor board members can follow the proceedings. Both may lose control of policy under such circumstances, allowing policy proposal functions to be assumed by people without any vestige of public accountability.

Although collective bargaining obviously is a major problem for school districts, it is a problem so concealed from public or board scrutiny that no accountability is feasible. In our study of eleven school districts, we searched in vain for any discussion of collective bargaining at board or administrative cabinet meetings. When administration assumed control of policy, there was at least the possibility of board veto, although veto rarely occurred. Now, even such weak constraints are removed. Policy and implementation, once blurred because nominally administrative implementation made policy, is further blurred because nominal delivery agents are acquiring policy responsibilities. Thus, the chain of accountability is further weakened.

Review

The final step in the policy-making process is review and evaluation of past decisions and programs. Of necessity, review must follow implementation. But as we shall see, the review process is continuous, and for some actors is concurrent with other steps in the policy-making process. Internal review is undertaken by school board members and district employees. External review involved participation by those outside the governmental unit.

INTERNAL REVIEW   There are two major types of internal review: executive review and legislative review. Most executive review occurs within the context of the executive recommendation step, with participation limited to school district administrators. This process is personified in most large districts by an administrator in charge of research and evaluation. There is also an ongoing process of executive review in the context of policy implementation management. On the micro level, principals review the performances of teachers. On the macro level, superintendents meet with their cabinets to assess district-wide programs.

Evaluation involves comparing actual performance with an expected performance or goal. The summary goal of public schools is to educate children. There are, however, a number of indicators of success, such as enrollments, promotions, test scores, and student-teacher ratios, as well as indicators relating benefits to costs. Furthermore, because many evaluation indicators are technical or extremely detailed, they are difficult for the untrained and uninitiated to interpret.

Legislative review occurs within the context of the legislative action step. Because school board members are part-time, amateur, and voluntary, they have neither the time nor the expertise to carry on an effective review and evaluation program. The time lag between legislative authorization, implementation, and assessment often spans several years and several school boards, which further impedes the effectiveness of legislative review in school districts.

State legislatures are increasingly turning to outside experts to help them review and evaluate programs. There does not seem to be a parallel trend in school districts. School boards do not have staff research support and have not secured experts independent of executive employees to aid them in the review process. School boards have relied on their own limited expertise and the expertise of lay people from the public who attend meetings and contact them in private. As a result, legislative review is weak in school districts.

EXTERNAL REVIEW   External review of school district policies involves actors from other governments. As we have seen, participation of representatives of other governments is extremely rare. However, as the popular and professional administrative literature attests, this participation is extremely important when it does occur. Although external review can come from the executive and judicial branches of state and federal government, judicial review is presently of greater concern to school districts.

Ironically, judicial review is, in a sense, much less isolated from the general public than are the steps in the policy-making process that occur entirely within the school districts. The courts are always responsive to the extent that suits are either accepted for consideration or rejected; those accepted are subject to decision. The courts cannot table, bury in committee, ignore, or otherwise avoid the matters they accept for consideration. Though gaining a place on the judicial agenda may be difficult, those who do so are assured that some timely action will be taken.

The well-known result is that minority groups, whose limited access and success in local school districts reduces incentive to participate at that level of government, have requested the intervention of state and federal authorities on their behalf. Certainly the issue of equality of educational opportunity looms large in the review process. Not only is the maze of litigation surrounding federally mandated busing a prominent example of this issue, but the litigation involving finance also reflects this concern. The defense in such cases usually invokes the principle of local control as a justification for not achieving equal educational opportunity. Indeed, local control has even achieved statutory legitimacy.

Title IV of the Elementary and Secondary Education Act states, "the school . . . is most effective when the school involves the people of that community in a program designed to fulfill their education needs." But, to date, the principle of equality of opportunity has taken precedence over that of local control. Local options have given way to standardized procedures and programs enforced by the courts.

The other most conspicuous public debate, involves the *Serano* and *Rodrigues* decisions. In *Serano* v. *Priest* (California 1971) property taxes were ruled inherently unconstitutional according to the state constitution. The California State constitution requires equal education, and property taxes had allowed rich districts to spend more. However, in *Rodrigues* v. *San Antonio Independent School District* (1973), the U.S. Supreme Court ruled that property taxes do not violate the equal protection clause of the Fourteenth Amendment to the U.S. Constitution. The impact of *Serano* was widely viewed as one of threatening local control, while *Rodrigues* was viewed as restoring local control. In fact, the former interpretation is more accurate. Federal courts are certainly likely to avoid school finance issues since *Rodrigues*, but state courts are not. Additionally, the impact of both decisions is likely to shift the burden of financial reform to the state legislature, which can expect its remedies to be subject to judicial review. Thus, continued litigation concerning educational equality will have the effect of removing the local board (and even the superintendent) from the policy process.

The thrust of legal challenges, whether financial or with regard to racial imbalance, is against local participation. Because the largest source of school revenue is local property taxes, wealthy districts can spend more than poor districts. Thus, equality of financial resources for education can only be achieved by statewide distribution programs. Further, because the wealth of states varies substantially, the goal of equality may ultimately require a national system of school finance. As state and federal governments assume more control over financing education, opportunity for local populations to influence educational policy by voting for or against budgets will diminish, as will the opportunity for local administrators to set budgetary priorities.

The courts seem to be moving toward an unrealistic separation of policy-making and spending. The two clearly cannot be separated, and the policy implications of reduced local control of spending priorities are conspicuous. Further, there is a spillover effect from increased litigation. Administrators, finding their districts involved in litigation, can seek judicial remedies for board action viewed as unreasonable. Thus, cases of superintendents successfully challenging a board decision not to renew their contracts and lower level administrators challenging similar decisions (especially those involving reassignment) are becoming more prevalent. The upshot is that judicial review weakens the policy-making authority of all officials at the local level. Additionally, minority groups, who correctly perceive more access to nonlocal (federal) decision arenas, use the review process to augment their influence. Such augmentation, achieved at the expense of local officials, further ensures their insulation.

Summary

We have used a six-step model of school district governance to examine the role of six potential types of participants in the policy-making process. Different actors are eligible to participate at different steps; and the process is least insulated, in theory, from those outside the school district establishment at the proposal development and legislative action steps. However, few outsiders do participate directly. Furthermore, at each step in the policy-making process, administrators—especially superintendents—dominate school board members. Empirical data support neither a traditional model of governance from democratic theory, nor a democratic model of administrative representation. Again, the answer to the question, Who governs public schools? is superintendents and their professional staffs.

Such a conclusion is, certainly, not without exceptions. Superintendents have to manage conflict, and some fail. Hence, superintendent turnover is a topic attracting increasing attention. Still, the fact that superintendents can be (and are) removed does not negate our argument. Indeed, the mere fact that the only solution to superintendent dominance is removal is testimony to our argument. The belief that boards should either support or remove superintendents poses extreme alternatives for boards and makes a normal bargaining process even more difficult. Superintendents spend less than four hours per week in private communications with boards, hardly indicative of a sustained process of negotiation and compromise.

More effective challenges to administrative dominance are likely to come from efficiently organized teachers and, especially, from forces originating from outside the local district. Such challenges, however, only exacerbate the insulation of educational policy-making from community politics.

SOME POLICY ISSUES

THE NATURE of the issue to be resolved is, as we have argued, a crucial variable. The currency of the expert applies only when the issue is technical; hence superintendents try to define all issues as technical. We can contrast the resource-utilization process of boards and superintendents in two areas: curriculum, which is generally regarded as technical, and racial conflict, which, from the point of view of nearly everyone but the superintendent, is not technical.

Curriculum Development

Concerning curriculum, the American Association of School Administrators is unequivocal:

> Curriculum planning and development is a highly technical task which requires special training. . . . Board members do not have and cannot be expected to have the technical competence to pass on the work of expert teachers in this field. . . . Nor can the board pass upon specific textbooks.[88]

Obviously, such claims for a scientific curriculum run into occasional trouble. The perennial battles over sex education and new math bear witness to the fact that even the most allegedly scientific issue can arouse passions. Further, curriculum decisions are faddish. As Kirst and Walker note, when immigration was a national issue, "Americanization" was a curriculum goal.[89] Since World War II, when various forms of totalitarian government have challenged American international superiority, "democracy" has been the focus. When Sputnik wounded American pride, math and science became the objects of curriculum reform. Nevertheless, curriculum issues rarely become weighted with emotional content sufficient to plunge them into a community-wide conflict.

Although no national governmental units establish curriculum, the curriculum of public schools is remarkably similar, largely because of the influence of private accrediting associations. These agencies, though private, have universal influence with administrators because they can assert the imprimatur of professional support for a curriculum, thus helping to neutralize potential board level opposition. National testing services also constrain local initiative, because schools strive to best the national norm by emphasizing subjects that testing services deem important.[90] University entrance requirements and state departments of education also influence curriculum, again limiting local options.[91] There is, in brief, a well-integrated curriculum establishment beyond the reach of local school officials or publics. With the entry of the National Science Foundation, U.S. Office of Education, and Office of Economic Opportunity into the curriculum business, further nationalization is occurring.

Nationalization of interest-group activity parallels the nationalization of curriculum policy. Local interest groups do not view curriculum as a salient issue.[92] The Council for Basic Education, a group stressing the traditional curriculum, is almost never seen locally. Other organizations—the NAACP, AFL-CIO, John Birch Society—are only occasionally concerned. As Kirst and Walker observe: "These not specifically educational interest groups would probably be relatively weak forces in normal policy-making, but extremely powerful in crisis policy-making."[93] The professional strategy is, naturally, to exclude groups rather than compete with them. Further, lay knowledge of curriculum is minimal. Numerous polls have revealed that the members of the public know almost nothing about the substance of education. Discipline bothers the lay community, but curriculum does not. However, although the public is ignorant of the control of education, there is evidence that they would like to know more, but are not frequently given access to information: "there is great interest in the very areas that most school publicity neglects—the content of courses and the educational process. . . ."[94]

The evidence suggests, then, that curriculum experts prevent the development of external or episodic issues by reducing the flow of information to potentially active publics.[95] Curriculum issues are clearly a reservoir for episodic issues.[96] Children are sacred objects; the possibility of conflict is always present. School boards do not fare any better than individuals or organizations. As we have seen, they have been declared incompetent and usually accept this judgment. Election campaigns, as bland as they are, almost never emphasize curriculum and rarely initiate discussions of it during board meetings: "research has shattered the myth of lay control of schools . . . in the area of curriculum."[97]

Superintendents and their staffs, then, are (except as they feel intimidated by nonlocal sources) unchallenged in curriculum policy-making. The curriculum-centered bureaucracy is expanding: even small districts are hiring curriculum specialists, and courses in curriculum planning are increasing in colleges of education. Thus, not only boards and interest groups are excluded; in most cases teachers who are not curriculum specialists are uninvolved. In more bureaucratically complex school systems, even the superintendent defers to the experts.

Racial Conflict

Racial conflict is the "external" issue *par excellence.* One is tempted to describe racial conflicts as episodic, but in this case the episodic has become almost routine. The racial issue in public education has always been a question of how the school system will respond to external demands. The court system, followed belatedly by Congress and the U.S. Office of Education, has required that schools achieve integration, even if pupils must be bused from one school to another. The issue is one that superintendents and school board members would not have raised; it is one to which they have no option but to respond. It arouses fierce antagonism, propels interest groups into the educational policy-making process, and provides little opportunity for professional resources to be exchanged. Racial problems, along with financing schools, stimulate more intense interest-group activity than do any other issues.[98] Unlike most issues, furthermore, the federal government is—through the judicial system—providing a serious challenge to the insularity of school systems. Superintendents see federal intervention as a seriously disruptive force, even more of a threat than militant civil rights organizations.[99]

Crain's explanation for the superintendent's reluctance to engage the problem is persuasive. Because of various factors linked to recruitment and professional image, superintendents are likely to reject the demands of civil rights groups without consulting the boards.[100] Their reaction to racial strife is to treat it as a normal issue. They assert themselves to be color blind, stress a narrow definition of the function of schools as educational rather than social, and stress the illegitimacy of the claims of external groups.[101] In short, they try to use their traditional resources, defining the issue in such a way that they are likely to maintain their authority by reason of their expertise. When confronted with demands by civil rights organizations, superintendents react in hostile self-defense not so much because of racial bias but because they "literally do not speak the same language."[102] Thus, what the administration might want to treat as a routine matter balloons into a confrontation when the resources of the superintendent have no value.[103] The more hostile superintendents become, the more expensive becomes the conflict.

As the superintendent loses control of the conflict, the school board increases its power and ultimately takes the responsibility for racial policy away from the superintendent. Crain identifies, in most cases, a point when "the major decision which most influences the outcome of the integration issue was made not by the superintendent but by the board."[104] It seems that in issues where expertise is not a useful commodity, superintendents do not have either political resources or political skills to fall back on.

THE PAST
AND THE FUTURE

AS WE watch the civic disarray associated with federally mandated busing unfold, we are led to ask the questions: What is wrong? Why does government policy clearly contradict expressed public desires? In short, why is government unresponsive? These are hardly new questions. They have been asked each time the public education system is made the object of public scrutiny.

According to popular analysis—as reported by the various media providing coverage of the most recent outbreaks of violence in Boston and Louisville—parental objections to busing are generated by a perceived loss of control over the education of their children. However, our thesis is that, whatever parents may believe, the process whereby parents lost control of education began well before the current dispute over busing. It may be true, of course, that the helplessness of parents first became obvious to them when the buses began to roll. Indeed, a more dramatic demonstration of political impotence can hardly be imagined. However, we believe it is helpful to view the process of parental political disenfranchisement as one that has occurred in phases. Accordingly, we offer the following sketch of what has happened to American education: Phase 1, the first period of "maximum feasible participation" (circa 1835 to circa 1900); Phase 2, the period of "reform" and "efficiency," (1900 to circa 1968); Phase 3, the period in which the school became viewed as an agent of social and economic change (1954 to 1975); and, finally, Phase 4, which started in 1975, and by its end the aspirations of Phase 3 will be proven unachievable, albeit laudable. We will argue that the loss of control currently being protested actually began at the beginning of Phase 2, the period of reform, at the turn of the century.

Phase 1:
Lay Control

During Phase 1, the control (actual as well as legal) of American education rested, in general, with local boards of education. Furthermore, in Phase 1, community members had substantial opportunity to interact with and influence the members of their boards of education for several reasons. First, there were more school boards at that time. As late as 1930 there were approximately 130,000 independent school districts; now there are about 15,000. Because each school district had a school board—many districts even had multiple boards—the opportunity for participation by either holding office or voting was substantial in Phase 1.

Second, there were more school board members per district during Phase 1. For example, in 1895 there were 28 cities with populations of 100,000 or more. These 28 cities had a total of 603 central school board members, an average of 21.5 per city. In addition, some of the larger cities had hundreds of neighborhood boards. By 1913 (Phase 2), the 28 cities had only 264 central school board members, an average of 10.2 per city, and neighborhood boards had been abolished. Finally, in Phase 1 most school boards were elected on a ward basis and were, by today's standards, decentralized. Each school board member had an unambiguous constituency to represent and be held accountable by. By 1913 most board members were elected at large. Neighborhoods had lost their spokesmen because, according to reformers' plans, school board members were to be responsive to a much larger and heterogeneous constituency.

Although patterns of school governance varied considerably, especially with regard to the problem of division of labor between central and ward boards, it is a fair generalization to say that lay boards ran the schools. Most school board members believed their responsibility to be that of the *administration* of schools. In larger cities, these duties were shared between central and ward boards. In such cities, the central boards were frequently subdivided into smaller committees to manage specialized tasks (such as curriculum and finance).

ORIGIN OF THE SUPERINTENDENT POSITION   As school systems increased in size—partially because of the rapid influx of immigrant groups—lay boards found that they could not effectively keep up with the day-to-day operation of schools, such as checking attendance and recording examinations. They reasoned that they were quite capable of performing such routine tasks, but simply lacked the time. Thus they generally appointed superintendents. However, the superintendent's responsibilities were usually strictly clerical (many superintendents still retain the title "superintendent-clerk") and did not involve participation in such policy decisions as staffing and curriculum. Clearly, the norm of active lay administration was powerful.

It is a well-known axiom of politics that ward-based electoral systems favor the lower or working classes because they generally live in distinct sections of a city. By providing each section with a representative, an elected body can become more representative. That is, its social composition is a relatively accurate reflection of the composition of the city as a whole. Such appears to be the case with school boards in Phase 1. Some scholars have argued that the working class had captured many city wards by the 1880s. In Pittsburgh, for example, the school system consisted of thirty-eight subdistrict boards. Each board possessed authority to levy taxes and to appoint administrative and teaching personnel. The central board, composed of one representative from each subdistrict, was virtually powerless. An analysis of the social composition of the subdistrict boards indicates that the socioeconomic status of board members was roughly congruent with the status of the people of the subdistrict they represented.

RESPONSIVENESS   In addition to achieving representation, Phase 1 boards were responsive to a greater extent than is true today. Ward boards governed areas small enough to permit personal attention to problems. To modern readers familiar with the late 1960s argument for community control, such a system may seem ideal. A lay board, responsible to a small constituency, able to give personal attention to individual needs, governed education. Who could object?

Reformers objected, and the reform movement in urban politics (Phase 2) marked the beginning of the decline of lay control. Before turning to Phase 2, we should note that the reformers' objections to the nineteenth-century pattern of community control were not without substance. The ward-board electoral system shared all the advantages and disadvantages of the urban political machines of the era. Urban machines, in performing the function of integrating the millions of immigrants into political life, rewarded votes with jobs. Because most local school districts were coterminous with municipal wards, there was naturally a substantial amount of patronage in awarding teaching and administrative positions.

The currency of political machines was patronage, and in those cities in which machines dominated school politics, patronage played a major role in the schools. On the positive side, political machines were acutely sensitive to the potential alienation of the various ethnic minorities that formed the majority coalition. In New York, Boss Tweed's ward board of education, for example, did not bother to enforce Protestant values in Catholic neighborhoods, allowed the various native tongues to be taught, and removed textbooks that contained alleged slurs about immigrant groups. Tweed's school system sounds like the promised land to modern critics who decry the loss of cultural identity among minority groups.

On the negative side, machines were—as the reformers charged—corrupt. They siphoned off funds from building contracts, awarded contracts on the basis of political influence rather than competitive bidding, allowed bribery by textbook salesmen, and in general behaved like machines are alleged to have behaved. Teachers had to pay machine functionaries for positions, and academic qualifications played a minor role. Thus, school politics, like the machine politics of the urban area of which it was a part, provided responsiveness *and* corruption. Nevertheless, school policy-making reflected the values of the subgroups within the community. In working-class areas, working-class values prevailed. In upper-class areas, upper-class values prevailed. In any case, the people, for better or worse, were not excluded from making educational policy.

Phase 2: Control by Local Professionals

As was discussed in chapter 2, the political reform movement that began around the beginning of the twentieth century can be accurately described as one of WASP elite response to lay control. By fostering major structural changes in the governing structure of education, the movement was consciously designed to reduce lay responsibility for education. It was clearly a class-based movement to shift the response of schools from laymen to experts, and it succeeded.

THE GROWTH OF EDUCATIONAL PROFESSIONALISM   To return to one of the points with which this section began, the loss of parental control lamented in 1975 began long before busing, and was in fact almost complete by the 1920s. However, the enemy of local control during the years of Phase 2 was not the federal government, but rather the growth of educational professionalism within the local community. Lay control was first assaulted by professionalism, and only later by state and national bureaucracies.

The reform movement's major structural modifications were (1) the centralization of school administration, to be accomplished both by the destruction of the authority of community boards and by merging small districts into larger ones, (2) the substitution of a smaller central board, elected at large, for the large, ward-based central board, (3) the election of board members by nonpartisan ballots, and (4) the separation of board elections from other municipal and state elections. The major philosophical thrust behind these structural changes was to substitute scientific management for political influence. Thus, a necessary corollary for the structural changes was an expansion of the role of the superintendent, to be achieved by a contraction of the role of the board. Reliance on experts, then, played as large a role in the reform movement as the structural modification to reduce the influence of political machines.

If the political machines, with their strong immigrant base, were designed to give power to the people, the upper-class response was to provide power to *their* people. Though some reformers couched their bias against the lower classes in phrases such as efficiency, others were quite open in their assertion that only successful people should serve on school boards. Such people, presumably from businesses and professions, could be expected to defer to the expertise of the superintendent.

Indeed, an essential ingredient to the understanding of Phase 2 is the growth of the superintendency as the major source of educational decision-making.

SUPERINTENDENTS: FROM CLERKS TO POLICY-MAKERS   To understand how superintendents moved from clerks to dominant policy-makers, we first need to note the dramatic shift in the composition of boards of education. Not only did they become fewer and smaller; they also lost the representative character typical of Phase 1. In St. Louis, reformers were successful in persuading the Missouri legislature to press a new charter designating the nonpartisan at-large election of twelve (as compared to twenty-eight) school board members. The purpose of this new charter—a purpose that soon became the keynote of the school reform movement—was to take the schools out of politics—that is, to remove the influence of the machine. The charter was approved in 1897. In 1896, professionals and businessmen constituted 14 percent of the board; in 1897 they constituted 83 percent of the board. By 1927, the year of the first systematic national survey of the origins of board members, the St. Louis pattern was the norm.

Reformers had succeeded in eliminating the working class by substituting the previous politics of patronage with the apolitical politics of upper-class public-regarding behavior. Upper-class domination of school board members meant that 90 percent were male; 96 percent were white; 70 percent were college graduates; 36 percent earned incomes in excess of $30,000; 66 percent were from business and professional occupations; and 85 percent were Protestant. The reformers had clearly done their work well.

Not only did local boards of education reflect the social biases of the reformers, but their willingness to yield authority to the superintendent, a natural consequence of the business-efficiency orientation of the upper classes, was congruent with the tenets of sound management so clearly a part of the reform ideology. Superintendents moved from clerks to policy-makers because boards wanted them to do so. As the ideological descendant of the reformers, Phase 2 board members were doing a good job; they were leaving the governance to the experts.

But what of the experts? Where did they come from, and how did they become experts? As the reform movement achieved its goals, colleges of education began to produce and distribute experts in educational administration. By 1913 schools of education had become cohesive in their philosophy of education and well connected with urban reformers. A handful of highly influential educators took the lead in developing an ideology of administration, instilling the ideology in the instruction of future superintendents and placing their students in key superintendencies. The key points of the ideology, efficiency, unity (for example, minimization of conflict), and professionalism, were welcomed by upper-class boards. Schools, like businesses, should be managed by experts. By 1920, the norm of school board nonparticipation in administration had become so pervasive that superintendents protested lay influence, which would have been customary before the turn of the century, as encroachment.

CONTINUING ACQUIESCENCE OF THE BOARDS   As schools grew larger and more complex, an administrative structure equal to the task was generated. First, the boards acquiesced in the superintendent's influence; then boards acquiesced in the superintendent's delegation of authority to middle-level administrators. The expert appointed more experts. Boards of education found nothing objectionable. By the 1960s, the average school district employed 150 administrators. This professional staff administers the largest and most costly governmental activity in most communities, and consequently the position of the superintendent is, in comparison to his local counterparts, visible and prestigious. By way of contrast, most people cannot name anything their school board has done in the last year. Most do not identify the board as responsible for public representation within the school system, and a substantial minority (44 percent) do not think school boards have legal authority over school administrators.

Such confusion is reflected in the behavior of board members. Most board members do not view their role as representing, or speaking for the public: rather they view their role as speaking *for* the administration *to* the public. Such views are a natural consequence of reform. Lacking a constituency (as a consequence of at-large elections) and lacking a systematic recruitment mechanism (as a consequence of nonpartisanship), they are normally recruited through the civic-business elite, sometimes by the existing board. They view their service as one of the civic responsibilities of the guardian class. Because in most cases boards have no independent staff, the agenda for meetings is set by the administration. Setting the agenda is a highly significant political function, as it defines what is to be decided. It is therefore not surprising that school boards solicit and defer to policy recommendations from superintendents. School boards typically enact policies suggested by their professional staff in over 90 percent of the recorded votes. Such a percentage of success would be the envy of any president, governor, or mayor.

STABILITY THE GOAL   The bureaucratic system that characterized Phase 2 worked quite well as long as the goals of education were
narrowly defined. When the shift from Phase 1 to Phase 2 began, the
basic problem to be solved by educational planners was the homogeniza-
tion of an immigrant population, to infuse it with a consistent set of
values, to reduce conflict—in short, to manufacture a cohesive society.
The problem was comparable to the problem of new nations of today:
how to create a nation from disparate groups with only a tenuous identification with the concept of a nation. In this situation, it was
reasonable to replace community control of schools, which did not
homogenize, with a central administration, which could. As the late V.
O. Key remarked, "All national educational systems indoctrinate the
oncoming generation with the basic outlook and values of the political
order."[105]

The goal of Phase 2 was stability, not social change. Thus, the schools,
as agents of the transmission of knowledge, culture, and social norms,
became conservative in that they served the function of maintaining the
social order. However, in the last stages of Phase 2, new demands (and
revivals of old demands) were placed on schools. From the federal
government came the demand (beginning with *Brown* v. *Board of
Education* in 1954, but not achieving full articulation until the mid-
1960s) that schools serve as agents of social change. Minority populations within local communities demanded that schools be responsive.
These demands ultimately took the form of the quest for community
control, and hence were not new; they were an inadvertent plea for a
return to Phase 1. (Ironically, teachers vigorously resisted demands for
community control. They had resisted with equal vigor the abolition of
community schools by the reformers.)

Phase 3:
Nationalization

During the twilight of Phase 2 the radical critiques of educational
bureaucracy reached fever pitch. The proliferation of books critical of
education achieved saturation level before tapering off in the early
1970s. As Phase 2 drew to a close, two irreconcilable sets of demands
were being placed on schools: that they serve as agents of social change,
and that they return the schools to the people. To meet the latter goal
was to deny the former, as the major thrust for social change has never
originated locally. In both sets of demands, however, the dominance of
the superintendent was threatened.

As it turns out, the federal government proved more difficult for schools to resist than minority groups. The federal government was not interested in a shift in the structure of school governance, but in a transformation of the primary goal of public education. The federal government decided to use schools as instruments to achieve economic equality.

EROSION OF LOCAL AUTHORITY   Phase 3, then, is characterized by an erosion of the legal authority of the local school administration by the imposition of federal (and occasionally state) mandates. To place the problem in perspective, the consequence of Phase 2 was a loss of lay control to the local superintendent who then, during Phase 3, lost control to extralocal units of government.

The intervention of the federal government in education has had a consistent pattern, whether the source of the intervention is the courts, the Congress, or the Department of Health, Education and Welfare. The national government has intervened to increase the educational, and by inference economic, opportunity of deprived populations. In becoming the spokesmen for the underprivileged, the national government was responding to demands that local schools in Phase 2 could not meet. Deliberately designed as nonresponsive and insulated, they had little communication with established spokesmen of undereducated populations. As perpetuators of the status quo, schools had a vested interest in preferential education. Hence the federal government, the traditional defender of the downtrodden against the conservatism of local community power structures, took the role of advocacy for the underdog.

Though the immediate effects of the 1954 *Brown* decision (separate but equal facilities were ruled unconstitutional) were largely symbolic, they eventually contributed greatly to the black sense of self-esteem and to a growing dissatisfaction with the discrepancy between the stated purpose of the *Brown* decision and the reality of continued segregation. In addition to providing the stimulus for more radical black movements, the *Brown* decision shifted the arena of conflict and decision from local to national government. Henceforth, school administration devoted an increasing amount of energy into legal defense before federal courts. With each adverse decision they lost the power accumulated during Phase 2.

Local (that is, administrative) authority was further constrained by the establishment of desegregation guidelines in 1965 and 1966 by the Department of Health, Education and Welfare. Legal action initiated by HEW and the Justice Department established a highly visible base of federal influence. But even more important were the widespread but less publicized disputes over implementation between local districts and the mammoth HEW bureaucracy. The federal bureaucracy involved itself still further with the passage of the Elementary and Secondary Education Act of 1965 (ESEA), which doubled the federal contribution to educational funding and placed a strong monetary emphasis upon its concern with equality of educational opportunity. ESEA provided grants to local schools to meet the needs of "educationally deprived children" (Title I) and grants for "supplementary education centers and services" (Title III).

ESEA implementation created a new pattern of interaction that made the notion of lay control through school boards obsolete. To compete for Title I and Title III grants, local schools felt compelled to hire more administrators to establish and maintain the programs. Thus, the local bureaucracy expanded to do business with a national bureaucracy. It is estimated that 25 percent of Title I and Title III money was spent on administrative salaries. In one urban district, the size of the administrative staff tripled between 1966 and 1975, while the number of students and staff remained constant. Relationships between the new sets of local and HEW bureaucrats were cordial; the influx of federal funds was welcome. For example, although audits have revealed gross misuse of Title I grants, such funds were rarely withheld. Because of this misuse of funds, national interest groups who spoke for the underprivileged threatened legal action. Once again, administrators began to prepare their defense; once again the school board became an irrelevant appendage. The game was being played in another ballpark.

THE BUSING CONTROVERSY   The issues in Title I were those of compensatory education, a concept which had guided most federal efforts. However, at the same time, the efficacy of compensatory education was severely challenged by the Coleman Report.[106] The assumption behind ESEA (and indeed the assumption underlying any intervention on the part of the undereducated) was that improving the quality of educational services (for example, by reducing teacher-pupil ratio or increasing library resources) affected the achievement of students and, ultimately, their economic opportunities. The *Brown* decision might have gone the other way if it could have been demonstrated that separate facilities were not inherently unequal. Blacks wanted to go to previously all-white schools because they thought their economic opportunities would be enhanced if they received the same education as whites. ESEA was based upon an assumption that, even if integration did not occur as rapidly as was hoped, compensatory education would fill the void.

The Coleman Report revealed, however, that differences in school facilities and curriculum were not related to the achievement of students. Logically, therefore, increased expenditures and the various innovations supported by Title III of ESEA were pointless. The most important single factor affecting achievement was family background *and the family background of fellow students.* Further analysis revealed that black children attending predominantly black schools had lower achievement scores and lower aspirations than black students *with comparable family backgrounds* who attended predominantly white schools. The policy implications were clear. The only way to improve the educational and hence economic opportunities of blacks was to assign them forcibly to middle-class white schools, or to assign middle-class whites to black schools, or both.

Thus began the busing controversy. The leading advocate of busing was the U.S. Civil Rights Commission. Executive and legislative support ranged from neutral to obstructionist. However, the legal argument was sound and court-ordered busing began along with the attendant violence and protests. There was no point in protesting to the superintendent, who could do nothing, so parents tried to influence the federal bureaucracy and courts. They finally emulated the blacks of the 1960s and took to the streets. Their rhetoric was quite similar to the black demands of the late 1960s: Give us back our schools. However, as we have seen, this demand was three-quarters of a century too late.

FINANCING EDUCATION   Authority over school desegregation had been preempted from local school districts by the federal government. Other factors contributed to the nationalization of schools during Phase 3. Successful challenges to local finance are becoming more frequent, although the issue is far from resolved. The thrust of these challenges uses the same rationale that underlies compensatory education. Because the largest source of school revenue is local property taxes (about 50 percent), wealthy districts can spend more per pupil than poor districts. Thus, equality of financial resources for education can only be achieved by statewide redistribution programs. Furthermore, because the wealth of states varies substantially, the goal of nationwide equality of educational opportunity may ultimately require a national system of school finance. As state and federal governments assume more control over financing education, opportunity for local populations to influence educational policy by voting for or against budgets will diminish, as will the opportunity for local administrators to set budgetary priorities.

COLLECTIVE BARGAINING   Local administrators are experiencing an additional constriction of influence by the escalation of collective bargaining agreements between teachers' associations and administrations. Such agreements are being expanded to include not only salary, but also course content, curriculum change procedures, teachers' evaluation, community participation, teaching procedures, and grievance procedure. As such agreements become more prevalent, the range of issues left for even the superintendent to discuss with the board will diminish. As the professional associations expand their collective voice, they are also moving to increase teachers' organizational roles in certification. Again, the authority of the superintendent is reduced.

Phase 4:
the Social Goal

Our sketch of the history of education in America has advanced the thesis that the pattern of authority over schools has changed in response to an expanding mandate given to public education. The mandate in Phase 1 was to pursue limited educational goals that would enable individuals to function in their small communities. Administration was the province of local lay school boards that were representative of their communities. The mandate was expanded in Phase 2: schools must provide skills and values necessary to construct a homogeneous, larger society. Administrative responsibility shifted to local professionals who had the alleged expertise to achieve this goal. The mandate in Phase 3 was expanded further: schools must provide a basis for nationwide economic equality, or at least equal economic opportunity. A corps of national educational professionals has grown in size and authority as a result of this most ambitious social goal.

There is a supreme irony about the struggle for influence during Phase 3. Despite the Coleman Report's conclusion—admittedly subject to many interpretations—that schools and individual achievement are unrelated, the contestants in the struggle continue to assume that they are. The evidence which has been gradually accumulating strongly implies that using schools as agents of social change, specifically for the equalization of economic opportunity, cannot be successful. In 1972, Jencks's analysis concluded that school reform "cannot bring about significant social changes outside the schools."[107] Jencks explicitly addressed the goal of equal economic opportunity. Boudon offered the astonishing conclusion that "educational growth as such has the effect of increasing rather than decreasing social and economic inequality, even in the case of an educational system that becomes more equalitarian."[108]

If these researchers are right—and we believe that they are—Phase 3 was misguided. If schools cannot serve as agents of social change, then the philosophical underpinnings of the federal intervention are flawed. What, then, for the future?

The first issue that must be resolved is the status of the social goal of economic equality. If we retain the social goal, there are two options:

1. Accept the judgment that schools as now constituted cannot reduce inequality of economic opportunity, but also assume that they could if they were allowed to expand their sphere of control over the child. Specifically, schools would have to combat the disabling effects of class and family by assuming more control over the child at an earlier age. Formal schooling would have to begin as soon as cognitively feasible, and the role of the family would have to be minimized. School administration would, of necessity, be conducted at the national level by educational professionals.

2. Accept the judgment that schools cannot reduce inequality of economic opportunity and abandon them as a means to this end. The goal could be achieved by several other means. We could establish political controls over economic institutions, a process normally referred to as socialism. Alternatively, we could simply reduce actual inequality by legislative fiat. For instance, Congress could legislate that no individual can receive less than $10,000 or more than $50,000 in annual income, and institute a system of reverse taxation to achieve this goal, bypassing the process of education entirely.

If we retain the social goal and insist on achieving it through the schools the consequence for school governance is increased centralization of decision locus and expansion of authority. If, however, we either abandon the social goal or abandon schools as the means of achieving it, several options for school governance are possible:

1. We can retain the primacy of professional educational standards, while increasing the importance of local concerns by returning to Phase 2. We can return the superintendent and local educational professionals to their former positions of influence and accept minimal parental control of the educational process.

2. We can regard schooling as an end in itself and seek to make it as pleasant as possible for the student and parents. One way this can be achieved is by undoing the work of the reformers—that is, halt centralization and professionalization and return the schools to the conditions that existed prior to 1900. The result would be community control.

3. Another option is to assume that, though education is a public good and hence subject to public finance, the content and process of education are private matters. Thus, a system of vouchers could be instituted. Every parent could be given a governmental education voucher to be used for the child's education in any school, freely chosen by parents. Schools that could not successfully compete for vouchers would be closed. Private choice would thus be substituted for public choice. The result would be individual control.

American education is in an untenable position because Phase 3 governance cannot achieve its mandate. Whether the goal of economic equality is retained or abandoned, a change in the pattern of control over education seems inevitable. The options range from extreme centralization to maximum individual control. However, in no case should the choice be clouded by unrealistic expectations about what formal education can accomplish.

CONCLUSION

ALTHOUGH THIS chapter has been limited to educational policy, its message has wide applications. First, the finding that participation is constrained applies in all policy areas and all levels of government. Second, the pattern of executive domination over both laymen and other governmental actors can be found in municipal and state governments as well as in school districts. Third, the erosion of local authority and the imposition of state and federal mandates that originated in educational policy are now manifest in virtually all policy areas. The phenomenon of centralization affects states as well as school districts, municipalities, and other local governments. The experience in education is likely to serve as a precedent in other policy areas.

These three factors act to inhibit state and local governments from being responsive to their constituents in terms of either the representational or congruence models. Low public participation prevents the communication of demands and expectations necessary for responsiveness. Executive domination over laymen and legislative representatives makes expressions of public preferences irrelevant. The transfer of authority from local to central levels of governments makes local response to local demands impossible. These and other barriers to state and local government responsiveness are the subject of the next chapter.

NOTES

1.

David Easton, "An Approach to the Analysis of Political Systems," *World Politics* 9 (1957): 383–400; and Harmon Zeigler and G. Wayne Peak, "The Political Functions of the Educational System," *Sociology of Education* (1970): 115–42.

2.

NIE Planning Unit, *Program Planning Notes from the Interim Report of NIE Planning Unit* (unpublished report, 1972), pp. 10–11.

3.

William G. Walker, *Centralization and Decentralization: An International Viewpoint on an American Dilemma* (Eugene: Center for the Advanced Study of Educational Administration, University of Oregon, 1972).

4.

Anthony Downs, *Inside Bureaucracy* (Boston: Little, Brown, 1967), pp. 167–68.

5.

R. E. Agger, D. Goldrich, and B. E. Swanson, *The Rulers and the Ruled: Political Power and Impotence in American Communities* (New York: Wiley, 1964), p. 45.

6.

Roscoe C. Martin, *Government and the Suburban School* (Syracuse, N.Y.: Syracuse University Press, 1962), p. 61.

7.

Reuben Joseph Snow, *Local Experts: Their Roles as Conflict Managers in Municipal and Educational Government* (Evanston, Ill.: Northwestern University Press, 1966); and Martin, *Government and the Suburban School,* p. 62.

8.

David W. Minar, "Community Characteristics, Conflict, and Power Structures," in Robert S. Cahill and Stephen P. Hencley (eds.), *The Politics of Education in the Local Community* (Danville, Ill.: Interstate Printers and Publishers, 1964), pp. 132–33.

9.

Arthur J. Vidich and Joseph Bensman, *Small Town in a Mass Society* (Garden City, N.Y.: Doubleday-Anchor, 1960).

10.

Ralph B. Kimbrough, *Political Power and Educational Decision-Making* (Chicago: Rand-McNally, 1964).

11.
Martin, *Government and the Suburban School,* p. 50.

12.
Minar, "Community Characteristics, Conflict, and Power Structures," p. 141. Italics added.

13.
Robert H. Salisbury, "Schools and Politics in the Big Cities," *Harvard Education Review* 37 (1967): 408–24.

14.
Robert D. Hess and Michael Kirst, "Political Orientation and Behavior Patterns: Linkages Between Teachers and Children," *Education and Urban Society* 3 (1971): 453–77.

15.
Harmon Zeigler and Michael Baer, *Lobbying: Interaction and Influence in American State Legislatures* (Belmont, Calif.: Wadsworth, 1969).

16.
Robert L. Crain, *The Politics of School Desegregation* (Chicago: Aldine, 1968), pp. 115–28.

17.
M. Kent Jennings and Harmon Zeigler, "Response Styles and Politics: The Case of the School Boards," *Midwest Journal of Political Science* 15 (1971): 290–321.

18.
Marilyn Gittell, *Educating an Urban Population* (Beverly Hills, Calif.: Sage Publications, 1967), p. 209.

19.
Michael Lipsky, "Protest as a Political Resource," in Betty H. Zisk (ed.), *American Political Interest Groups: Readings in Theory and Research* (Belmont, Calif.: Wadsworth, 1968); and James Q. Wilson, "The Strategy of Protest: Problems of Negro Civic Action," *Journal of Conflict Resolution* 3 (1961): 291–303.

20.
M. Kent Jennings and Harmon Zeigler, *The Governing of School Districts* (Ann Arbor: Institute for Social Research, University of Michigan Press, 1969), p. 4.

21.
David W. Minar, "The Community Basis of Conflict in School System Politics," *American Sociological Review* 31 (1966): 822–35; and Louis H. Masotti, "Political Integration in Suburban Education Communities," in Scott Greer and others (eds.), *The New Urbanization* (New York: St. Martin's Press, 1968).

22.

M. Kent Jennings and Harmon Zeigler, "Avenues to the School Board and Political Competition," paper read at the American Educational Research Association, Chicago, Illinois, 1972.

23.

Ibid.

24.

Crain, *The Politics of School Desegregation,* p. 196.

25.

Jennings and Zeigler, "Avenues to the School Board and Political Competition."

26.

Ibid., p. 54.

27.

Ibid., p. 29.

28.

Crain, *The Politics of Social Desegregation;* Keith Goldhammer, *The School Board* (New York: The Center for Applied Research in Education, 1964); and Jennings and Zeigler, "Response Styles and Politics."

29.

Richard O. Carlson, *School Superintendents: Careers and Performance* (Columbus, Ohio: Charles E. Merrill, 1972), pp. 7–37; and Crain, *The Politics of School Desegregation,* pp. 116–17.

30.

Ronald G. Corwin, *Staff Conflicts in the Public Schools* (Columbus: Department of Sociology and Anthropology, Ohio State University, 1966); and M. Kent Jennings and Harmon Zeigler, "The Politics of Teacher-Administrator Relations," *Education and Social Science* 1 (1969): 73–82.

31.

Harmon Zeigler, *The Political Life of American Teachers* (Englewood Cliffs, N.J.: Prentice-Hall, 1967).

32.

Burton R. Clark, "Sociology of Education," in Robert E. L. Faris (ed.), *Handbook of Modern Sociology* (Chicago: Rand McNally, 1964), pp. 734–69.

33.

Carlson, *School Superintendents,* p. 9.

34.

Zeigler, *The Political Life of American Teachers,* p. 28; and Julius S. Brown, "Risk Propensity in Decision Making—A Comparison of Business and Public School Administrators," *Administrative Science Quarterly* 15 (1970): 473–81.

35.
Carlson, *School Superintendents,* p. 25.

36.
Crain, *The Politics of School Desegregation,* p. 117.

37.
Ibid.

38.
Martin, *Government and the Suburban School,* p. 89. See also Salisbury, "Schools and Politics in the Big Cities," pp. 408–20.

39.
Jennings and Zeigler, *The Governing of School Districts,* p. 4.

40.
Jennings and Zeigler, "Response Styles and Politics."

41.
Vidich and Bensman, *Small Town in Mass Society,* pp. 194–201.

42.
M. Kent Jennings and Harmon Zeigler, "Interest Representation in School Governance," in Harlan Hahn (ed.), *People and Politics in Urban School Government* (Washington, D.C.: U.S. Office of Education, Cooperative Research Project S-029, 1965).

43.
Ibid., p. 180.

44.
Smoley, *Community Participation in Urban School Government;* Neal Gross, *Who Runs Our Schools?* (New York: Wiley, 1958); and, Jennings and Zeigler, "Interest Representation in School Governance."

45.
Smoley, *Community Participation in Urban School Government,* p. 180.

46.
Harmon Zeigler and M. Kent Jennings, with G. Wayne Peak, *Governing American Schools: Political Interaction in Local School Districts* (North Scituate, Mass.: Duxbury Press, 1974), p. 99.

47.
Laurence Iannaccone, "School Board Conflict is Inevitable," *American School Board Journal* 154 (1967): 5–9; and Alan K. Campbell, "Who Governs the Schools?" *Saturday Review* 64 (1968): 50–52.

48.
Jennings and Zeigler, "Response Styles and Politics" and "Interest Representation in School Governance."

49.

Harry L. Summerfield, "Cuing and the Open System of Educational Politics," *Education and Urban Society* 3 (1971): 425–39.

50.

Jennings and Zeigler, "Interest Representation in School Governance."

51.

James Lipham, Russell T. Gregg, and Richard A. Rossmiller, *The School Board as an Agency for Resolving Conflict* (Bethesda, Md.: Educational Resources Information Center, 1967).

52.

Robert A. Dahl, *Who Governs?* (New Haven, Conn.: Yale University Press, 1961), p. 155; and James D. Koerner, *Who Controls American Education? A Guide for Laymen* (Boston: Beacon Press, 1968), p. 26.

53.

Jennings and Zeigler, "Interest Representation in School Governance."

54.

Daniel E. Griffiths, *Human Relations in School Administration* (New York: Appleton-Century-Crofts, 1956), p. 106.

55.

Alan Rosenthal, *Pedagogues and Power* (Syracuse, N.Y.: Syracuse University Press, 1969), p. 154.

56.

Keith Goldhammer, John E. Suttle, William D. Aldridge, and Gerald Becker, *Issues and Problems in Contemporary Educational Administration* (Eugene, Oregon: Center for the Advanced Study of Educational Administration, 1967).

57.

Corwin, *Staff Conflicts in the Public Schools,* p. 107.

58.

Harmon Zeigler, "Teacher Militancy: An Analysis of the Strike-Prone Teacher," in James E. Bruno (ed.), *Emerging Issues in Education* (Lexington, Mass.: D. C. Heath, 1972), pp. 103–22.

59.

Robert E. Doherty and Walter E. Oberer, *Teachers, School Boards, and Collective Bargaining: A Changing of the Guard* (Ithaca: New York State School of Industrial and Labor Relations of SUNY, 1967).

60.

Myron Lieberman and Michael H. Moskow, *Collective Negotiations for Teachers: An Approach to School Administration* (Chicago: Rand McNally, 1966).

61.
National Education Association, "Teachers Strikes and Work Stoppages," *Research Memo* (1968): 1.

62.
Zeigler, "Teacher Militancy."

63.
Timothy A. Almy and Harlan Hahn, "Public Perceptions of Urban Conflict: The Case of Teacher Strikes," *Education and Urban Society* 3 (1971): 440–52.

64.
Hess and Kirst, "Political Orientation and Behavior Patterns."

65.
Norman Luttbeg and Harmon Zeigler, "Attitude Consensus and Conflict in an Interest Group: An Assessment of Cohesion," *The American Political Science Review* 60 (1966): 655–66.

66.
Clark, "Sociology of Education."

67.
Doherty and Oberer, *Teachers, School Boards, and Collective Bargaining.*

68.
Paul F. Lazarsfeld and Wagner Thielens, Jr., *The Academic Mind: Social Scientists in a Time of Crisis* (Glencoe, Ill.: Free Press, 1958); and M. Kent Jennings and Harmon Zeigler, "Political Expressivism Among High School Teachers," in Roberta S. Sigel (ed.), *Learning About Politics* (New York: Random House, 1970), pp. 434–53.

69.
Jennings and Zeigler, "The Politics of Teacher-Administrator Relations."

70.
Rosenthal, *Pedagogues and Power,* p. 19.

71.
Both William Boyd, "The Public, The Professionals, and Educational Policy-Making: Who Governs?" (unpublished manuscript), and Paul E. Peterson "The Politics of American Education," in Fred N. Kerlinger (ed.), *Review of Research in America* (Itasca, Ill.: F. E. Peacock Publishers, 1974), are among those who challenge the notion of insulation as advanced in Zeigler, Jennings, with Peak, *Governing American Schools.*

72.
E. E. Schattschneider, *The Semi-Sovereign People* (New York: Holt, 1960), p. 68. The analogy of the battleground is suggested in Roger W. Cobb and Charles D. Elder, *Participation in Politics: The Dynamics of Agenda-Building* (Baltimore: The Johns Hopkins University Press, 1972).

73.

Original data reported in this chapter were collected in two sequential national studies of educational governance. The first was a cross-sectional study based primarily on survey research. For this data, see Zeigler, Jennings, with Peak, *Governing American Schools.* The second was a longitudinal study that included both observational and interview data. For this data see, L. Harmon Zeigler, Harvey J. Tucker, and L. A. Wilson II, in The National Society for the Study of Education, 1977 Yearbook (Chicago: University of Chicago Press, 1977), pp. 219–54.

74.

Boyd, "The Public, The Professionals, and Educational Policy-Making," p. 31.

75.

Some of these data were reported in Zeigler, Jennings, with Peak, *Governing American Schools.* A more exclusive analysis was undertaken by Michael O. Boss who tragically died before his manuscript was complete. These remarks are drawn from Boss's incomplete notes.

76.

This analysis is taken from Boss's notes. It was found that the more a district spends (as indicated by per-pupil expenditure), the higher the salience of curriculum issues to the public. Further, the salience of curriculum issues among the public seems more volatile than with decision-makers. Hence, the correlation between per-pupil expenditures and citing of curriculum problems is higher (0.41) with the public than with the board (0.24) and superintendent (0.11). In suburban schools, fully 77 percent of the public cite curriculum problems, a percentage that exceeds that of the board and administration. Thus, although the education program is of low salience, it need not be so.

77.

See, for example, Dale Mann, *The Politics of Administrative Representation* (Lexington, Mass.: D. C. Heath, 1976).

78.

See M. Kent Jennings, "Patterns of School Board Responsiveness," in Peter J. Cistone (ed.), *Understanding School Boards* (Lexington, Mass.: D. C. Heath, 1975), pp. 246–49 for an explanation of this idea.

79.

See Zeigler, Jennings, with Peak, *Governing American Schools,* pp. 95–105, for a discussion of the dominance of supportive groups in the communication pattern of school boards. Boss found superintendents to be even less diverse.

80.

National School Boards Association, *The People Look at Their School Boards* (Research Report 1975-1), p. 31.

81.

The idea of a defensive response is developed in Crain, *The Politics of School*

Desegregation, pp. 115–24. The data about superintendents, education and conflict management skills are found in Michael O. Boss, Harmon Zeigler, Harvey Tucker, and L. A. Wilson II, "Professionalism, Community Structure, and Decision-Making: School Superintendents and Interest Groups," *Policy Studies Journal* (Summer 1976): 360.

82.
Archie Dykes, *School Board and Superintendent: Their Effective Working Relationships* (Danville, Ill.: Interstate Printers and Publishers, 1965), pp. 132–33.

83.
Lipham, Gregg, and Rossmiller, "The School Board as an Agency for Resolving Conflict."

84.
James W. Guthrie, "Public Control of Schools: Can We Get It Back?" *Public Affairs Report* 15 (June 1974): 3.

85.
National School Boards Association, *The Impact of Collective Bargaining on Curriculum and Instruction* (Research Report 1975-2), p. 6.

86.
Ronald G. Corwin, "The Organizational Context of School in Board-Teacher Conflict," in Peter J. Cistone (ed.), *Understanding School Boards* (Lexington, Mass.: D. C. Heath, 1975), pp. 31–158.

87.
Lawrence C. Pierce, "Teachers' Organizations and Bargaining: Power Imbalance in the Public Sphere," in National Committee for Citizens in Education, *Public Testimony on Public Schools* (Berkeley, Calif.: McCutchan, 1975), p. 124.

88.
Thomas H. Eliot, "Toward an Understanding of Public School Politics," *American Political Science Review* 53 (1959): 1037.

89.
Michael W. Kirst and Decker F. Walker, "An Analysis of Curriculum Policy-Making," *Review of Educational Research* 41 (1971): 479–509.

90.
Koerner, *Who Controls American Education?*

91.
Kirst and Walker, "An Analysis of Curriculum Policy-Making."

92.
Jennings and Zeigler, "Response Styles and Politics."

93.

Kirst and Walker, "An Analysis of Curriculum Policy-Making."

94.

George Gallup, *How the Nation Views the Public Schools* (Princeton, N.J.: Gallup International, 1969), p. 2.

95.

Kirst and Walker, "An Analysis of Curriculum Policy-Making."

96.

Martin, *Government and the Suburban School.*

97.

Kirst and Walker, "An Analysis of Curriculum Policy-Making," p. 481.

98.

Zeigler, Jennings, with Peak, *Governing American Schools.*

99.

Harmon Zeigler and Michael O. Boss, "Racial Problems and Policy-Making in the American Public Schools," *Sociology of Education* (1974): 319–36.

100.

Crain, *The Politics of School Desegregation.*

101.

Ibid.

102.

Ibid., p. 123.

103.

Zeigler and Boss, "Racial Problems and Policy-Making in the American Public Schools."

104.

Crain, *The Politics of School Desegregation,* p. 124.

105.

V. O. Key, Jr., *Public Opinion and American Democracy* (New York: Knopf, 1961), p. 316.

106.

James S. Coleman and others, *Equality of Educational Opportunity* (Washington, D.C.: Government Printing Office, 1966).

107.

Christopher Jencks and others, *Inequality: A Reassessment of the Effect of Family and Schooling in America* (New York: Basic Books, 1972), p. 255.

108.

Raymond Boudon, *Education, Opportunity, and Social Inequality: Changing Prospects in Western Society* (New York: Wiley, 1973), p. 187.

6

BARRIERS TO
RESPONSIVENESS

IN THIS chapter we amplify our central theme, responsiveness of state and local governments to their clientele. We have argued that, for a number of reasons, governments cannot be responsive to the preferences of all citizens, or even the more limited population of voters. Governments are systems of elites who are responsive to articulate minorities. The present chapter will review previously developed reasons and present additional explanations to support our arguments.

Our discussion of barriers to state and local governments' responsiveness to clientele will begin with noninstitutional factors. Complexity, uncertainty, organizational behavior, heterogeneity of preference, and public apathy are elements of twentieth-century America that impede all governments from knowing and acting on clientele preferences. These barriers make responsiveness difficult no matter how strongly governing elites desire to do what the people want. We will then consider barriers to responsiveness in the common institutions of state and local government: mechanisms of mass-elite linkage, public administration procedures, and intergovernmental relations. We shall see that the institutions of state and local government have been evolving, but that the

255

evolution has by no means enhanced responsiveness. On the contrary, the growth of noninstitutional barriers to responsiveness has not stimulated institutional change to overcome the barriers, but rather institutional change which, in many cases, reinforces the barriers.

NONINSTITUTIONAL BARRIERS

Complexity

The increasing complexity of the matters government officials must deal with is the major noninstitutional barrier to governmental responsiveness to clientele. Government decision-making is complex, largely because of the complexity of modern life. The most easily documented aspect of increasing complexity for state and local governments lies in the increasing number of their clients—that is, individuals and businesses. The number of individuals has increased from 132 million in 1940 to over 215 million in the mid-1970s. The number of businesses increased 360 percent in the same period to a figure of over 12 thousand in the 1970s. State and local governments reacted to their expanded constituency by spending more money, employing more people, and enacting more statutes and resolutions, as shown in tables 6.1 and 6.2. Yet, while clientele and activities were increasing, the number of state

Table 6.1.   Government Expenditures and Employees

	Expenditures (millions of dollars)		Employees (thousands)	
	State	Local	State	Local
1940	5,209	7,685	—	—
1950	15,082	17,081	1,057	3,228
1960	31,596	39,056	1,527	4,860
1970	85,055	92,522	2,755	7,392

Source: *1972 Census of Governments,* Vol. 6, No. 4, U.S. Bureau of the Census.

governments increased from 48 to 50, and the number of local governments actually decreased by about one-half (see table 6.3). Thus, for
local governments, complexity has increased both as a function of increasing clientele and activities and as a function of decreasing numbers
of units to undertake activities.

Table 6.2.   Enactments of State Governments

1945	26,864[a]
1950	25,357
1960	37,599
1970	56,436

Source: *The Book of the States, 1948–49, 1952–53, 1962–63, 1972–73,* (Lexington, Ky.: The
Council of State Governments).

[a] 48 states.

A second aspect of complexity is the increasing availability of information. Never before has there been such a proliferation of information,
which makes possible—although certainly not feasible—consideration of
a virtually limitless number of alternatives for every decision. The
average citizen and the average semiprofessional state or local legislator
simply does not have the time to evaluate competing proposals and
plausible alternatives.

Table 6.3.   State and Local Governments

	State	Local
1942	48	155,067
1952	50	116,756
1962	50	91,186
1972	50	78,026

Source: *1972 Census of Governments,* Vol. 6, No. 4, U.S. Bureau of the Census.

TECHNICALITY OF INFORMATION   The situation is further
complicated by the fact that much of the information relevant to
government decision-making is highly technical. The vast majority of
citizens are unable to interpret and evaluate alternative policy recommendations made by two architectural consultants concerning the optimum size and cost of a new county jail. Citizens are unable to predict
the impact on the state economy of alternative programs of tax incen-

tives to new businesses or welfare reform or changing the basis of state and local financing of schools. The average citizen lacks the expertise to participate in a discussion with the local school district superintendent on the comparative merits and weaknesses of proposed curricula for elementary school reading and social studies.

The average citizen cannot determine whether the municipal water district's proposed purification facility will meet federal technical standards for water purity. Just as major appliances, automobiles, and houses have become so complex and intricate that the individual consumer cannot adequately compare and evaluate the goods in the marketplace, the affairs of state and local government have become complex. As consumers of government goods and services, citizens must rely on experts to help them evaluate policy alternatives. When so many issues must be decided by state and local governments, responsiveness to constituent preference is impossible because constituents are not and, practically speaking, cannot be sufficiently informed to indicate policy preferences.

The political maxim that knowledge is power has important implications as government officials increasingly attempt to base their public policy decisions on technical criteria. The ability of concerned citizens to get the knowledge they need to participate in matters of concern decreases in direct proportion to the increasing dependence of those with political power on those with technical knowledge. In economic terms, the costs of information are so high that constituents and their elected representatives must rely on experts in and outside government.

The increasing role of technical knowledge in government threatens the decision-making ability of legislators and executive officials as well as members of the public. The threat is twofold: not only must government officials often turn to outside experts for information on policy choices, in many cases government officials lack the expertise necessary to evaluate the recommendations of their own employees. Wildavsky has given an example of this latter problem at the federal level:

> Suppose that you were a Congressman or a Budget Bureau official interested in the leukemia research program and you wondered how the money was being spent. By looking at the National Cancer Institute's budget presentation you would discover that $42,012 is being spent on a project studying "factors and mechanisms concerned in hemopoiesis," and that $5,095 is being spent for "a study of the relationship of neutralizing antibodies for the Rous sarcoma virus to resistance and susceptibility for visceral lymphomatosis." Could you tell whether too

much money is being spent on hemopoiesis in comparison to lymphomatosis or whether either project is relevant for any useful purpose? You might sympathize with Congressman Laird's plaintive cry, "A lot of things go on in this subcommittee that I cannot understand." It is not surprising, therefore, that one runs across expressions of dismay at the difficulties of understanding technical subjects.[1]

Experts within government attempt to secure and expand their own bases of power and influence by presenting as many matters as possible as essentially technical. We noted in chapter 5 how school superintendents and their administrative staffs have transferred such issues as curriculum from the arena of public discussion and school board decision-making to the arena of discussion by experts and school board endorsement of professional recommendations. School board members' counterparts in municipal and state government are similarly subject to the argument that their role is to ratify public policy decisions made by experts.

Not only top administrators but also the rank and file of state and local government employees increasingly possess professional credentials. Advanced degrees in public administration, engineering, agriculture, law, business administration, education, and social services are becoming prerequisites to government employment. Chief executives are either promoted specialists of limited expertise or administrative generalists; legislators are part-time or amateur servants whose experience is in the private sector. Neither can be expected to have the extensive technical background necessary to deal with the cadre of experts they nominally control.

BIASED EXPERTS   The public and their elected representatives often turn to experts outside of government for technical information and advice. Unfortunately, outside experts also have professional orientations and important vested interests that prevent them from being entirely impartial. The consulting engineer employed by a municipality to evaluate the technical merits of competing plans for a bridge also derives his income from consulting with the construction industry. A governor's commission appointed to recommend changes in existing state insurance regulations invariably is composed largely of insurance company executives. Similarly, the university professor hired as an educational consultant by a local school district is not an entirely independent expert because of his interest in the district's continuing to hire graduates of the university.

The problem of biased reviews of employee proposals and biased information has enormous significance for the majority of state legislatures and nearly all city councils, school boards, and other legislative bodies because they lack independent fact-gathering facilities. Thus, they must rely largely on lobbyists and interest groups for evaluation of technical proposals and collection of reference information. A former state legislator cites a typical example:

> When I was in the legislature, a highway was being built through my district, and I started getting complaints from farmers that they weren't being adequately paid for damage to their land. To get a law correcting the situation, I first needed a lot more evidence but I had no way of getting it myself. So I asked the Farm Bureau, a lobby group, to go out and interview farmers along the route. It came up with a fine report and the law got passed, but I never did feel comfortable about having to depend on a farmers' lobby for the facts in this kind of a bill.[2]

Similarly, state and local legislatures must rely on such biased organizations as state bar associations, chambers of commerce, and local teachers' organizations for information and evaluation of policy proposals.

A crucial element of the paradigm of rational decision-making is the assumption that an individual can evaluate alternative courses of action in terms of the costs and benefits he expects from each. Complexity prevents the individual citizen from recognizing the costs and benefits of alternative policies and communicating his preference to government officials. Complexity also prevents many government officials from recognizing the costs and benefits of alternative policy proposals. Citizen and official alike are forced to rely on experts in government and outside of government. Unfortunately, there is no guarantee that the recommendations of experts will always be value-free. In any case, the existence of complexity prevents direct government responsiveness to citizen preference.

Uncertainty

Uncertainty is a special type of complexity that is worthy of separate mention as a noninstitutional barrier to governmental responsiveness. Complexity can prevent constituents and government officials from being able to discern both desired policy goals and suitable policy actions. The problem of uncertainty is mainly that of finding appropriate policy actions that will achieve desired goals.

CHANGING TECHNOLOGIES   The uncertainty that inevitably accompanies changing and improving technology is a major impediment to the general goal of efficiency in government. National defense is a classic example of this dilemma. Huge capital investments are necessary on a continuing basis to keep pace with advancements in weapons technology. Entire systems or generations of weapons can be rendered obsolete without warning. Thus, there is no reliable way of calculating the life expectancy of an antiballistic missile system, a B-1 bomber, or a nuclear-powered aircraft carrier and no reliable way of matching cost with expected benefit. This uncertainty makes responsiveness to citizen demand for cost-efficiency virtually impossible.

Although state and local governments do not participate directly in setting national defense policies, they must make major capital expenditures in response to changing technologies that make responsiveness to the goal of efficiency difficult. Should the source of energy for heating a new school building, city library, county courthouse, or state office building be electricity, natural gas, or fuel oil? Which energy source offers the greatest likelihood of future availability at the lowest cost? Should a technology of the past—the coal furnace—be considered? Should a chance be taken on the underdeveloped technology of solar energy? Perhaps the building should be delayed in the hope that future advances in modular construction techniques will reduce construction costs. Perhaps the building should be constructed in anticipation of increased future demand because, in light of rising costs of construction and general inflation, present costs are a bargain. The uncertainty of changing technology is a barrier to efficiency in all areas of capital expenditure.

ECONOMIC DISRUPTIONS   State and local governments have recently come to recognize that economic uncertainty is a major impediment to responsiveness. Unanticipated inflation has caused major cost overruns on extended construction projects, such as the domed stadia in New Orleans and Seattle. When government officials cannot be sure of the expense associated with the proposals they endorse, they and their constituents cannot evaluate alternative proposals on the basis of efficiency.

Economic disruptions create uncertainty for state and local government income as well as expenditure. Economic recession results in decreasing revenues for governments dependent on personal income taxes and general sales taxes. Ironically, these seemingly unpredictable economic conditions at once reduce state and local resources and create demand for increased expenditures for unemployment compensation, public welfare assistance, and government employment in general.

POPULATION SHIFTS   State and local governments have traditionally been responsive to popular demand for free or inexpensive public primary, secondary, and higher education. Using the number of children born in one year, it is possible to estimate the demand they will create for public education in the next twenty years. It is more difficult to predict the distribution of that demand over the next twenty years. Thus, when the general population of Seattle declined in the early 1970s, largely as a result of unexpected employment reductions at the Boeing Corporation (as a result of a general decline in the aerospace industry), the Seattle School District was left with buildings and administrative capacity for over 100,000 students, and a clientele of fewer than 70,000 students. Could the district best serve the present and future educational needs of the community by reducing excess capacity—and possibly having to repurchase at higher cost—or by maintaining excess capacity in the expectation of increased future enrollments—and bearing greater costs per pupil in the meantime?

Boom towns like Odessa, Texas, created by the sudden demand in the mid-1970s for increased production of domestic oil, face the opposite problem. Should new facilities be delayed in the expectation that the population increase is temporary, should temporary facilities be built, or should permanent facilities be constructed? Though it is possible to anticipate population size and the corresponding level of demand for government services, the distribution of population is subject to rapid change. The burden of this uncertainty obviously falls on state and local levels of government.

Higher education has recently been through a period of unexpectedly high enrollments resulting from student deferments of military service and the Vietnam war. The end of the war, the failure of a college degree to guarantee a high-paying job, and the popularity of alternative life-styles have all contributed to an unexpected decline in university enrollments in the mid-1970s. Furthermore, a fluctuating birth rate indicates that there will be fewer candidates for higher education twenty years later. Because the major ingredients of higher education—buildings, libraries, laboratories and other capital facilities, and tenured faculty—cannot easily be increased and decreased by state government to match unexpected changes in demand, it is extremely difficult to avoid being either underresponsive or overresponsive to the demand for higher education.

ENERGY AND POLLUTION   The unexpected oil crisis of the early 1970s stimulated a wide range of demands on federal, state, and local governments. The federal government responded by influencing

states to lower maximum highway speeds to 55 miles per hour, by requiring that new cars meet higher standards of energy efficiency, and by
increasing research and development of mass transit systems. State and
local governments were responsive to popular demands by strictly enforcing reduced speed limits and by providing increased mass transportation services. The major manifestations of the oil crisis are sharply increased prices for petroleum products and predictions that another,
more serious petroleum shortage is imminent. At the same time, the
best-selling American-made automobiles provide the least fuel economy,
the 55-mph speed limit is poorly enforced, and many observers speak of
the "so-called energy crisis."

There is considerable ambiguity about the nature of the energy problem and about the policy preferences of the masses. The uncertainty of
future petroleum availability makes prediction of public demand for
restrictions on private automobiles, development of mass transit
facilities, and energy rationing virtually impossible. Yet, if governments
are to be responsive to such demands in the near future, certain preliminary actions must be taken at once.

Uncertainty is a major barrier in issues such as scarcity of energy
resources and environmental pollution because the problems seem to
involve two important thresholds: first, the threshold of public
awareness and demand for government action, and second, the
threshold of effective policy response, beyond which no government action is possible to solve the problem quickly. When the threshold of effective government action precedes the threshold of public awareness
and demand, responsiveness to clientele preference is impossible. If
government is to be in a position to be responsive to anticipated demands in the future, it must initiate unpopular policies today.

Government officials find themselves in a paradoxical position—they
are damned if they do and damned if they don't. The choice is between
being responsive today and unable to be responsive tomorrow, and being
unresponsive today and potentially responsive tomorrow. For example,
Oregon has imposed unpopular restrictions on private ownership of
ocean beach property and forbidden the use of aerosol propellant con-
tainers to meet anticipated future demand for public beaches and environmental cleanliness. California and other states are considering
limiting the development of needed nuclear power facilities because of
the unknown possibilities of future catastrophic accidents. Federal,
state, and local governments undertook an emergency program in 1976
to produce sufficient swine influenza vaccine to inoculate all Americans
—which decreased the availability of other vaccines—to be responsive to public demand had an epidemic occurred in 1977. Because

the future is uncertain, public policy choices must be made that sacrifice responsiveness to current demands for responsiveness to future demands or vice versa.

Governmental responsiveness to clientele can be defined as a state in which the supply of goods and services of government equals the demands for those goods and services. Uncertainty is a barrier to this kind of responsiveness because demand is subject to sudden, unpredictable change. Even were demand perfectly predictable, a barrier to responsiveness exists when government is uncertain as to how to meet the demand. The problem is particularly acute in policy areas in which long-term commitment of resources is necessary, such as public health, education, transportation, and environmental quality. These policy areas have traditionally been and continue to be primarily the responsibility of state and local government.

Organizational Behavior

Another important barrier to governmental responsiveness is the fact that government organizations—as do all organizations—tend to engage in patterns of behavior that serve their own self-interests above all else. Many students of organization theory and behavior believe that no matter what the origin or purpose of an organization, its primary goals soon become survival and growth. Providing the goods or services for which it was brought into being becomes secondary to the goals of survival and growth.

It is not uncommon for an organization to survive despite fulfillment of its original mission. A classic example is the March of Dimes organization. Originally, it was formed to support medical research to cure and prevent poliomyelitis. When this goal was achieved with the development of the Salk and Sabin vaccines, the organization shifted to a new class of diseases: birth defects.

SURVIVAL   The missions of governmental organizations are normally to deal with ongoing problems and therefore are rarely achievable. However, as the survival of the federal and state selective service system—despite the abolition of military conscription—illustrates, government organizations also tend to transcend their reason for existence. Herbert Kaufman has asked the provocative question: are government organizations immortal? In a comparison of federal agencies in 1923 and 1973 Kaufman concluded that government organizations display impressive powers of endurance. Only a little over 15 percent of a sample of agencies in existence in 1923 had disappeared by 1973.[3] A comparison of death rates of government organizations with business failure rates for the same period revealed that the annual rate of business failures was more than twice the annual death rate of the government units.[4] Thus, the impressive ability of government agencies to stay alive once they have been launched is not mere conjecture.[5]

Kaufman provides a list of factors that tend to keep every federal agency alive indefinitely. The factors are equally applicable to state and local governments and provide insight into how these organizations seek to ensure their own survival.

1. *Most agencies are established by statute or accorded statutory recognition.* An agency established by statute is more secure than one established by executive or departmental order because it can be altered or abolished only by another statute. As Kaufman notes:

   > Enacting a significant piece of legislation in a representative body is a lengthy, tortuous process requiring extensive bargaining and trading to assemble a supporting majority; having achieved sufficient consensus to pass a bill, legislators are not ordinarily disposed to reverse themselves quickly. Moreover, the legislative process makes it easier to block action than to carry proposals to function. . . . The legislative setting tends to favor the defenders of the status quo—especially if the defenders have recently overcome the previous status quo to produce the current one.[6]

   The stronger the instrument of creation, the greater the life expectancy of the agency. Many state, municipal, and special district governments have the components of their executive departments specified in their constitution, charter, or enabling document. Thus, many state and local government agencies enjoy even stronger bases than statutory law.

2. *Positive and protective attitudes are developed by legislative committees toward the agencies they oversee.* This effect is probably most pronounced in the federal government where members of Congress serve longer terms and develop personal relationships with leaders of administrative agencies. The greater rate of turnover of state and local legislators means that personal relationships between administrators and legislators are of shorter standing, but probably not diminished in frequency or importance. As Kaufman points out, a

congenial agency can do as much for a cooperative legislator as the legislators can do for the agency.

> A cooperative agency, for example, may exercise its discretion about the location of facilities and about program emphases in such a way as to increase jobs, expenditures, and services in the states and districts of committee members. . . . An agency may also take favorable and speedy action for clients on whose behalf strategically placed legislators intervene. . . .[7]

This latter point is of paramount importance to state and local legislators, who, as part-time and amateur officials of government, live and do business in the community that is served by the agencies they oversee. Friendly relationships with agency administrators are particularly important to those state and local legislators who hope to serve as consultants or lobbyists for private or government interests after they retire from legislative service.

3. *Established agencies benefit from the process of budgetary decision-making.* Federal, state, and local government's budgets are so large and complex that legislatures and senior executive officials cannot treat it as a totally new document each year. (Governments such as the states of Georgia, New Jersey, Idaho, Texas, Rhode Island, and others that employ "zero-base budgeting" do purportedly review every program financed by government for every fiscal period.) Thus, the decision-making process tends to be incremental in nature. Recent appropriations or expenditures are generally treated as an acceptable base. Budget participants limit their consideration to moderate changes in the base: increases to meet increased costs or number of clients or service reductions. For all practical purposes, massive reductions or total budget eliminations for existing agencies are extremely rare. In Kaufman's words, "once an agency receives appropriations, it is apt to be borne along by the sheer momentum of the budgetary process."[8] Because most state and local legislative bodies are composed of members who serve only part-time, they are even more dependent on the incremental method of budgetary review and more subject to defer to the opinion of professional administrators about the scope of an agency's program and budget.

4. *Some agencies are further sheltered by their comparative invulnerability to executive control.* Many state and local agencies —regulatory boards and commissions, for example—are deliberately insulated from executive influence. Other state and local agencies gain a measure of independence because their existence and

form are required to receive matching funds from another government agency. State departments of employment security and fish and wildlife are required to receive federal funds, and county or regional welfare organizations are often required for state funds.

Yet other state and local agencies maintain independence of executive control because of the independent selection of the agency head. In many states lieutenant governors, secretaries of state, treasurers, auditors, and other department heads are chosen by popular election or appointed by commissions independent of the governor. Similarly, important local government officials such as law enforcement chiefs, local attorneys general, and tax assessors are selected independently of the chief executive. Independent selection tends to provide a measure of insulation from the influence of chief executives.

Agency heads also enjoy some freedom from executive control by virtue of their own longevity. It is not unusual for several years to pass between the original proposal and the final implementation of a major program. Chief executive tenure in office is inevitably limited by constitution, partisan competition, or fatigue; agency personnel enjoy greater longevity. Time is therefore on the agencies' side. Delay of policy implementation may have the same effect as a formal veto.

5. *Agency personnel are motivated to preserve the organization to which they belong.* Job security, a preference for the familiar over the unknown, and the mysterious force of organizational loyalty are three incentives Kaufman mentions as applicable to all agency employees. The leaders are further motivated by considerations of professional status, reputation, and future employability. Agency personnel are not passive spectators when executive and legislative officials contemplate their fate, they are active participants who can make use of extensive resources in their struggle to preserve their organization.

6. *Agencies have clientele that support their continued survival.* Clients for such service agencies as public schools are self-evident. Clientele support for regulatory agencies is also strong, partly because of the "capture" phenomenon or industry orientation that occurs in most regulatory agencies. State agencies for inspection, industry regulation, and occupational licensure are particularly likely to develop close ties with those they nominally control. For one thing, agency personnel are in daily contact with those they are regulating; contact with the general public or executive and legislative officials is much less frequent. This fraternization leads to common perceptions and attitudes between agency and industry.[9]

In many cases dominant occupational groups are associated with government agencies. For example, many top state department officials for public mental health and medical examining and licensing boards will also belong to state and national medical associations. Industry orientation is enhanced in those agencies in which a professional degree or experience in the regulated area is a prerequisite to government service. In such cases there are likely to be strongly held professional values common to agency and industry members, particularly when professional or trade associations are active. These ties are strengthened by the frequently documented practice of interchange of personnel between regulating agencies and regulated industries.

Aside from the capture phenomenon, regulated interests often recognize benefits from the controls enforced by regulatory agencies. Though agencies may control prices and profits, they also restrict competition by restricting entry into the marketplace and prohibiting destructive practices. Indeed, industry itself may seek the establishment of a regulatory agency as a means of securing a state-enforced monopoly.[10] Thus, state and local service and regulatory agencies tend to develop the support of the clients they serve by being responsive to them.

Unfortunately, being responsive to the desires of their immediate clientele will not always lead an agency to pursue policies in the interest of the larger population. For example, a member of a state insurance commission who shares the professional values and viewpoint of the companies he is regulating and who is looking forward to resuming his career in private industry is not likely to be entirely impartial when reviewing a citizen complaint against an individual company or an industry practice. Similarly, licensure boards composed entirely of professionals will tend to promote the views of their professional organization over the interests of the general public.

It is easy to see that the factors which tend to keep agencies alive also tend to insulate agencies from the general public they nominally serve. To be sure, agencies must be responsive to survive. But their survival is ensured by responsiveness to selected government officials, direct clientele, and professional associations. The interests of an agency's select clientele and its larger clientele will not necessarily be in conflict, but whenever they are, the desire for organizational survival dictates that the agency will choose to be responsive to the smaller, more immediate clientele.

GROWTH   If the first goal of an organization is survival, its second goal is growth. The growth rate of state and local government employees and expenditures exceeds that of the federal government. This is one aspect of growth. A less frequently observed aspect of increased state and local government activity is the increasingly direct involvement of state and local government in the provision of goods and services.

James M. Buchanan has pointed out that it is useful to distinguish between governmental support or financing of a particular service and the actual governmental operation or provision of a service.[11] The actual operation may be carried out by governmental agencies—for example, local government provision of public primary and secondary education services and state provision of higher education services—or by private firms hired through government funds—such as state and local government financing of building and road construction contracted to private firms. Buchanan and other economists argue that there is little intrinsic reason why publicly financed activities should also be produced by government: the decision between public and private operation should rest solely on grounds of efficiency.

Thomas E. Borcherding has asked, have the proportions of public and private supply of public services through government been changing over the last seventy years?[12] Borcherding presents data on public and private provision of services by governments in the United States (see table 6.4) that indicate, except for the defense sector which relies heavily on private contractors, there has been a slight tendency to produce more goods "in-house." Furthermore, this trend is more pronounced in state and local governments than at the federal level.

Thus, it appears as though state and local governments are not only realizing growth by undertaking new activities, but they are realizing

Table 6.4.   Exhaustive Government Expenditures Provided by the Private Sector (in percentages)[a]

| | Total expenditures | Total excluding defense | | |
	All governments	All	Federal	State and local
1903	51	50	48	52
1913	52	52	39	57
1963	54	55	50	43
1970	48	45	47	44

Source: Thomas E. Borcherding, "One Hundred Years of Public Spending, 1870 to 1970," Simon Fraser University Department of Economics and Commerce, *Discussion Paper*, Feb. 9, 1974, p. 41.

[a] The sum of public payrolls and direct government purchases: the actual payments for the state resources used in the production of public services.

growth by increasing their role in directly providing goods and services. Like survival, growth is a documented attribute of government organizations.

The logic of organizational behavior dictates that government agencies will seek growth. It is not necessarily true that growth will mean increased quantity or quality of goods or services provided to clientele. Growth may be in response to clientele demand or in spite of clientele demand. Furthermore, strong, established agencies tend to receive resources at the expense of weaker, infant agencies.

It is a paradox of government activity that once an organization is established, its original mission becomes subordinate to the common organizational goals of survival and growth. Public service and satisfaction soon become means to these organizational goals. This organizational behavior is a barrier to responsiveness to the extent that the organization develops alternative means of achieving survival and growth.

Heterogeneity of Preference

Heterogeneity of preference is a barrier to governmental responsiveness almost by definition. In a situation where there is unanimity of policy preference, action can be taken that is responsive to everyone. Wherever opinion is divided, responsiveness to everyone is impossible; and the greater the heterogeneity of preference, the smaller the maximum overall responsiveness.

Heterogeneity of preference is commonly associated with size of governmental units. For example, as Dahl and Tufte have posited:

> Smaller democracies are likely to be more nearly homogeneous with respect to beliefs, values, and goals. *Conversely:* Larger democracies are likely to exhibit more diversity in beliefs, values, goals, social and economic characteristics, occupations, etc.[13]

A key tenet underlying various proposals to decentralize government decision-making or reduce the size of existing governments is the presumption that smaller units will be more homogeneous. Thus, in his presidential address to the 1967 meeting of the American Political Science Association, Robert Dahl called for breaking down large cities into smaller self-governing units of 50,000 to 100,000 persons.[14] The

Bundy Commission, established in 1967 to suggest ways of reforming the massive New York City public school system, recommended that the system be decentralized, and that thirty to sixty school boards be created with authority over the schools in their districts. Such districts, presumably, would be sociologically homogeneous.

William Appleman Williams has recently suggested that the federal government in the United States could largely be dissolved in favor of associations of states with strong regional ties.[15] Williams argues that regional homogeneity would facilitate consensus on necessary uniform standards for business regulation, educational services, and other activities of central government. It stands to reason that the evidence of increasing numbers of businesses and individuals and decreasing numbers of local governments cited in the earlier discussion of complexity is also evidence of increasing heterogeneity of opinion within local units of government.

PUBLIC OPINION   Public opinion is heterogeneous, not only because of the heterogeneous sociological, political, and economic makeup of the population, but also because of the complexity of the issues of modern government. As V. O. Key explained:

> While the simple yes-no division is the form most commonly referred to in everyday discourse, the actual distribution of opinion within the public usually takes on a more complex form. Instead of a yes-no dichotomy, attitudes toward a public issue may be ranged along a scale represented by a series of different ways of dealing with the question. For example, assume that the problem of relief for the destitute is at issue. At one extreme some people may hold the view that destitution is a product of shiftlessness or of divine will and that the poor deserve to starve. Further along the scale others may be of the opinion that the destitute should receive from the public treasury the minimum necessary to maintain life. A more liberal attitude would be that they should receive a decent maintenance. And still others might hold that they deserve generous support, for their difficulties are but a consequence of the evil workings of the economic system.[16]

Most issues facing state and local governments involve choice between numerous alternatives, not a simple yes-no dichotomy.

Tables 6.5, 6.6, and 6.7 summarize contemporary data concerning the heterogeneous nature of public opinion relevant to state and local governments. As shown in table 6.5, Americans distribute themselves

272   Chapter 6

Table 6.5.   Political Ideology in the United States (in percentages)

Ideology	Response
Left	18
Far left	3
Substantially left of center	4
Moderately left of center	11
Middle of the road	53
Just slightly left of center	13
Middle of road	11
Just slightly right of center	19
Right	20
Moderately right of center	13
Substantially right of center	3
Far right	4
No opinion	19

Source: *Gallup Opinion Index* (Princeton, N.J.: The American Institute of Public Opinion, 1975), November–December 1975, Report No. 125.

across the entire range of the general liberal-conservative continuum of political ideology. The greatest proportion identify themselves as favoring middle-of-the-road positions. Unfortunately for state and local government officials, proponents of the political left and right are much more active in articulating their policy preferences; the middle-of-the-

Table 6.6.   Most Important Problem for Local Government (in percentages)

Problem	Response
Crime	15
Unemployment	11
Transportation	9
High cost of living	5
Education needs	5
High taxes	4
Drug problems	4
Poor housing/slums	4
Unsanitary conditions	4
Ineffective police	3
Other problems	39
No major problems	7
No opinion	6

Source: *Gallup Opinion Index* (Princeton, N.J.: The American Institute of Public Opinion, 1975), October 1975, Report No. 124.

Table 6.7.   Most Important Problem for Local Public Schools (in percentages)

Problem	Response
Lack of discipline	23
Integration/segregation problems	16
Lack of proper financial support	13
Use of drugs	13
Difficulty of getting "good" teachers	11
Size of school/classes	6
Parents' lack of interest	6
School board policies	4
Poor curriculum	3
Lack of proper facilities	3
Pupils' lack of interest	2
Miscellaneous	4
There are no problems	3
Don't know/no answer	17

Source: *Gallup Opinion Index* (Princeton, N.J.: The American Institute of Public Opinion, 1975), May 1975, Report No. 119.

road majority too often does not make their preferences known. Moreover, because the policies advocated by the left and right are often mutually exclusive, it is not possible to find the middle position by "averaging" extreme proposals. When the preferences of left, middle, and right are known, the problem of heterogeneity is clear: if the 53 percent in the middle of the road can be satisfied, chances are that the 38 percent on the left and right and at least some of those with no constant ideological position will be dissatisfied.

Tables 6.6 and 6.7 document that there is great division of opinion on the most important problems that municipal or community governments and school districts should deal with. Whatever the agenda priorities set by county, municipal, and school district governments, the wide heterogeneity of opinion among their constitutents means that a majority will inevitably be dissatisfied. Obviously, government cannot be responsive to a majority if there is no majority opinion. At present, there is nothing close to a majority consensus among members of the public on the proper agenda for local governments.

Heterogeneity of preference is a stronger barrier to governmental responsiveness in view of evidence that greater homogeneity of public opinion than a simple majority is necessary for policy change. Key noted that markedly unimodal distributions of supportive opinion are associated with most public policies and services. Furthermore, the files of opinion surveys contain many instances of the existence of an approving opinion long before the related statute was enacted. Examples include pluralities of 72 percent favoring admission of Hawaii to statehood, and 75 percent favoring home rule for Washington, D.C., before the policies in question were adopted.[17]

In a study of nine different policy areas, Anne H. Hopkins found that there are thresholds of public opinion other than simple majority, which increase the likelihood that given policies will be enacted by state governments.[18] The thresholds varied by policy area from a minority of 32 percent to a majority of 70 percent. Hopkins also found that thresholds for later time periods were substantially higher than for earlier periods.

There is further evidence for the "larger than majority consensus" hypothesis in the division of opinion on some contemporary issues of concern to state and local governments. As table 6.8 indicates, a referendum survey revealed majorities of approximately two-thirds and three-fourths on five of six issue areas. Ironically, in four of the five areas in which preferences are so homogeneous, most state and local governments have policies that contravene the popular mandate. State and federal agencies and courts pursue busing of school children to achieve racial balance despite the opposition of 65 percent of American citizens. Only a few states have passed new laws invoking the death penalty for persons convicted of murder that meet recent U.S. Supreme Court requirements. Only a few states and communities have passed legislation requiring universal registration of firearms. At this writing, it appears as though the Equal Rights Amendment to the U.S. Constitution will fail to be ratified by three-fourths of the states even though 78 percent of citizens nationwide favor its adoption. On the other hand, a few states

Table 6.8.   Referendum Results on State and Local Issues (in percentages)

	Favor	Oppose
Busing school children to achieve better racial balance in schools	35	65
Death penalty for persons convicted of murder	64	36
Registration of all firearms	72	28
Legalize the use of marijuana	27	73
Abortions through the third month of pregnancy should continue to be legal	51	49
Equal rights amendment	78	22

Source: *Gallup Opinion Index* (Princeton, N.J.: The American Institute of Public Opinion, 1975), November 1974, Report No. 113.

have in effect legalized the use of marijuana in spite of 73 percent nationwide opposition to such a policy.

It should be underlined that these surveys are based on national samples, and that variation is likely among states and localities. However, margins of difference between nationwide approval at 66 percent and a majority of disapproval in a single state should be rare. Disapproval in a majority of states in light of such high nationwide approval is virtually impossible. Clearly, a majority of state and local governments find it possible to resist mandates of popular opinion in high ranges.

Obviously overwhelming majority opinion favoring a policy does not guarantee governmental responsiveness. It may be that stability of a super-majority over a considerable period is necessary for some policy actions. In any case, issues of concern to state and local government that provoke homogeneous public opinion are rare. Thus, it is ironic that homogeneity of preference is a necessary condition for responsiveness, but it is by no means a sufficient condition for responsiveness.

Assessing Popular Preferences

Public apathy is a barrier to responsiveness because government officials cannot be responsive to popular preference if they do not know what those preferences are. As explained in chapters 1 and 2, the channels of communications commonly employed by government officials are inadequate to provide an accurate and timely account of public opinion. Knowledge of constituent preferences is a necessary condition for both the representational and congruence models of responsiveness. The failure of the public to articulate policy preferences to government officials is a barrier to responsiveness.

INSTITUTIONAL BARRIERS

WE NOW turn our attention to institutional barriers to state and local government responsiveness to the preferences of their constituents. Some institutions and procedures commonly found in state and local government create barriers to responsiveness by exacerbating the non-institutional barriers. Others inhibit responsiveness independently. Our consideration of institutional barriers to responsiveness will be organized by the following categories: formal institutions of linkage between constituents and governments, institutions of public administration, and intergovernmental relations.

LINKAGE INSTITUTIONS

IN CHAPTERS 2–5 we discussed the problems of linkage mechanisms that communicate information from masses to governing elites. The present discussion focuses on linkage mechanisms intended to stimulate decision-makers to be attentive and responsive to the desires of their constituents.

The underlying tenet of these linkages is that decision-makers will be responsive to their constituents only insofar as incentives are enforced. Public officials must be held accountable for their public acts. The electorate must be given frequent opportunity to review performance and frequent choice between maintaining or replacing the leadership. In short, an officeholder's major incentive to be responsive is the theoretical consequence of nonresponsiveness: loss of office.

Our examination of linkage institutions designed to promote accountability brings us back to the theme of conflict between the norms of expertise and responsiveness to constituent preferences as guides to public policy decision-making. Of course, the norms of expertise and responsiveness do not always indicate mutually exclusive institutions. But, as we shall presently see, these norms do conflict in terms of linkage mechanisms and thus offer a convenient scale to assess whether they promote accountability of state and local government officials to experts or to the general public.

Form of Government

The first linkage mechanism is form of government. The norm of responsiveness favors maximum opportunity for mass participation. The norm of expertise favors limited opportunity for mass participation, so decisions can be made in isolation from the disturbances of the uninformed masses.

The division of decision-making authority in state governments has been patterned after the federal executive-legislative-judicial trichotomy. Generally speaking, state governments have been remarkably similar and stable in the selection and duties of chief executive and legislators. On the other hand, cities have not evolved a single form of government. Table 6.9 reflects the widely accepted fivefold classification of city government types. As the table indicates, important shifts in city government form have occurred in recent years.

Table 6.9. Form of City Government in Cities of 5,000 or More (in percentages)

	Mayor-council	Council-manager	Commission	Town meeting	Representative town meeting	Sample size
1951	55.0	26.1	15.3	2.5	1.1	2,525
1953	52.7	28.9	14.7	2.6	1.1	2,527
1957	49.4	34.6	12.5	2.3	1.2	2,559
1959	48.3	36.3	12.1	2.0	1.2	2,562
1963	52.3	38.6	8.1	0.4	0.6	3,044
1967	48.6	41.2	6.1	2.9	1.2	3,113
1971	44.0	47.3	5.9	1.8	1.1	1,875
1974	46.0	47.0	3.0	*	*	6,254

Source: *The Municipal Year Book*, *1952*, *1954*, *1958*, *1960*, *1964*, *1968*, *1972*, *1976* (Washington, D.C.: International City Management Association).

*Breakdown not available.

The two forms of government with greatest opportunity for mass participation, town meeting and representative town meeting, have maintained their small numbers since 1951. The mayor-council form of government, which allows for popular selection of executive and legislative leadership, has declined from 55 percent in 1951 to 44 percent of city governments in 1971. The commission form of government, which places central authority in a directly elected council, has declined from 15.3 percent to 5.9 percent. The council-manager form of city government has taken up the slack, increasing its share from 26.1 percent in 1951 to 47.3 percent in 1971.

Only the town meeting and representative town meeting forms solicit active citizen participation in day-to-day decision-making, and their number has remained small. The mayor-council and commission forms, which permit citizen participation in choosing major leaders, are both declining in percentage. The council-manager form, where the public elects the council but does not choose the city manager, is rapidly growing in popularity. Thus, the trend is decline of forms with direct popular selection of major leaders, and increase in the form where a major decision-maker, the city manager, is not popularly selected. Furthermore, many mayor-council governments include a city administrator in their executive department. Fifty-three percent of mayor-council cities in 1971 had administrators. The overall trend is toward professional administration and important decision-makers who are chosen for their knowledge and experience. Recent changes in form of municipal government indicate that the norm of expertise is being promoted at the expense of the norm of responsiveness.

Terms of Office

The accountability model holds that terms of office serve as linkage mechanisms affecting responsiveness. Two important dimensions are associated with office terms: first, the length of elected officials' terms; and second, the overlap or concurrence of elected officials' terms.

The norm of expertise is best served by long terms. The expertise argument holds that elections are exercises that distract officials from

Table 6.10.   Length of Term for Mayoral Terms (median number of years)

	All	Mayor-council	Council-manager	Commission	Town meeting	Representative town meeting
1951	2	2	2	4	2	2
1957	2	2	2	4	2	2
1959	2	2	2	4	2	2
1963	2	2	2	4	a	a
1967	a	4	2	4	a	a
1974	2*	a	a	a	a	a

Source: *The Municipal Year Book, 1952, 1958, 1960, 1964, 1968, 1976* (Washington, D.C.: International City Management Association).

a Data not available.
*Mean.

their policy-making duties. Thus, long terms reduce the interruptions and demands of electoral politics and allow the decision-maker to concentrate on broad consideration of the general welfare rather than on narrow partisan consideration. The expertise argument also favors long terms because tenure in office is postulated to increase the officials' familiarity and ability to deal with the issues of public policy. Infrequent elections allow officials to build up their expertise and base their decisions on expertise rather than political considerations.

The norm of responsiveness is best served by short terms. The popular control argument holds that elections are linkage institutions which provide a regular opportunity for constituents to review and evaluate the performance of government and to communicate current preferences to representatives. Short terms and frequent elections stimulate this interaction between governing elites and masses and help ensure that leaders will be attentive to their constituents.

Data on terms of office for governors, mayors, and state and city legislators are presented in tables 6.10 through 6.12. Table 6.10 indicates that the median term for mayors has remained virtually unchanged from 1951 to 1967; only the mayor-council form shows an increase in length of term. Table 6.11 indicates that there has been an increase in the median term for city councilmen overall, which is caused by increases in terms of council-manager and town meeting cities. The norm of expertise is served by these increasing terms of city legislators.

Table 6.12 reveals that in the states the terms of governors and senators have increased in the 1950–1974 period. In 1950 governors in twenty-nine states were elected to four-year terms. The four-year term quickly became the norm, with only four states still retaining the two-

Table 6.11.   City Council Terms (median years in office)

	All	Mayor-council	Council-manager	Commission	Town meeting	Representative town meeting
1951	3	3	3	4	2	3
1953	3	3	3	4	2	3
1957	3	3	4	4	2	3
1959	3	3	4	4	2	3
1963	4	3	4	4	3	3
1967	4	3	4	4	3	3

Source: *The Municipal Year Book, 1952, 1954, 1958, 1960, 1964, 1968* (Washington, D.C.: International City Management Association).

Table 6.12.   Terms of Office

	States with four-year governor term	States with four-year senate term	States with four-year representative term
1950	29	34	4
1954	30	34	4
1958	31	34	4
1962	34	35	4
1966	36	36	4
1970	39	38	4
1974	46	38	4

Source: *The Book of the States* (Lexington, Ky.: The Council of State Governments).

year term in 1974. The number of states with four-year senate terms increased from thirty-four in 1950 to thirty-eight in 1974. The number of states with four-year terms for representatives has remained constant at four throughout the period. Nevertheless, a distinct trend of increased terms for top state-elected officials is evident. Again, the norm of expertise is served and the norm of responsiveness is weakened.

The norms of expertise and responsiveness also prescribe different procedures for the timing of elections. Expertise is best served by staggering the terms of elected officials. Staggered terms ensures a carryover of experienced leaders who can pursue current policy concerns and initiate and guide the newcomers. Representativeness is best served by concurrent elections of all officials. Elections are postulated to provide an opportunity to present the political leadership with a policy mandate and to reject discredited programs and leaders at the polls. Staggered terms deny the voting public the opportunity to pass judgment on the entire leadership. And any mandate gained by newly elected members will not necessarily be heeded by previously elected members.

Data on overlapping terms of office in city and state government are presented in tables 6.13 and 6.14. A sharp increase in overlapping terms has occurred at both levels of government in the period from 1951 to 1974. Legislative overlap in city councils has increased overall from 57.7 percent in 1951 to 72 percent in 1971, because of increased overlap in council-manager and town meeting forms of city government; overlap in the other forms has decreased.

Data are available on state governments for overlap in legislative terms and in legislative and gubernatorial terms. Again, the pattern is increased overlap: a rise in legislative term overlap from thirty states in

Table 6.13. City Councils with Overlapping Terms in Cities with Population over 5,000 (in percentages)

	All	Mayor-council	Council-manager	Commission	Town meeting	Representative town meeting
1951	57.7	56.4	71.9	43.1	30.6	51.9
1953	60.4	57.2	72.1	43.5	28.8	53.6
1957	60.6	56.4	75.4	43.4	30.5	48.4
1959	61.3	56.1	76.0	44.0	32.7	43.8
1963	64.0	55.0	79.0	46.0	54.0	58.0
1967	66.2	54.6	82.2	40.4	86.8	28.6
1971	72.0	a	a	a	a	a

Source: *The Municipal Year Book, 1952, 1954, 1958, 1960, 1964, 1968, 1972* (Washington, D.C.: International City Management Association).

[a]Data not available.

1950 to thirty-five states in 1974, and a rise in gubernatorial and legislative overlap from thirty-four states in 1950 to forty-four states in 1974.

Selection of Officials

The third linkage mechanism of the accountability model is the means of choosing governing officials. The norm of responsiveness favors choosing leaders by direct election. The reasoning is well known: elections give the governed masses an opportunity to choose their leaders. The

Table 6.14. Overlap in State Elections

	States with overlap in legislative elections	States with overlap in gubernatorial and legislative elections
1950	30	34
1954	30	35
1958	30	36
1962	31	38
1966	31	39
1970	33	41
1974	35	44

Source: *The Book of the States* (Lexington, Ky.: The Council of State Governments).

norm of expertise favors indirect elections or appointment as a means of selecting leaders. The reasoning is that a smaller group of experts is better qualified to evaluate the performance of incumbents and the credentials of newcomers than is the mass public. Concentrating the selection power will cause leaders to be selected on the basis of merit, rather than on the basis of popularity, in this view.

DIRECT ELECTION   Of the major executive and legislative leaders of cities and states, only mayors are not all chosen by direct election. In some municipalities the mayor is the councilman who receives the most votes; in others, the council chooses the mayor from its members. As table 6.15 indicates, 73 percent of all mayors in cities with populations of 5,000 or more were chosen by direct election in 1974. The percentage of direct elections overall has declined from 77 percent in 1951. And the decline has occurred over all categories of city government with the exception of the council-manager form. Although the council-manager form shows an increase of 10 percent in the proportion of directly elected mayors, this increase is augmented by the fact that those mayors must share their authority with the council-selected city manager. It is not unusual for the manager's tenure to be longer than the mayor's in council-manager governments. So, even though a directly elected council-manager mayor may win a popular mandate, his power of implementation is restricted by the manager.

Table 6.15.   Direct Election of Mayors in Cities of 5,000 or More (in percentages)

	All	Mayor-council	Council-manager	Commission	Town meeting	Representative town meeting
1951	77.0	95.0	41.7	73.2	68.2	60.9
1953	76.5	95.3	43.8	73.1	68.1	65.2
1957	74.0	95.0	47.0	71.0	51.0	65.0
1959	74.0	96.0	48.0	69.0	67.0	51.0
1963	76.1	95.5	50.1	76.5	a	a
1967	a	96.6	50.1	77.5	a	a
1971	71.0	92.2	51.0	72.0	a	a
1974	72.9	93.8	51.4	72.6	50.0	50.0

Source: *The Municipal Year Book, 1952, 1954, 1958, 1960, 1964, 1968, 1972, 1976* (Washington, D.C.: International City Management Association).

aData not available.

APPOINTMENT   The principle of direct election is often frustrated when a vacancy occurs in a position normally filled by popular election. Typically, the vacancy is filled, not by a special election, but by an appointment made by the chief executive or the legislative body. Thus, when an elected school board member resigns or dies, the remaining board members interview candidates and appoint a replacement to serve either the remainder of the vacant term of office or until the next regular election. Over two-thirds of cities with populations greater than 5,000 fill vacancies for councilmen through appointment by the council; only one-sixth of the cities hold special elections.[19] Vacancies in elected state judicial and administrative offices are usually filled by a gubernatorial or commission appointment with or without legislative confirmation.

Data concerning the frequency of elected posts being filled by appointment are rare. A national survey of school board members found that 23 percent of respondents serving on elective boards originally obtained their seats by appointment.[20] Once on the school board appointees enjoy the advantages of incumbency: the same study reported an average rate of incumbent removal of 34 percent.[21]

A sample of city council members in eighty-seven cities in the San Francisco Bay Area showed that nearly one-fourth initially reached office by appointment.[22] Seventy-nine percent of council members who sought to be elected after being appointed to office won elections.[23]

These data on school board members and Bay Area city council members cannot be generalized to all state and local legislators, but they do suggest that the number of elective positions being filled by appointment is by no means insignificant. At any rate, though the vast majority of state and local legislative and top executive officials are selected by election, most midterm vacancies are filled by appointment. The accountability mechanism of direct election is therefore mainly inoperative when official vacancies occur, and declining in importance for chief executives of municipal government.

The effectiveness of direct election of officials as a mechanism of linkage and responsiveness can be impaired by certain features of the electoral system. Three typical elements of state and local election procedures inhibit accountability by preventing voters from selecting legislators who reflect their preferences. The elements are the plurality vote rule, multimember districts and at-large elections, and malapportionment.

PLURALITY VOTE RULE   Representative government will inevitably fall short of perfect responsiveness because the variety of preferences in a large population can never be reflected by a limited number of legislators. This basic problem is exacerbated by the process of selecting representatives from separate districts under a rule of plurality. As Patterson explains:

> The plurality vote formula produces results in legislative elections such that political parties accumulating large proportions of the popular vote tend to acquire even larger percentages of legislative seats. This regularity in the performance of the electoral system on the basis of which most American legislatures are chosen sometimes is called the *Matthew effect,* after the ukase in Matthew 13:12 that, "to him who has will more be given, and he will have abundance; but from him who has not, even what he has will be taken away." The Matthew effect in state legislative elections is illustrated in [figure 6.1]. . . . Each dot on the figure represents the share of both votes and seats accruing to the Democratic or Republican party candidates in a legislative election. Notice that, in general, a party that wins 55–60 percent of the votes in a state wins roughly 65–70 percent of the legislative seats, while a party that wins only 40–45 percent of the statewide vote wins only about one third or less of the seats in the legislature.[24]

The election process utilized by most European parliamentary systems to elect legislators is much more representative. The principal is proportional representation. Legislative seats are distributed among political parties according to their share of the popular vote. Under the plurality system, the party composition of the legislature will reflect the make-up of preference in individual districts, which may or may not reflect the aggregate preference within the entire policy. It is possible that a party that attracted 51 percent of the voters could win 100 percent of the seats. On the other hand, it is possible that a party that attracted a majority of the voters in a polity could win a minority of the legislative seats. (The principle is that of the electoral college or scoring in tennis. In the electoral college, presidential candidates gain individual votes toward a "winner take all" system at the state level. In tennis, players win individual points toward a "winner take all" system for games and sets. Thus, a presidential candidate can win a majority of electoral votes with a properly divided minority of popular votes, and a tennis player can win games and sets with a properly divided minority of individual points.) Thus, the plurality rule can be a barrier to representativeness and accountability to majority and minority preferences.

Figure 6.1.   Votes and Seats in Four State Legislative Houses

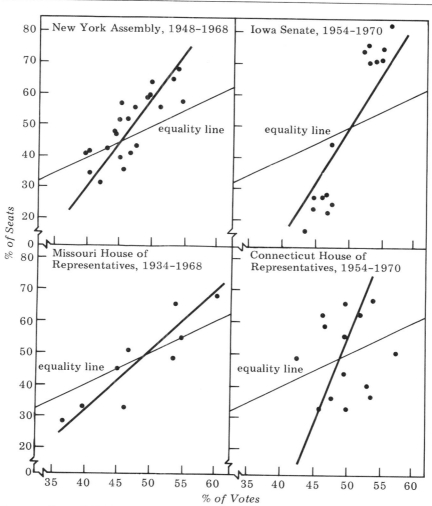

Source: Samuel C. Patterson, "American State Legislatures and Public Policy,"
in Herbert Jacob and Kenneth N. Vines (eds.), *Politics in the American
States*, 3rd ed. (Boston: Little, Brown, 1976), p. 154.

MULTIMEMBER DISTRICTS AND AT-LARGE ELEC-
TIONS   The single-member district, plurality-vote system can
prevent the selection of a legislative body that reflects the prefer-

ences of voters within the polity as a whole. Multimember districts and at-large elections can prevent the selection of legislative representatives that reflect the preferences of voters within individual districts. Again, the principle of majority party dominance and minority party exclusion is operative. In multimember and at-large election districts, the plurality formula tends to mean that all the legislators who win election in any one district will be the candidates of the political party that polls a plurality of the votes—more votes than any other party.[25]

Thus, a district that elects four representatives to a state legislature will tend to elect four Democrats if the Democrats win over 50 percent of the votes in the district. Nearly half the residents may have voted Republican, but this proportion of party preference will probably not be reflected in the district's delegation to the legislature. Similarly, a party or faction that can command a majority of votes in an at-large city council or school board election can easily elect its candidates for all contested positions. Minority preferences, no matter how strong the minority, will not be represented on the legislative body.

At-large elections may also bar responsiveness by discouraging potential candidates from running for office:

> At-large elections appear to scare potential candidates away from competing for office. Prospective officeholders are less sure of their goals and strategies when operating outside home area. They may be intimidated by the candidacies of local notables, whereas the potential aspirants in the ward system will compare themselves with local fellows who do not appear to be giants. It may be easier for people to encourage political candidates in the more familiar confines of the ward than in the more inclusive ones of the entire district.[26]

This thesis is supported by the finding that in school board elections, at-large elections depress levels of competition.[27]

The plurality system is nearly universally used in American state and local government legislative elections. At-large and multimember districts are also predominant. Fully 67 percent of cities with population over 5,000 elect city council members on an at-large basis,[28] and 73 percent of school districts elect board members on an at-large basis. On the state level, 42 percent of representatives and 18 percent of senators were elected in multimember districts in 1973.[29] Thus, most state and local legislators are elected on a basis other than the single-member district. As a result, the problem of legislators who may not reflect the division of preferences within election districts is considerable.

Electoral systems contain two major sets of rules about electing legislators. One set governs the conditions under which legislative seats are won by the contestants. Plurality winner-take-all elections, multi-member districts, and at-large elections are selection rules that may be barriers to responsiveness.

MALAPPORTIONMENT   The other set of rules has to do with how the number of legislators is to be distributed over the government's territory by drawing legislative district boundary lines. This issue is salient in the 33 percent of cities and 27 percent of school districts that elect legislators on a ward basis and for all fifty state legislatures. There has to be some system of apportionment of legislative districts among constituents in these governments. Unfair apportionment, or malapportionment, is a barrier to legislative representativeness and responsiveness that has long been recognized by political scientists and political practitioners.

Figure 6.2.   Inequalities in State Legislative Apportionments

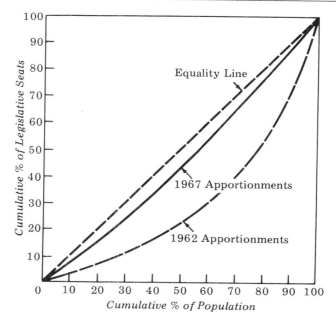

Source: Samuel C. Patterson, "American State Legislatures and Public Policy," in Herbert Jacob and Kenneth N. Vines (eds.), *Politics in the American States,* 3rd ed. (Boston: Little, Brown, 1976), p. 151.

The two types of malapportionment are population malapportionment and partisan malapportionment. Population malapportionment in state legislatures has been the subject of controversy and reform during the past twenty years. Before the one man–one vote decision in *Baker* v. *Carr* in 1962, some state legislatures were considerably malapportioned. The decision meant that all legislative districts were to be equal in population. However, the interpretations of *Baker* v. *Carr* by the courts have not been consistent, particularly in settling the issue of providing minority groups representation. Some of the variations in state legislative apportionments are shown in figure 6.2. According to Samuel Patterson:

> In 1962, before the reapportionments, in general there existed very substantial inequality in the relation between legislative seats and population. By 1967, after all states had been reapportioned, only fairly trivial inequalities remained. The completion on the 1970 census necessitated realignments of legislative district boundary lines in many states to reduce whatever inequalities might have resulted from population movement between the 1960 and 1970 censuses. During the 1972–1973 legislative sessions, reapportionments occurred in twenty-eight states for at least one legislative house. Although additional challenges in the courts may well bring about further reapportionments of the legislatures before the 1980 census, it is reasonable to claim that the small existing deviations from pure population equality in legislative districts in the states, difficult to eradicate completely, are of no important political consequence. In general, the legislatures are now reasonably well apportioned on a population basis.[30]

Unfortunately, no comprehensive study of population malapportionment in local governments has been undertaken, so parallel information is not available. Likewise, there are no comprehensive data on the extent of partisan malapportionment in state and local governments. Unlike population malapportionment, partisan malapportionment has not been dealt with by the courts.

Nearly all state legislatures are charged with the responsibility of establishing and modifying state and congressional district boundary lines. Local legislative bodies with ward elections typically determine district boundaries themselves. In states and local governments with ward-based partisan elections, the party in control of the legislature at the time of redistricting can draw district lines to its own political advantage. By carefully distributing voters of the various parties among districts, the majority party can win a disproportionate share of the districts in spite of a modest advantage on a state, city, or school district-wide basis. The art of drawing up such legislative districts is known as *gerrymandering,* and its practice is apparently universal. Gerrymandering can also be accomplished silently by failing to reapportion legislative districts to reflect population and partisan shifts.

Both population malapportionment and partisan malapportionment are barriers to responsiveness that result from selecting legislators by plurality vote. Population malapportionment at the state level is no longer a serious problem. Partisan malapportionment is a serious barrier that will remain so long as partisan elections are conducted on a winner-take-all basis and representative districts are drawn by those who have direct partisan interests at stake.

Partisanship

A fourth linkage mechanism of the accountability model of responsiveness is partisanship. The norm of responsiveness holds that political parties identify candidates with clearly articulated policy goals before elections and give them the necessary organization to implement their programs after elections. The norm of expertise favors nonpartisan elections and government. The preference is for men of quality to stand for election, rather than loyal party members who have paid their dues. The norm of expertise prefers nonpartisan government, free from the demands and limitations of a dogmatic party line.

All fifty states elect their governors on a partisan basis, and only Nebraska has nonpartisan election of state legislators. Table 6.16 summarizes partisanship in general city elections since 1951. The trend is for less partisan affiliation on city ballots overall, and in all governmental forms except council-manager. The decline of partisanship as a linkage mechanism in city government promotes the norm of expertise and weakens the norm of responsiveness.

Declining partisanship also characterizes the election of school board members. Before the municipal government reform movement around the turn of the century, virtually all metropolitan school boards were elected on a partisan basis. Today, approximately 25 percent of all school districts select board members by formally partisan elections. About 41 percent have either partisan or regularized slate competition.[31]

Partisanship is declining as a linkage mechanism promoting account-ability and responsiveness of local government officials. About one-third of city councils and one-fourth of school boards select members by par-tisan election.

Table 6.16.   Cities with Partisan Affiliation on General Election Ballots (in percentages)

	All	Mayor-council	Council-manager	Commission	Town meeting	Representative town meeting
1951	40.6	54.7	15.4	33.3	48.9	20.8
1953	39.8	54.6	15.6	34.3	52.0	25.0
1957	39.0	56.0	15.0	37.0	49.0	20.0
1959	39.0	56.0	16.0	39.0	55.0	23.0
1963	36.0	51.0	16.0	37.0	46.0	24.0
1967	35.1	50.8	17.7	30.5	43.5	39.3
1974	24.5	35.8	12.8	17.4	41.2	34.3

Source: *The Municipal Year Book, 1952, 1954, 1958, 1960, 1964, 1968, 1976* (Washington, D.C.: International City Management Association).

Competition

Competition among candidates for political office is seen by many obser-vers as an essential element that promotes accountability and respon-siveness to constituents:

> It is the struggle among candidates for the control of political of-fice that makes of elections not plebiscites but mechanisms for expressing voter choice. Competition for office is a minimum condition if elections are to establish the consent of the gov-erned. Unless men in office are challenged by others who want those offices, there is no way in which the electorate can threat-en eviction. And if eviction is not a potential threat, the chain of events which allows the governed to control the governors lacks a vital link. . . .

> Competition for office has a direct bearing on whether elections link the governors and the governed. We can suggest this by several reasonable assumptions. A competitive struggle for office generates greater interest among citizens than the noncom-

petitive election. The prospect of a change in personnel is sufficient in itself to attract the attention of the normally indif-
ferent citizenry. And in close elections it is thought that one's
own vote is more likely to make a difference. Moreover, the
behavior of the leadership echelon is affected by the prospect of
a close election. Those in office busy themselves taking their
case to the people. The challengers busy themselves by stirring
up constituency support. The election campaign is a period of
intense activity. All this makes for a greater variety and a larger
number of links between the normally distant governors and the
normally uninterested citizens.[32]

How much competition exists for legislative seats? Not as much as we
might expect.[33] We have already seen that a significant proportion of
state and local legislators are originally appointed to office, with no electoral competition. Units of government vary considerably in the proportion of legislators elected without competition. Of those elected to school
boards, fully 25 percent run unopposed.[34] The Bay Area study reported
that less than 7 percent of councilmen were elected without competition.[35] Malcolm Jewell reported that the proportion of uncontested seats
in general elections for eighteen state legislatures ranged from zero to 59
percent, with a mean of 19 percent.[36]

Mere competition for office may not be an accurate indicator of
whether or not eviction of the incumbent was a real possibility. Incumbents seeking reelection to state and local legislative office are generally
successful. The incumbent removal rate in school board elections is 34
percent.[37] The Bay Area Study found a wide range of eviction rates of incumbent city councilmen. In nearly a third of their cities fewer than one
in ten incumbents seeking reelection suffered defeat. In contrast, fourteen cities had electorates that evicted 40 percent or more of the incumbents attempting to be returned. The median incumbent eviction rate
was approximately 21 percent.[38] A recent study of lower houses in eight
state legislatures reported a mean eviction rate of 18 percent in 1967.[39]
Thus, a substantial minority of candidates for state and local legislative
office face no competition, and a majority of incumbents seeking reelection succeed. Competition for office is by no means universal or, when
present, always a threat to the incumbent.

Competition for office is generally thought to promote accountability
and responsiveness. Paradoxically, one form of competition may be a
barrier to responsiveness to mass preferences. Whenever more than two
candidates compete for a single position under a system of plurality election, the winner can be elected by a minority of voters. The greater the

number of candidates, the smaller the proportion of voters that can possibly elect the winner. When a plurality election occurs in a district with great heterogeneity of preference and many candidates, the election of a representative with less than a majority of the votes is almost certain. The accountability model holds that officeholders seek to maintain their electoral base by being responsive to the policy preferences of those who elected them. Obviously, the smaller the electoral base, the smaller the proportion of the electorate an officeholder can be responsive to and win reelection. Thus, competition in the form of many candidates running for the same office can act as a barrier to responsiveness.

Divided Party Control of Government

Those who believe that responsiveness of government to constituent preferences is served by responsible party government argue that three prerequisites are essential. First, of course, legislative and major executive positions must be chosen on a partisan basis. Second, there must be strong two-party competition, so that the majority party may be turned out when the voters decide it is time for a change. Third, the major party must control both the top executive office and the legislative body or else it cannot be collectively responsible for how the government is run.[40]

We have already reviewed the way partisanship and competition are thought to promote responsiveness. Competition provides the officeholder with strong incentives to be responsive to his constituents by threatening removal from office. Competition also provides a stimulus to the articulation of policy positions by candidates and motivates successful candidates to follow through on their promises. By simple aggregation, this model holds that competition on the level of individual candidates will promote responsiveness on the macro level. The ruling party's small margin of victory ensures that it will heed public opinion for fear of losing its majority. The secure individual or party is free to neglect constituency interests in favor of self-interests or the interests of the few. Competition among partisans supposedly leads to articulation of alternatives by candidates, opportunities for policy choice through the electoral process, and prompt attention by elected officials to their campaign promises and the continuing needs of their constituents.

Partisanship and competition thus are independent factors that promote linkage between governors and the governed. A provocative line of reasoning, however, argues that although the presence of either partisanship or competition may promote responsiveness, the presence of both simultaneously acts as a barrier to responsiveness.

This argument has two separate thrusts. First, on the micro level, the partisan candidates must win a healthy plurality to have a clear mandate about the policy preferences of his constituency. If competition between candidates implies electoral choice between competing policies, then the clarity of the choice made is directly proportional to the winner's margin of victory. Second, on the macro level, the argument focuses on the three prerequisites of responsible party government. Paradoxically, the first two prerequisites, partisanship and strong competition, together act as a barrier to the third, control of government by a single party. Several studies have documented that competition is directly related to divided party control of government.[41] Though partisan competition may provide a means of communicating constituent preferences and may serve as an incentive for officials to act on those preferences, it simultaneously may withhold the power necessary for elected officials to enact coherent programs.

Divided party control of government is most serious at the state level. From 1946 to 1974 no fewer than forty-four of the fifty states experienced at least one period, and usually more, in which control of the governorship and legislature was divided between the two parties.[42] Thus, at the state level, divided party control is frequent. What are the consequences?

> A governor facing a legislature controlled by the opposition party does not invariably mean angry partisan wrangling and deadlock. If the governor carefully cultivates the opposition's legislative leaders, proposes a moderate program to which they have agreed, and in general plays down party politics and the independence of his office, the government may proceed about as smoothly as if all concerned were members of the same party. But people are not angels and politicians have to fight elections, so such cross-partisan harmony is rare. A more common story has been the bitter partisan conflict and resultant near-total deadlock, typically between Republican governors and Democratic legislators, that marked such administrations as those of Ronald Reagan in California in the 1970s. All resulted in deadlocks over such basic matters as taxation, legislative apportionment, and executive appointments; and for a good part of the time the governments of such states were brought to nearly complete standstills.[43]

Divided party control acts as a barrier to responsible, responsive party government and may well lead to interparty deadlock.

Malapportionment and staggered terms of office also contribute to divided party control. Partisan malapportionment can result in minority party control of the state legislature so strong that only the most extraordinary popular gubernatorial majority brings with it legislative control.[44] Nonconcurrent terms for legislators and governors prevent the electorate from simultaneously choosing or replacing all major officeholders. Staggered terms cause changes in party strength in state senates and governorships to lag behind those in state houses of representatives and can result in divided party control.

V. O. Key observed that the instances in which the electorate intentionally chooses a governor of one party and a legislature of another are quite rare. Division of executive-legislative control stems in far higher degree from factors of institutional design.[45] Joint partisanship and close competition for office, partisan malapportionment, and staggered terms of office, for example, contribute to divided party control and act as barriers to governmental responsiveness to constituent preferences.

Ratio of Representatives to Constituents

The accountability model holds that responsiveness is served by a small number of constituents for each representative. The reasoning is essentially the same as that advanced earlier for small governments: increased homogeneity of constituent preference and increased opportunities for communication between constituents and representatives. The greater the number of representatives, the greater the probability that they will accurately reflect the preferences of the general public. The norm of expertise favors fewer representatives for three reasons. First, a smaller number of representatives can interact more closely as professional administrators and eventually develop expertise themselves. Second, a smaller number of representatives can reach decisions by more rational processes—such as consensus through discussion rather than voting the supposed interests of a limited constituency. Third, a smaller number of representatives means that each will represent a larger, more heterogeneous constituency and will be forced to seek policy alternatives that promote the general welfare. Large constituencies will prevent the formation of coalitions that seek to trade off policies which maximize benefits for small isolated interest groups.

Table 6.17.   Median Number of Councilmen

	All	Mayor-council	Council-manager	Commission
1951	a	7	5	5
1953	a	7	5	5
1957	a	7	5	5
1959	a	7	5	5
1963	a	7	5	5
1971	6	7	5	4
1974	6	6	5	5

Source: *The Municipal Year Book, 1952, 1954, 1958, 1960, 1964, 1968, 1972, 1976* (Washington, D.C.: International City Management Association).

[a] Data not available.

The number of legislators in the states has not changed significantly in the past four decades. In 1950 there were a total of 1,839 senators and 5,754 representatives in state legislatures. In 1975 the numbers were 1,982 and 5,583. Table 6.17 indicates that the number of city councilmen has remained virtually unchanged from 1951 to 1974. In the same period the number of school board members has declined drastically because of school district consolidation. The number of school districts has declined from 67,346 in 1952 to 15,781 in 1972.

At the same time that state and municipal governments have been maintaining a constant number of legislators and school districts have been decreasing legislators, the constituents of these governments—individuals and businesses—have been increasing. As we documented earlier in this chapter, the private population increased 54 percent and the business population increased 300 percent from 1950 to 1970. These figures indicate a severe decline in the ratio of representatives to constituents and a parallel weakening of this mechanism of accountability and responsiveness.

Summary

We have examined six mechanisms that are commonly thought to link governing elites and governed in state and local governments. On the local level, trends in form of government, the processes by which leaders are selected, and terms of office promote the norm of expertise and erode the norm of responsiveness. Partisanship is rarely present in local governments, and competition is quite often weak or even nonexistent. The declining ratio of representatives to constituents indicates that this linkage mechanism is also eroding.

On the state level, there has been no recent change in forms of government, selection of leaders, and partisanship. Competition is by no means universal, and its status as a mechanism of linkage is questionable. Trends in terms of office and the declining ratio of representatives to constituents promote the norm of expertise and weaken the norm of responsiveness. Divided party control is a major barrier to responsive state government and is a consequence of the failure of some linkage mechanisms.

Of course, the linkage mechanisms by themselves cannot guarantee accountability but can only provide conditions that permit or promote accountability. Nevertheless, it is interesting that some linkage mechanisms are surprisingly weak at the state and local level, and others seem to be eroding.

INSTITUTIONS OF PUBLIC ADMINISTRATION

FOR WANT of a better label, we will group the next institutional barriers to responsiveness under the heading of public administration. Some are formal institutions, whereas others are commonly employed standard operating procedures. Unlike some of the previously discussed barriers that impeded the communication of preferences from constituents to governors, all the following institutions of public administration impede government officials from fulfilling their constituents' policy preferences. In a thoughtful essay, Ronald E. Weber discusses five institutions of public administration that act as barriers to responsiveness in state and local governments: antiquated state constitutions, state control of local government, nonprofessionalized legislatures and bureaucracies, inflexible fiscal systems, and diffusion of executive power.[46] We add a sixth barrier to Professor Weber's list: overlapping cycles of decision-making.

ANTIQUATED STATE CONSTITUTIONS   The essential problem with state constitutions and their impact on governmental responsiveness is that public opinion on various policy matters may change much faster than state constitutions. State constitutions, historically, have been limiting or constraining documents. Once embodied in a state constitution, any particular provision is hard to change or remove; procedures for amending constitutions are generally more cumbersome than the procedures for changing statutory law. Although amendment of state constitutions is an ongoing process, it is instructive to note that of current state constitutions, three first took effect in the eighteenth century, twenty-eight in the nineteenth century, and nineteen in the twentieth century.

STATE CONTROL OF LOCAL GOVERNMENT   In a strict legal sense, all units of local government in the American political system are creatures of the state and therefore subordinate to state governments. Local governments must have the cooperation of state governments in developing the autonomy and capability to respond to the wishes and needs of their citizens. Localities have been slowly winning their struggles for broad home-rule powers of self-determination: approximately forty of the fifty states permit some form of municipal home rule and about fifteen states allow some type of home rule for counties. The overall picture is still one of widespread state government control of local governments, but the trend is toward permitting more meaningful home rule for general purpose local governments.

NONPROFESSIONAL LEGISLATURES AND BUREAU-CRACIES   When compared to their counterparts at the federal level, state legislatures and state bureaucracies have not attracted as many of the "best and the brightest" personnel as the Congress and the federal bureaucracy. The norm at the state and local levels all too often has been the amateur legislature and the patronage-based bureaucracy. Professionalization of state and local public service is expected to lead to the recruitment of people who wish to pursue long-term careers in the bureaucracy or the legislature. Professionalization, in turn, might increase the *potential* for responsiveness to the wishes of the public in three ways. First, professional legislators and bureaucrats would be more knowledgeable and would have the expertise necessary to design and implement policy programs according to the desires of the masses. Second, the long tenure of professionals will ensure that decision-makers have the time necessary to design and implement long-range policy programs. And third, the professionals' long tenure and their desire to continue in office will ensure that those who initiate policy can be held accountable when the results of policy are known.

INFLEXIBLE FISCAL SYSTEMS   So much of what government does involves the expenditure of money that fiscal systems which constrain the ability of state and local officials to raise and spend funds also constrain their ability to be responsive to their clientele. Weber points to three major sources of inflexibility in state and local fiscal systems: constraints on revenue sources, emphasis on inelastic revenue sources, and constraints on expenditures. Local government revenue sources are determined by state governments and usually limited to property taxes. State revenue sources are established in state constitutions, and it is not uncommon for state constitutions to prescribe income taxes, graduated tax rates for private and commercial income or property. State constitutions may also restrict the legislature's ability to reform property taxes. To the extent that state constitutions contain provisions on taxation, state and local governments are denied flexibility in raising revenue to respond to demands.

The second source of inflexibility is emphasis on inelastic revenue sources. An elastic tax will be responsive to changes in taxpayers' incomes. Income taxes, particularly those with graduated rates, are the most elastic forms of taxation. State and local governments rely most heavily on the most inelastic forms of taxation: local governments depend almost entirely on property taxes, and state governments depend mainly on sales and excise taxes. As of 1970, only three states derived more than 50 percent of their revenue from individual and corporate income taxes. The upshot is that state and local revenues do not keep pace with increasing wealth and demands for services. Inflexible revenue systems keep state and local governments in the unenviable position of having either to dissatisfy some constituents because there are not enough resources to go around or to dissatisfy all constituents by increasing tax rates.

The third source of inflexibility is the widespread practice of earmarking tax revenues for specific purposes. All states earmark some of their revenue: for example, highway programs are often financed by motor vehicle and fuel taxes, conservation programs are supported by the proceeds from fish and game licenses, and mental health services may be funded by taxes on alcohol and tobacco products. Some states have tended to earmark over 70 percent of their revenues; others have earmarked less than 10 percent. Obviously, a government that earmarks most of its revenue has little discretion to shift funds in response to new demands.

DIFFUSION OF EXECUTIVE POWER   The problem, which is more serious in state than at local levels, is that executive *responsibility* is vested in a governor or mayor but executive *power* is shared by other officials who are chosen and may operate independently of the chief executive. Quite commonly, a state will have a popularly elected secretary of state, attorney general, treasurer, and auditor who are responsible, not to the governor, but to the people who have elected them. Election of plural executives has not been the only reason for the diffusion of executive power. In some governments, major department heads are appointed by legislative bodies, independent boards, or commissions over which chief executives have little control. In addition to the problems growing out of restricted appointment powers, chief executives usually find it difficult to change the administrative structure of their organizations. Specific organizational schemes may be prescribed by constitutional or statutory law; changes can be made in these situations only by constitutional amendment or by persuading the legislative body to rewrite the relevant statutes. Both these routes are time-consuming and often unrewarding. Diffusion of executive power is an impediment both to the efficiency and the responsiveness of state and local governments.

OVERLAPPING CYCLES OF DECISION-MAKING   A number of overlapping decision-making cycles in state and local governments complicate the coordination of activities within and among governments. These different cycles are illustrated by the various calendars employed by government officials. The *fiscal year* for most state and local governments runs from July 1 to June 30, while the fiscal year for individuals and businesses runs from January 1 to December 31. The *political year* for most governments begins with campaigns starting in March and ends with elections in November. Many local governments do not hold elections in November—for example, school board elections are commonly held in May. New governments begin their *administrative year* within sixty days of their election—most typically in January or July. State, local, and federal governments have peak hiring periods in June and September, so it is possible to speak of a *personnel hiring year.* The personnel year somewhat coincides with the September to June *academic year* of school districts.

Although city councils and school boards meet year-round, only thirteen state legislatures have annual sessions of unlimited length. Most state legislatures' regular sessions are completed by the end of June, and fourteen state legislatures meet in regular sessions only every other year. Thus, it is also possible to speak of a *legislative year.*

The different fiscal, administrative, and political cycles cause problems of coordination both within and between governmental units. The overlap period between the political, legal, and fiscal years is a prime example of a barrier to efficiency within a governmental unit. Consider a governor who is newly elected in November 1980. Because of the discrepancy between the political and legal calendars, he or she must wait approximately two months before taking office. Many commentators have pointed out that the negative aspects of having a "lame duck" administration for this sixty-day holding period are balanced by beneficial aspects. The governor-elect can relax and recover from the campaign, choose top advisors and staff members, and arrange for an orderly transfer of government.

However, the discrepancy between the legal and fiscal calendars means that it will be another six months until the new governor begins his first new fiscal year. For the first six months of his administration the governor must implement the budget passed by the previous governor and legislature. Moreover, because agency budget requests and the governor's executive budget document were due in September 1980 and January 1981 for the fiscal year beginning in July 1981, the new governor's first fiscal year budget is largely developed under the previous predecessor. As a result, the first fiscal year in which the new governor can influence the entire budgetary decision-making cycle begins twenty months after his or her election.

The problem is exacerbated in the twenty-one states that have biennial budgets. Newly elected mayors and new school district superintendents have similar difficulties. A new chief executive who seeks to implement new programs that involve major redistribution of ongoing allocations or the development of new revenues cannot do so immediately on assuming office.

Discrepancies between the various governmental calendars also cause problems for relations between governmental units. Consider a hypothetical community that elects a slate of school board members in May 1980 who promise to attempt to reduce local school taxes by increasing state and federal funds coming into the district. Perhaps they even hire a new superintendent in July who joins the board in campaigns to acquire more federal grants and to influence state government to increase aid to local schools. The superintendent and school board members probably will be hampered in their efforts by overlaps in the state and federal political and administrative calendars. For example:

1. Officials of state and federal education administrations were probably appointed by a chief executive elected in November 1976. Hence, their policy mandate is four years out of date with that of the new school board and superintendent.

2. State and federal elected officials may be up for reelection or about to retire, and appointed officials may also be uncertain about their roles in the administration to be elected in November. As a result, the superintendent and school board members may have limited success in gaining the attention and support of state and federal officials whose terms may end in January 1981.

3. Even if school district officials do succeed in winning friends and influencing people in state and local government, they will have to reestablish relations with the new administrations starting in January 1981.

4. Because the school district is asking for major changes in budget allocations and perhaps in revenue structure, state officials cannot implement the desired changes until July 1981. The school district will be asking the new federal administrator for grants beginning with the next academic year in July or September 1981. Thus, different cycles of decision-making can inhibit intergovernmental cooperation necessary for responsiveness to clientele for up to ten months.

INTER-GOVERNMENTAL RELATIONS

OUR LAST category of institutional barriers to responsiveness is intergovernmental relations. The American system of federalism provides for some division of labor between local, state, and national levels of government. There is also considerable overlap of authority, which leads to competition between levels of government. As a result, intergovernmental relations include elements of cooperation and conflict. Some of these elements promote responsiveness to mass preferences, others inhibit responsiveness.

Most discussions of intergovernmental relations focus on federal-state and federal-local interactions. This limited definition of federalism ignores important state-local, state-state, and local-local relationships. Our consideration of intergovernmental relations will be in the broader sense of all interactions of federal, state, and local governments.

Multiple Levels
of Government

American federalism is largely the result of historical circumstances
such as the character of European colonization of North America, the
American Revolutionary War, the philosophies of our founding fathers,
the Industrial Revolution, and the worldwide rise of the nation-state.
Undoubtedly, our system of multiple levels of government persists partly because of inertia. However, multiple levels of government have certain structural advantages that also account for the persistence of
American federalism for over two hundred years. Though our major concern here is with how intergovernmental relations act as a barrier to
responsiveness, we will briefly consider the advantages of multiple
governments to provide the proper context for a discussion of how multiple levels of government inhibit responsiveness.

EQUITY   Multiple levels of government permit the equitable sharing of the costs of government.[47] Let us return to our premise that
governments exist to provide goods and services. The advantages of
goods and services extend to different populations. For example, the
policeman on the corner protects the jewelry store as well as the hard-
ware store; the deterrent protection offered by a nuclear-powered sub-
marine extends to all citizens in the United States. The existence of
multiple levels of government makes possible an equitable allocation of
the costs of various government goods and services. Each good has a
geographic range over which its benefits extend. Multiple levels of
government allow the responsibility of providing goods and services to
be matched with their range of benefits. The cost of the policeman can
be shared by the locality he patrols, and the costs of the nuclear sub-
marine can be shared by the nation it protects. Multiple levels of
government make it possible for citizens to share the costs of the benefits they receive, and only the benefits they receive.

EFFICIENCY   Multiple levels of government allow units of different size to take advantage of various economies of scale.[48] For example,
administrative costs per client can often be reduced if the administrative unit is enlarged. Thus, state administrative offices can
oversee the activities of locally based offices for such diverse activities as
employment services, public welfare, and registration of motor vehicles.
Several schools can join together in a school district and share the costs
of a computer, a director of research, and a lawyer. Furthermore, govern-

ments can realize economies by buying supplies in large quantities. A school district can purchase thousands of textbooks at a lower unit price than individual schools can each purchase several hundreds. Similarly, a state motor pool can purchase and maintain a large fleet of automobiles at a lower unit cost than a series of smaller county or municipal motor pools. There are different economies and diseconomies of scale associated with various goods and services. The existence of governments of different size allows a division of labor according to the economic size of the government unit.

DECISION COSTS   There are political benefits parallel to the economic benefits of equity and efficiency in a system of multiple units of government. Decisions can be made by—and the costs of making decisions limited to—those who will be affected by the decision. Thus, the existence of small units of government makes a national referendum unnecessary to resolve the question of whether the police forces in Detroit, Providence, Atlanta, Houston, Phoenix, San Jose, and Grand Rapids should be expanded or reduced. Large units of government allow more widespread participation in decisions that affect greater numbers.

DIVERSITY   The existence of multiple levels of government makes it possible to accommodate heterogeneity of preferences: different governments can pursue different policies. Thus, a school district in rural Illinois can emphasize agricultural subjects in its curriculum that are largely ignored in Chicago. Gambling can be legal in Nevada and illegal in Utah. School districts, municipalities, and states can impose different tax burdens and provide different levels of public goods and services. To an extent, the freedom of migration among the separate states and local units in the nation allows individuals a choice among the different combination of public costs and benefits roughly analogous to their choice in the market. Of course, there are costs involved in moving from one jurisdiction to another. The existence of multiple units of government pursuing heterogeneous policies permits individuals to assess the costs and benefits of migration and to make choices consistent with their preferences.

PARTICIPATION   Many small units of government allow a greater number of citizens to participate directly in government. Nearly a million people hold some kind of public office in the United States in states, counties, municipalities, school districts, and other government units. Furthermore, state and local elections to choose officials, consider initiative and referendum measures, decide on bonding and tax measures and other issues also present the opportunity for direct citizen participation in government decision-making. These opportunities for citizen participation are widely thought to bring government "closer to the people," generate popular support of government, and make government responsive to mass preferences.

The advantages of multiple units and levels of government are rooted in the outlets they provide for heterogeneity. Unfortunately, this heterogeneity is often a disadvantage when diverse units of government have to interact with each other. Intergovernmental relations often inhibit responsiveness by exacerbating the noninstitutional and institutional barriers already extant in state and local governments. Thus, our discussion of intergovernmental relations as a barrier to responsiveness can be organized by the noninstitutional and institutional barriers considered earlier.

Intergovernmental Problems and Noninstitutional Barriers

COMPLEXITY   The existence of multiple levels of government multiplies the problems of *complexity* for all governments. Federal, state, and local governments do not control separate, well-defined areas of public policy. There is considerable overlap between levels of government with respect to both programs and power.

Some education and law enforcement programs include all three levels of government. In programs such as those under the Elementary and Secondary Education Act (ESEA) and the Law Enforcement Assistance Administration (LEAA), federal funds are distributed to local units of government through state governments. Programs under the Economic Development Administration have been carried out by federal and local governments.[49] Programs such as unemployment compensation and construction of interstate highways involve federal and state governments. State and local governments also cooperate in such areas as school finance and public welfare.

Multiple levels of government increase complexity by complicating the environment in which individual governments must operate. In many ways, governments of different levels have a clientele relationship with each other. The preferences of other governments may conflict with those of a government's constituents. This conflict has increased with the growth of parallel, functionally defined bureaucracies across units of government. For example, experts with common duties, backgrounds, and interests exist in state departments of environmental protection and the federal Environmental Protection Agency (EPA). These technical experts have as much—or more—in common with their counterparts in other governments as they do with the state and local administrators, legislators, and citizens they work with.

It is similarly possible to speak of an educational establishment. Professional expertise links professional administrators in school districts, state departments of education and the federal Office of Education. The professional network of communication, personnel transfer, and common interest extends across levels of government. Thus, the problem of complexity giving rise to a powerful elite whose resource is professional expertise, discussed earlier, has its counterpart in intergovernmental relations.

Multiple levels of government create a barrier to state and local government responsiveness by increasing complexity. Other units of government act as clients that compete with residents for influence over state and local decision-makers.

UNCERTAINTY   Intergovernmental relations pose a barrier to responsiveness when more central governments create or increase *uncertainty* for more local governments. Many problems state and local governments are expected to deal with extend across the artificial boundaries of municipalities, counties, and states. Such diverse problems as pollution, unemployment, and crime can be dealt with by programs at the local, state, or federal level. Uncertainty occurs when more local governments do not know what programs state and federal governments contemplate. Uncertainty is a barrier to responsiveness when state and local governments fail to initiate action to meet popular demands in anticipation of future action by a more central government.

Uncertainty is not only a barrier when new programs are at stake, but ongoing intergovernmental programs also cause considerable uncertainty. Administrative rules and regulations inevitably accompany any intergovernmental program. These provisions are usually written in highly technical terms or legalistic language. Such rules and regulations not only add to complexity for participating governments but also may create uncertainty.

The ambiguity of highly technical regulations in intergovernmental programs is felt most strongly by extremely small units of government that do not have large professional staffs which can understand them or ask their colleagues in other governments about their meanings. Uncertainty can also be a problem in large units of government with an abundance of full-time experts.

It is not uncommon for key terms to be ambiguously defined in federal or state intergovernmental legislation and administrative regulations. And even where rules are straightforward, there may be considerable ambiguity concerning how strictly they will be enforced. The Title I program of the Elementary and Secondary Schools Act of 1965 is an example of both kinds of uncertainty. Its goal was to establish a program of compensatory education for deprived children. Federal funds were to be distributed to state education agencies which would authorize programs in local education agencies. A major ambiguity developed over the definition of deprived children. Federal regulations called for concentration of funds in poverty areas, implying an economic definition of deprivation. However, some states and school districts applied a standard of educational deprivation. Thus, there was ambiguity over whether funds were meant for all students in poor schools, educationally deprived students in poor schools, or educationally deprived students in all schools.

Environmental protection also raises considerable uncertainty about intergovernmental programs. Of necessity, the rules and regulations of the federal Environmental Protection Agency concerning acceptable and unacceptable levels of air and water pollution must be drafted in highly technical terms. Federal officials perceive the guidelines they issue to be clear. However, state and local officials who must apply the guidelines perceive them to be unclear and open to multiple interpretations. Furthermore, state and local officials see the federal regulations as unstable—subject to revision and reinterpretation without warning.[50]

Law enforcement is a policy area shared by state and local governments in which the problem of uncertainty is prominent. Local police are expected to enforce state and federal laws as well as local ordinances. However, there are several areas of ambiguity for the local policeman. What exactly is the content of the state law? What procedures of arrest must be followed for a case to be admissible? What rules of evidence will be imposed by state courts? Under what circumstances will a state attorney prosecute a case submitted by local police?

These examples suggest that ambiguity is an ongoing problem in intergovernmental relations in selected policy areas. Another area of ambiguity in intergovernmental relations affects all policy areas: uncertainty in the budgetary process. The budgetary process is both the collection of revenue, mainly through taxes, and the allocation of public funds. Both areas contain uncertainty.

For example, governments cannot project with certainty the amount of revenues they will receive in a given fiscal year. This is a major problem for federal and state governments because their tax revenues fluctuate with unpredictable levels of personal income and sales.

Resource allocation decisions are political decisions that are strongly contested by government executives and legislators and nongovernmental personnel. Budgetary decisions are usually compromises agreed to at the last possible moment. Indeed, it is not uncommon for federal and state governments to enter a new fiscal year without a budget. Governments pass continuing appropriations legislation to authorize spending at the previous year's level until a budget can be passed. In the meanwhile, new and continuing programs are in limbo. The uncertainty created by late budgets affects other governments that participate in intergovernmental programs.

The problem of uncertainty occurs in many areas of intergovernmental relations for many reasons. Uncertainty acts as a barrier to responsiveness when a government does not know if, when, and how an intergovernmental program will be implemented. Without that information it is not possible to know whether or not an intergovernmental program will fulfill constituent preferences.

HETEROGENEITY   We observed earlier that multiple units of government facilitate the accommodation of heterogeneous preferences by permitting different governments to pursue different policies. Cities, counties, and states are not entirely homogeneous units of government, of course. But, generally speaking, smaller units are more homogeneous than larger units, and multiple units permit diversity.

Intergovernmental programs, for the most part, involve a centralized level of government administering a fairly uniform policy across many more local units of government. The federal government carries out programs for state and local governments, and states carry out programs for local governments. The heterogeneity that multiple units of government permits is all but forbidden in the context of intergovernmental relations. Whenever many preferences are present, a single policy cannot be responsive to all. Uniform intergovernmental programs can only be responsive to a plurality of smaller governments, which may or may not comprise a majority of citizens. Programs designed to achieve equality among local governments often employ standardization. Intergovernmental relations invariably require rules imposed by central governments on local governments. The result is the familiar complaint that the federal and state programs for other levels of government reduce local control and responsiveness to local preferences.

The barrier of heterogeneity of preferences to responsiveness within governments is a more serious barrier in the context of intergovernmental relations. Intergovernmental programs act as a barrier to responsiveness insofar as they impose uniform policies on governments whose constituents prefer alternatives. By their nature, intergovernmental programs inhibit local options. The only choice that may be available to the local unit of government is whether or not it should participate in the intergovernmental program.

ORGANIZATIONAL BEHAVIOR   The same phenomenon that causes an organization to subordinate its original mission to the goals of survival and growth acts as a barrier to responsiveness in intergovernmental as well as intragovernmental organizations. This problem often takes the form of competition between agencies in different levels of government with similar missions.

A number of policy areas can be served at the local, state, and federal levels. In an age of scarcity of public resources, similar organizations at different governmental levels must compete for resources and, at the extreme, for survival. As a result, the temptation exists for intergovernmental competition when the interest of the public calls for cooperation.

Local, state, and federal law enforcement agencies are expected to cooperate by enforcing laws of different governments, cooperating in the apprehension of criminals in other jurisdictions, and so forth. However, each agency's desire to build favorable records of arrests and convictions may lead to unilateral investigations when cooperation is desirable. The result may be the refusal of one level to share information with or even enforce the laws of another level of government.

Another area of possible conflict is environmental protection. A recent study has shown that the education, career patterns, and attitudes of federal and state and local level environmental protection agency employees are quite different.[51] They disagree about which level of government should perform certain functions. The most notable conflict in the area of water purity is the issue of planning, where the states wish to retain their present responsibility. Federal officials, on the other hand, prefer to see planning executed at the local level.[52] It is possible that officials at one level of government might resist loss of power to serve better the interests of their constituents. It is equally possible that constituent interests might be served better by the transfer of power from one level of government to another. In those latter cases, the forces that cause agencies to compete with their counterparts in other governments to achieve survival and growth act as a barrier to responsiveness.

Intergovernmental Problems and Institutional Barriers

OVERLAPPING TERMS   Intergovernmental relations exacerbate the problem of overlapping terms of office as a barrier to responsiveness. It will be recalled that responsiveness is promoted by concurrent election of all officials. Staggered elections deny the voting public the opportunity to pass judgment on the entire leadership at a single election.

Though overlapping terms of office might not occur in any one government, relations between elected officials of different levels of government almost always involve overlapping terms of office. Most state elections are concurrent with federal elections; most local elections are held at different times than state and federal elections. Thus, term overlap in local-state and local-federal relations is nearly inevitable. Because federal representatives are elected to two-year terms, the president to a four-year term, and senators to six-year terms, there is always overlap within the federal government. As noted earlier, forty-six state governors are elected to four-year terms, thirty-eight states elect senators to four-year terms, and forty-six states elect representatives to two-year terms. Thus, term overlap is always a characteristic of state-federal relations.

DIVIDED CONTROL   Intergovernmental relations also magnify the problem of divided party control of government. The problem of divided control does not occur very often in local governments because most elect officials on a nonpartisan basis. Divided party control is characteristic of most state governments and was characteristic of the federal government for sixteen of the twenty-four years between 1952 and 1976. As is the case with overlapping terms, divided party control is virtually inevitable when more than one level of government must interact.

Table 6.18 characterizes the fifty states according to interparty competition in the 1962–1973 period. It is instructive that twenty are designated one-party Democratic or modified one-party Democratic, and seven are designated modified one-party Republican. Interstate relations are highly likely to involve representatives of both major parties; the probability increases with the number of states involved.

Because of the division of party strength across levels of government, intergovernmental relations almost certainly will involve interaction of

Table 6.18. The Fifty States Classified According to Degree of Interparty Competition, 1962–1973

One-party Democratic	Modified one-party Democratic	Two-party		Modified one-party Republican
Louisiana (.9930)	North Carolina (.7750)	Nevada (.6057)	Delaware (.4947)	North Dakota (.3463)
Alabama (.9520)	Maryland (.7647)	California (.6020)	Michigan (.4903)	Idaho (.3445)
Mississippi (.9145)	Virginia (.7543)	Alaska (.5760)	Pennsylvania (.4705)	Colorado (.3390)
South Carolina (.8935)	Tennessee (.7443)	Connecticut (.5670)	Utah (.4647)	Kansas (.3380)
Texas (.8780)	Florida (.7410)	Montana (.5553)	Arizona (.4377)	South Dakota (.3373)
Georgia (.8710)	Hawaii (.7313)	New Jersey (.5437)	Illinois (.4245)	Vermont (.3307)
Arkansas (.8645)	Oklahoma (.7297)	Washington (.5420)	Wisconsin (.4245)	Wyoming (.3205)
	New Mexico (.7107)	Nebraska (.5127)	Indiana (.4160)	
	Missouri (.7085)	Oregon (.5075)	Iowa (.4113)	
	Kentucky (.7037)	Minnesota (.5037)	New York (.4053)	
	West Virginia (.6945)		Maine (.4045)	
	Rhode Island (.6860)		Ohio (.3693)	
	Massachusetts (.6730)		New Hampshire (.3600)	

Source: Austin Ranney, "Parties in State Politics," in Herbert Jacob and Kenneth N. Vines (eds.), *Politics in the American States*, 3rd ed., (Boston: Little, Brown, 1976), p. 61.

members of opposing political parties. Members of different parties generally support different philosophies and policies, respond to different constituencies, and regard each other as potential or active enemies. Intergovernmental relations increase the probability of partisan conflict, which acts as a barrier to responsiveness.

CYCLES OF DECISION-MAKING   As noted earlier, overlapping fiscal, administrative, and political cycles cause greater problems for responsiveness when cooperation across levels of government is required than when action by a single government is possible. As was the case with term overlap and divided party control, relations involving many governments or multiple levels of government inevitably exacerbate the problem of overlapping cycles of decision-making because those cycles vary markedly from government to government. Overlapping cycles act as a barrier to responsiveness by increasing complexity and uncertainty. They also inhibit responsiveness by increasing the time necessary for intergovernmental programs to move from proposal development to the implementation stage of policy-making. Even the most popular intergovernmental policy will require considerable time first to secure the consent of all parties and then to mobilize necessary resources. The greater the number of governments that must coordinate their activities, the greater the barrier of overlapping cycles of decision-making to responsiveness.

Barriers in the Federal System

In addition to exacerbating barriers to responsiveness that act within individual governments, the federal system of American government creates two additional barriers to responsiveness. The first barrier is that intergovernmental relations inhibit the development of new, more appropriate, and presumably more responsive levels of government. The second barrier is that intergovernmental relations prevent governments from becoming responsive to their clientele by intervening in their decision-making processes and by preempting areas of policy from their jurisdiction.

INAPPROPRIATE LEVELS OF GOVERNMENT   The advantages of multiple levels of government include (1) levels of government that can handle problems with maximum efficiency, (2) equitable distribution of costs and benefits, and (3) reasonable decision costs. However, there are a variety of problems for which existing levels of government are not of optimal size according to these criteria.

Environmental protection is an area where the effects of policy decisions spill over across existing levels of government. The smoke caused by burning agricultural waste in Oregon's Willamette Valley affects several counties, but not the entire state. Similarly, industrial pollution originating in major urban areas may affect several municipalities, counties, or states. California's decision on whether to construct nuclear power facilities may have severe consequences to neighboring states in the event of a catastrophic accident. Ideally, the policy should be agreed to by all whose interests are at stake. Yet, because residents of most states are completely unaffected by California's nuclear decision, a decision at the federal level is hardly necessary.

In the previous examples, new regional governments within and between states would seem to be logical institutions that could be given responsibility and authority to create policy responsive to those affected.

Existing governments are too large or too small, yet they prefer to take ineffective or inefficient action rather than assign responsibility and authority to new levels of government.

The problems of inappropriate government size to cope with traditional areas of responsibility are particularly severe for municipal governments. We have spoken earlier of the fiscal problems connected with the segregation of business and residential areas in separate municipalities. The problem is compounded by the accompanying class migration. Thus, such major urban areas as New York City and Detroit are simultaneously losing the upper- and middle-class residential tax base necessary to provide public services and gaining increasing proportions of lower-class citizens who require costly welfare services. Thus, many municipal governments have evolved into an untenable imbalance of resources and social need. New levels of government are necessary to distribute equitably and efficiently the wealth generated by urban complexes that spread over county and state boundaries to meet the demand for governmental services they create. Law enforcement, education, transportation—nearly all policy areas are affected. Intergovernmental approaches prevent the creation of more effective and responsive units of government.

INTERVENTION   The sharing of policy-making responsibility by multiple levels of government inhibits responsiveness when more central levels can intervene and impose decisions on more local levels of government. The principle of local control is violated when parties to a dispute can appeal to a more central level of government. The ability to appeal to another level reduces incentive for parties to resolve differences among themselves, and the frequent use of extragovernmental authorities by any group of citizens reduces the incentive for local government to be responsive to their demands.

Concurrent federal and state judicial authority is a major source of intervention. The ability of local and state governments to pursue independent and different policies is circumscribed by judicial decisions of state and federal courts that apply the standards of a larger government.

The same problem occurs when federal agencies intervene in the affairs of state and local bodies.

Court-ordered busing is largely the result of dissatisfied minority groups transferring their demands for desegregation of schools from school districts to state and federal arenas. The upshot is that different levels of government are being responsive to different clientele. In this particular case, the preferences of white majorities at the school district level are being overruled by more distant state and federal authorities.

No matter what the final disposition of the controversy, the act of intervention itself weakens the incentive for the local governmental unit to be responsive. Why try to accommodate majority preferences or attempt to develop compromises acceptable to all when minority factions can successfully obtain decisions by appealing to other levels of government? Similarly, the possibility of intervention reduces the need for those in the minority to seek to make state and local governments consider their preferences. Intergovernmental intervention acts as a barrier to responsiveness by reducing incentives for the politics of accommodation and increasing incentives for the politics of confrontation.

CONCLUSION

WE HAVE discussed numerous factors that inhibit state and local government responsiveness. Noninstitutional barriers, such as complexity, uncertainty, organizational behavior, heterogeneity of preference, and public apathy, make responsiveness to constituents virtually impossible. Furthermore, of these barriers only public apathy is malleable. Public apathy has always characterized state and local politics in America; it is likely to increase as government decisions become more complex and remote.

Institutional barriers are subject to change. Reform movements have occurred in the past, a series of institutional changes to enhance responsiveness to constituents is possible. But would such reforms be successful in view of the continuing presence of the noninstitutional barriers? Furthermore, would the effort be worth it? This problem is the substance of our final chapter.

NOTES

1.
Aaron Wildavsky, *The Politics of the Budgetary Process,* 2nd ed. (Boston: Little, Brown, 1974), pp. 8–9.

2.
Quoted in James Nathan Miller, "Hamstrung Legislatures," *National Civic Review* 54 (April 1965): 184.

3.
Herbert Kaufman, *Are Government Organizations Immortal?* (Washington, D.C.: The Brookings Institution, 1976), p. 34.

4.
Ibid., p. 54.

5.
Ibid., p. 64.

6.
Ibid., p. 4.

7.
Ibid., p. 6.

8.
Ibid., p. 7.

9.
Marver H. Bernstein, *Regulating Business by Independent Commission* (Princeton, N.J.: Princeton University Press, 1955), pp. 154–60, 295.

10.
Harold S. Cohen, "Regulatory Politics and American Medicine," *American Behavioral Scientist* 19 (September–October 1975): 122–36.

11.
James M. Buchanan, *The Public Finances,* 3rd ed. (Homewood, Ill.: Richard D. Irwin, 1970), p. 28.

12.
Thomas E. Borcherding, "One Hundred Years of Public Spending, 1870 to 1970," Simon Fraser University Department of Economics and Commerce; *Discussion Paper* (February 9, 1974).

13.
Robert A. Dahl and Edward R. Tufte, *Size and Democracy* (Stanford: Stanford University Press, 1973), pp. 13–14.

14.
Robert A. Dahl, "The City in the Future of Democracy," *The American Political Science Review* 61 (December 1967): 953–70.

15.
The Portland Oregonian, August 15, 1976, Northwest Magazine Section, pp. 10–12.

16.
V. O. Key, Jr., *Public Opinion and American Democracy* (New York: Knopf, 1967), p. 21.

17.
Ibid., pp. 31–38.

18.
Anne H. Hopkins, "Opinion Publics and Support for Public Policy in the American States," *American Journal of Political Science* 18 (February 1974): 167–77.

19.
The Municipal Year Book, 1972 (Washington, D.C.: International City Management Association, 1972), p. 26.

20.
L. Harmon Zeigler, M. Kent Jennings, with G. Wayne Peak, *Governing American Schools: Political Interaction in Local School Districts* (North Scituate, Mass.: Duxbury Press, 1974), pp. 32–33.

21.
Ibid., p. 56.

22.
Kenneth Prewitt, *The Recruitment of Political Leaders: A Study of Citizen-Politicians* (Indianapolis: Bobbs-Merrill, 1970), p. 132.

23.
Ibid., p. 137.

24.
Samuel C. Patterson, "American State Legislatures and Public Policy," in Herbert Jacob and Kenneth N. Vines (eds.), *Politics in the American States,* 3rd ed. (Boston: Little, Brown, 1976), p. 153.

25.
Ibid., p. 153.

26.
Zeigler, Jennings with Peak, *Governing American Schools,* p. 59.

27.
Ibid.

28.
The Municipal Year Book, 1972, p. 25.

29.
The Book of the States, 1974–75 (Lexington, Ky.: The Council of State Governments, 1974), pp. 66–67.

30.
Patterson, "American State Legislatures and Public Policy," pp. 149–52.

31.
Zeigler, Jennings with Peak, *Governing American Schools,* p. 55.

32.
Heinz Eulau and Kenneth Prewitt, *Labyrinths of Democracy: Adaptations, Linkages, Representation, and Policies in Urban Politics* (Indianapolis: Bobbs-Merrill, 1973), pp. 229–30.

33.
Thomas R. Dye, "State Legislative Politics," in Herbert Jacob and Kenneth N. Vines (eds.), *Politics in the American States,* 2nd ed. (Boston: Little, Brown, 1971), p. 182.

34.
Zeigler, Jennings with Peak, *Governing American Schools,* p. 56

35.
Eulau and Prewitt, *Labyrinths of Democracy,* p. 232.

36.
Malcolm E. Jewell, *The State Legislature: Politics and Practice* (New York: Random House, 1962), p. 36.

37.
Zeigler, Jennings, with Peak, *Governing American Schools,* p. 56.

38.
Eulau and Prewitt, *Labyrinths of Democracy,* pp. 234–35; and Prewitt, *The Recruitment of Political Leaders,* p. 137.

39.
David Ray, "Voluntary Retirement and Electoral Defeat in Eight State Legislatures," *Journal of Politics* 38 (May 1976): 426–33.

40.
Austin Ranney, "Parties in State Politics," in Herbert Jacob and Kenneth N.

Vines (eds.), *Politics in the American States,* 3rd ed. (Boston: Little, Brown, 1976), p. 81.

41.
See, for example, Richard E. Dawson and James A. Robinson, "Inter-Party Competition, Economic Variables, and Welfare Policies in American States," in Robert E. Crew, Jr. (ed.), *State Politics: Reading on Political Behavior* (Belmont, Calif.: Wadsworth, 1969), pp. 459–78.

42.
Ranney, "Parties in State Politics," p. 82.

43.
Ibid.

44.
V. O. Key, Jr., *American State Politics: An Introduction* (New York: Knopf, 1965), p. 65.

45.
Ibid., p. 73

46.
Ronald E. Weber, "The Political Responsiveness of the American States and their Local Governments," in Leroy N. Rieselbach (ed.), *People vs. Government: The Responsiveness of American Institutions* (Bloomington, Ind.: Indiana University Press, 1975), pp. 189–225.

47.
Buchanan, *The Public Finances,* pp. 417–32.

48.
Ibid., p. 427.

49.
See, for example, Jeffrey L. Pressman and Aaron Wildavsky, *Implementation* (Berkeley: University of California Press, 1973), which discusses an employment program in Oakland.

50.
Harmon Zeigler, *Attitudes of Selected Groups Toward Implementation of Public Law 92–500, The Federal Water Pollution Control Act Amendments of 1972* (Eugene: Oregon Research Institute, 1975).

51.
Ibid.

52.
Ibid., p. iii.

7

EPILOGUE

THIS BOOK began with a note of irony. On one hand, responsiveness is presumed to be a good thing. On the other hand, considerable confusion exists as to how to tell whether or not a government is responsive.

We proposed two models of responsiveness, one based on a representational relationship between leaders and led, the other based on a congruence between policy and mass preferences. We found both inadequate.

HOW RESPONSIVE ARE STATE AND LOCAL GOVERNMENTS?

REPRESENTATION   The representational model makes a clear distinction between acting in response to demands and acting in the interest of the represented. This distinction is necessary because those who make demands are not representative of the community at large. They are wealthier, better educated, and better informed than less active, underrepresented segments of the population. It frequently happens, therefore, that those governments most responsive to the active minorities are accused of being the captives of entrenched interests. In extreme cases—those in which a city or state economically depends on a single source of income—such claims are clearly justified. Even, however, when there is no such dependence, the problems of diversity loom large. The active demand articulators always constitute a biased sample.

We referred to the few who communicate (other than by voting) with decision-makers as the "attentive public." This public—whether speaking individually or through organizations—knows what it wants and knows how to get it. Its high level of information stems not only from its higher status, but also from its active involvement in governmental affairs. As a linkage between the passive majority and the legal decision-makers, the attentive public communicate, obviously, with decision-makers: they talk to each other, but they rarely have any contact with the inactive public. This is not to say, of course, that members of the attentive public are unaware of the needs (as they see them) of the masses. Indeed, the opposite is true. The attentive public tends to be public-regarding and takes a community-wide, rather than particularistic, view of policy. Still, a benevolent elite is an unstable linkage because benevolence can turn to malevolence under conditions of conflict.

It is quite probable that conflict in state and local politics will be intensified as redistributive policy problems become paramount. When resources are abundant, the active minority can afford to be public-regarding because such a posture is not costly. The poor can have playgrounds for their children and mental health clinics, because the expense is nominal. Despite inflationary erosion, income (especially that of the active minority) is at least 50 percent higher today than twenty years ago. Such economic good fortune, however, depends on growth. When growth slows down, because of shortage of resources and dangers of pollution, the struggle will be for the redistribution of existing goods. We alluded to the politics of redistribution in our discussion of race relations in chapter 2, noting that such political controversies reduce the support of normally public-regarding whites for black candidates.

Redistribution questions will become more frequent, thus precipitating a conflict between the well-off and the not so well-off. Because no social class will voluntarily reduce its income, public-regarding elites may become no more than an artifact of the age of abundance. Thus, if we are uncomfortable with the representational mode of responsiveness now, we are likely to become even more so in the future.

CONGRUENCE   The other model of responsiveness—that of congruence—is equally troublesome. If policy is to be congruent with mass preferences, preferences must be discernable. The traditional way to find out what the people want is to look at election results. However, state and local governments, presumably created to bring government closer to the people, do not turn out as many voters as national elections. Indeed, in an average turnout, 75 to 90 percent of the eligible population do not vote in local elections; 45 to 60 percent do not vote in state elections. Again, we are confronted with the problem of diversity and representation. "The voters" and "the people" are quite distinct, because many, if not most, people do not vote at all.

Even if elections were more representative, what would they tell us about voters' preferences, much less mass preferences? Elections decide personnel, not policy. Winners are free to interpret the results as they wish, to provide their mandate with whatever content they wish.

Candidates rarely provide, nor do voters perceive, clear policy alternatives. Differences between candidates are consciously blurred, as each seeks the vote of the same active electorate. Issue blurring is accentuated by the prevalence of nonpartisan local and state elections. Such elections, by eliminating partisan identification, make candidate image (as distinct from ideology) even more central than in national elections.

The information received by government officials concerning mass preferences is of insufficient quantity, quality, and diversity to support either the representative or congruence model of responsiveness. Policymakers, then, are left with two options: they can respond to the active few or they can ignore them and do what they think best. Obviously, only the former situation is a form of responsiveness to constituents, albeit a minority of constituents. State and local governments tend to be more responsive to organizations than to individuals, and more responsive to business and professional associations than to other organizations. Especially underrepresented at both levels of government are racial minorities and various antiestablishment organizations.

As we explored the policy-making process, we found even those who achieve access are ineffective. Policy choices are becoming increasingly complex. Legislators find themselves depending on experts supplied by administrative agencies for information. If nongovernmental organizations are to compete with such experts, they must supply their own expertise, a task which few can undertake successfully. This rise of experts as policy initiators is particularly well illustrated by the case of education.

As we saw in chapter 6, a plethora of factors—institutional and non-institutional—inhibits responsiveness. How responsive are state and local governments to their constituents? Probably as responsive as possible—which is to say, not very responsive.

HOW RESPONSIVE CAN GOVERNMENTS BE?

INSTITUTIONAL BARRIERS   Clearly, state and local governments could be more responsive if some barriers to responsiveness are removed. Existing institutional barriers to responsiveness are subject to manipulation. Municipalities could adopt more responsive forms of government. All terms of office could be made uniformly brief and concurrent. All elections could be contested on a partisan basis, either by wards or with distribution of legislative seats proportionate to popular votes. All forms of malapportionment could be eliminated. The ratio of representatives to constituents could be increased. Antiquated state constitutions and city charters could be rewritten. State and local government fiscal systems could be changed. Local governments could all be granted autonomy. Legislatures could be allocated greater research and support resources. Elected executive officials could be chosen on a partisan basis. Various governments could adhere to a single cycle of decision-making. However, such changes are undeniably numerous, complex, and costly. Furthermore, any or all changes would have unanticipated consequences. The uncertainty of such reforms is amply documented by the failure of the last reform movement to achieve responsiveness and the ongoing paradox of partisanship and competition in electoral competition.

NONINSTITUTIONAL BARRIERS   Even if these institutional problems could be overcome, noninstitutional barriers to responsiveness remain. Unfortunately, complexity, uncertainty, organizational behavior, and heterogeneity of preference are not subject to manipulation. Indeed, these barriers will probably become even greater in the foreseeable future as finite resources are exhausted, policy concerns shift to conservation and redistribution, and technical criteria for decision-making proliferate.

It is possible to argue that the noninstitutional problems in assessing popular preferences could be overcome. If state and local governments could afford to do so, they could rely exclusively on public opinion surveys for assessing public preference. Such an idea is given added feasibility by the gradual development of cable television, readily accessible data banks (or "information utilities"), and telecommunications. It is conceivable that these technological advances will make mass preferences easily obtainable. Thus, instant plebiscites may replace more traditional polling techniques, providing an approximation of the congruence model.

Before we invest in ATT or IBM, however, let us reconsider some major aspects of mass opinion. The public may not have policy preferences until the options are displayed for them by elites. Thus, such opinions are unstable—indeed, they vary randomly in many cases (except when the issue is unusually salient, a rarity in state and local politics). Although the technology exists for assessing mass preferences, there is no technology for generating mass preferences of sufficient quality to guide policy-makers. In other words, well-developed, detailed rather than generalized, opinions can only be voiced by very well-educated people. Hope as we might, there is no realistic way to increase levels of information or to reduce apathy among the masses. As one commentator remarked, "We should never plead with people to get out and vote. It is a perverted sense of civic duty to beg the uncaring, uninformed, and ignorant to 'Go to the polls and vote for the candidate of your choice.' "[1]

INTERGOVERNMENTAL RELATIONS   There is another class of institutional barriers to responsiveness that we frankly see as insuperable. We see no way of obviating the difficulties for responsiveness posed by intergovernmental relations. There is supreme irony in the fact that American federalism, originally established to maximize subnational flexibility, now exacerbates previously existing barriers to responsiveness and creates its own barriers. Multiple levels of government increase complexity, uncertainty, heterogeneity, organizational competition, term overlap, divided partisan control, and overlapping cycles of decision-making. The present system of federalism inhibits the creation of new, more appropriate units of government at regional levels. Intergovernmental relations also inhibit responsiveness by allowing more central governments to intervene in the affairs of more local governments, thus reducing incentives for negotiation and accommodation at the local level.

IS THE QUEST FOR RESPONSIVE GOVERNMENT FUTILE?

WHAT WOULD happen if state and local governments suddenly became completely responsive to mass preferences? In one sense, not very much would happen. If state and local policy-making were completely dependent on plebiscites for instructions, governments would be paralyzed. Mass opinion is insufficient to set the general policy agenda, to say nothing of making day-to-day decisions. The masses are simply uninformed and uninterested.

In another sense quite a lot would happen. For those few areas which are salient to a majority of citizens, responsiveness would mean substantially different policies. Generally speaking, the masses are less tolerant and public-regarding than are elites. They are more fearful of change. Recent events in such diverse locations as Boston, Louisville, and San Francisco suggest that, if racial policy were determined by the masses, de facto segregation would be the law of the land. Although mass attitudes toward integration have become more positive, white flight from central cities continues unabated.

It is realistic to say that progress toward integration has been the result of elite initiative, as opposed to elite response. Indeed, we are hard pressed to give an example of any reform that was not elite-initiated. If elites were completely responsive to masses, freedom of speech and all forms of dissent would be severely curtailed. Surveys have repeatedly demonstrated that the Bill of Rights is neither understood nor supported by the majority of Americans. In short, state and local governments completely responsive to contemporary mass preferences would subvert the individual freedom that is the philosophical base of American government. A large-scale program of civic education seems a necessary prerequisite.

But even if the problems of mass intolerance could somehow be solved, the problems of complexity remain. Participation as an ideology in American society seems to be of growing importance just when technical complexity threatens to limit effective political choice.[2] It is ironic that, as the presumed prerequisites for effective mass participation in government (such as universal suffrage or increased access to education) are realized, the new technology of government makes these prerequisites insufficient. Even if they had the desire and ability to learn, the common people lack the time necessary to master complex and often uncertain technical material. In short, it is unrealistic to expect that the masses can become experts.

Thus, for the foreseeable future, there is no alternative to government by experts. The experience in educational policy suggests that experts not only dominate at the local level, but that they are part of a network which is removing local initiative and transferring it to larger units. We think that such a trend toward nationalization of expertise will soon find other counterparts, especially in such policy areas as environmental protection, criminal justice, and public welfare where the problems cut across existing political boundaries. If the trend toward nationalization continues, the role of state and local governments will necessarily decrease.

The goal of matching decision-making in each policy area with an ideal level of government is unrealized. The problems that intergovernmental relations pose for responsiveness result from this failure. American federalism is a system of shared and overlapping policy responsibilities. As a result, governments are more responsive to other governments than to their constituents. In the best of all possible worlds, each policy area would be assigned to one appropriate level of government and would be excluded from all others. Unfortunately, units with the optimum capacity for solving problems may not be optimal with respect to responsiveness to constituent preferences.[3] Indeed, the trend toward nationalization of policy-making is a consequence of so many crucial problems being insoluble by state and local governments.

It would be unfortunate if nationalization of policy-making makes state and local governments obsolete. As the process of nationalization proceeds, elected elites that were initially responsive to articulate minorities shift their response to administrative bureaucracies with the requisite expertise to conduct them through the maze of intergovernmental regulations, guidelines, and mandates. Even though state and local governments, like all governments, are selectively responsive, they nevertheless reflect stable regional idiosyncracies. Policies initiated at the state level provide laboratories for evaluation. Oregon's success in outlawing nonreturnable bottles, California's and Oregon's decriminalization of marijuana, and Massachusetts' efforts at gun control provide an opportunity for other states to make a rational assessment of policy consequences. If these policies work, they will be adopted by other governments.

This brings us to a final dilemma. "From Aristotle to Jefferson it was axiomatic that you cannot maintain rule by the people except in a society where resources are rather equally distributed. . . . this country falls short not only of an ideal but of an actual condition of equality which was taken for granted by democrats like Jefferson and Madison in the early years of the republic."[4] Yet existing subnational idiosyncracies that lead to diversity in policy-making result in inequality. Sometimes the tradeoff between diversity and equality is acceptable: many applaud the Northwest's innovations in environmental policy. Sometimes the tradeoff is less appealing: many condemn the South's reactionary race relations policy. Communities that allow neighborhoods to establish zoning guidelines may permit another form of restrictive covenants. Allowing education to be financed and executed locally results in discrimination against lower classes. Allowing health and welfare benefits to be established by states results in nationwide inequality.

Thus, equality can be equated with nationalization and expertise and non-responsiveness to mass preferences. Inequality can be equated with decentralization and diversity and responsiveness. Responsiveness of state and local governments, either by congruence or representation, results in inequality in the distribution of resources and inequality of opportunity. It should be recognized that realizing the goal of responsiveness will be at the expense of economic and political equality. Paradoxically, reduction of inequalities by nationalization of decision-making would make the targets for participation more remote from masses and more responsive to experts. In this sense, the quest for responsive government is futile.

American state and local governments simply cannot be responsive in the sense of providing all things to all citizens; they cannot even provide most things to most citizens. State and local governments lack both the incentive and the means to be responsive to the so-called silent majority. They can only be responsive to the few who make their demands and preferences known. We see both irony and opportunity in this situation. The same factors that make responsiveness to the masses who do not actively seek it impossible make responsiveness a realistic goal for those who do seek it.

NOTES

1.

Francis P. Lynch, "Let's Not Get Out the Vote," *Newsweek,* October 18, 1976, p. 15.

2.

Dorothy Nelkin, "The Technological Imperative Versus Public Interests," *Society* 13 (September–October 1976): 6.

3.

Robert A. Dahl and Edward R. Tufte, *Size and Democracy* (Stanford, Calif.: Stanford University Press, 1973), pp. 41–65, 118–136.

4.

Robert A. Dahl, *After the Revolution* (New Haven, Conn.: Yale University Press, 1970), pp. 106, 113.

INDEX

AFL-CIO, 119, 229

Accountability, 166 - 168, 170 - 172, 276 - 296; and auditing, 177 - 178

Agenda setting, 10, 148 - 149; in school policy, 210 - 212

Agger, R. E., 191 - 192

Alabama, 90

Alaska, 151

Almy, Timothy, 43

Amateur government, 150 - 151

American Association of School Administrators, 142, 209, 228

American Federation of Teachers, 206, 208, 209

American League of Anglers, 93

Amicus curiae briefs, 181

Anaconda Co., 5, 91 - 94, 104

Antipollution laws, 89, 90, 96

Apathy, 17, 255, 275, 313

Associated Industries of Oregon, 104

Association of State School Officials, 142

At-large elections, 32 - 33, 35, 205, 286; and school boards, 236

Atlanta, 39, 67

Auditing, 177 - 178

Audubon Society, 112

Baer, Michael, 58, 107 - 108, 111, 119, 154 - 155

Baker v. *Carr*, 288

Baltimore, 67, 202 - 203

Banfield, Edward C., 35, 37 - 38, 39, 40, 57 - 58, 71, 74

Bauer, Raymond A., 94 - 95

Bay Area City Council Study, 63, 291

Bensman, Joseph, 193

Biemiller, Andrew J., 117

Bill of Rights, 324

Birmingham, 67

Black Panthers, 75

Blacks, 38 - 39, 41 - 44; and cities, 66 - 67; community activity, 54, 55; and labor, 65 - 66; politicial activity, 67 - 76; and schools, 240 - 241

Borah, William E., 92

Borcherding, Thomas E., 269

Boudon, Raymond, 242

Boyd, William, 211 - 212

Bradley, Thomas, 43, 44

Brandeis, Justice, 140

Bribery, 111, 113

Brown, Edmund, 102

Brown v. *Board of Education*, 68, 238, 239, 240

Buchanan, James M., 269

Buchanan, William, 99, 100

Budget: and agency survival, 266; biennial, 300; preparation, 144 - 145; and uncertainty, 306 - 307

Bundy Commission, 271

Bureaucrats: and accountability, 170 - 172; associations, 140 - 142; expertise, 169 - 170, 171, 297, 305; hierarchy, 170 - 171; mobility, 171 - 172; and policy, 165 - 166, 182; professionalism, 297

Burke, Edmund, 12

Business, 14; and civic associations, 62 - 63; conflict among, 60 - 62; vs. labor, 57 - 60, 92; and legislatures, 89, 94 - 95, 103, 116 - 117; and reform movement, 31; and taxation, 92 - 93, 94; and voting, 48

Busing, 76, 230, 231 - 232, 240 - 241; and courts, 137, 313; opposition to, 274

Butte, Montana, 93

COPE, 64 - 65

CORE, 70

California, 11; elections, 35, 46, 47; fair